Christian Belief
in a Postmodern World

Other books by Diogenes Allen

Philosophy for Understanding Theology
Love: Christian Romance, Marriage, and Friendship
The Reasonableness of Faith
Finding Our Father
Temptation
Traces of God in a Frequently Hostile World
Three Outsiders: Pascal, Kierkegaard, and Simone Weil
Mechanical Explanations and the Ultimate Origin
of the Universe According to Leibniz
Leibniz's Theodicy (edited and abridged)

Diogenes Allen

Christian Belief
in a Postmodern World

The Full Wealth of Conviction

WJKP

Westminster/John Knox Press
Louisville, Kentucky

Acknowledgment is made for permission to quote from the following sources:

To Cowley Publications for excerpt from Chapter Six, Diogenes Allen, *THREE OUTSIDERS,* copyright 1983. Used by permission.

To *Theology Today* for the last two-thirds of Chapter Ten from Diogenes Allen, "A Christian Theology of Other Faiths," *Theology Today* 38 (October 1981): 305–13. Used by permission.

To *Faith and Philosophy* for Chapter Eleven, which is based on Diogenes Allen, "Incarnation in the Gospels and the *Bhagavad-Gita.*" Reprinted from *Faith and Philosophy,* Vol. 6, No. 3 (July 1989), by permission of the Editor.

To Oxford University Press for the quotation from Christopher Fry, *SLEEP OF PRISONERS,* copyright 1951. Used by permission.

© 1989 Diogenes Allen
2 4 6 8 9 7 5 3
Printed in the United States of America
Westminster/John Knox Press
Louisville, Kentucky

Library of Congress Cataloging-in-Publication Data

Allen, Diogenes.
   Christian belief in a postmodern world : the full wealth of conviction / Diogenes Allen.
      p.   cm.
   Bibliography: p.
   Includes index.
   ISBN 0-8042-0625-2

   1. Apologetics—20th century.   I. Title.
BT1102.A398 1989
239—dc20   89-32281
                                                    CIP

For Jesse de Boer
Professor of Philosophy, Emeritus
University of Kentucky

"I strive for you . . .
that [you may] come to the full wealth of conviction
which understanding brings"

(Col. 2:2, NEB)

Contents

Acknowledgments   xi

Introduction   The End of the Modern World:
                   A New Openness for Faith   1

PART I: THE BOOK OF NATURE

Chapter One   The Christian Roots of Modern Science
                   and Christianity's Bad Image   23

Chapter Two   Has Science Replaced God?   35

Chapter Three   The Order of the World Points
                   to the Possibility of God   50

Chapter Four   The Existence of the World Points
                   to the Possibility of God   64

Chapter Five   The Need for God and the Book of Nature   85

PART II: THE BOOK OF SCRIPTURE

Chapter Six   The Experience of God's Grace:
                   Faith and the Book of Scripture   99

Chapter Seven   The Reasonableness of Faith   128

Chapter Eight   Reason and Revelation   149

Chapter Nine   Divine Agency in a Scientific World   165

PART III: CHRISTIANITY AND OTHER FAITHS

Chapter Ten   A Christian Theology of Other Faiths   185

Chapter Eleven   Incarnation in the Gospels
                   and in the *Bhagavad-Gita*   197

                   Conclusion   213

                   Notes   217

                   Index   233

Acknowledgments

I am deeply grateful to Thomas W. Gillespie, President of Princeton Theological Seminary, who allowed me a leave of absence to complete this book, which had been begun during an earlier sabbatical leave. On both occasions I was a member of the Center of Theological Inquiry, Princeton, New Jersey. I am very grateful to its Chancellor, James I. McCord, for the opportunity this gave me to discuss it with other members of the Center.

The manuscript was read in whole or in part by Edward H. Henderson, Professor of Philosophy, Louisiana State University; Daniel L. Migliore, Arthur M. Adams Professor of Systematic Theology, Princeton Theological Seminary; Basil Mitchell, Nolloth Professor of the Christian Religion, Emeritus, Oxford University; W. Jim Neidhardt, Associate Professor of Physics, New Jersey Institute of Technology; the late Paul Ramsey, Professor of Christian Ethics, Princeton University; Eric Springsted, Chaplain and Professor of Philosophy, Illinois College; Russell Stannard, Professor and Head of the Physics Department, Open University; and Eleonore Stump, Professor of Philosophy, Virginia Polytechnic Institute and State University. Timothy G. Allen spotted several opaque passages, and Jane M. Allen greatly improved my English prose. Their numerous suggestions helped make this a much better book. I am, of course, responsible for any of its inadequacies.

The End of the Modern World: A New Openness for Faith

I

To have a faith to live by is a great comfort and support, especially in times when there is great intellectual disagreement and rapid change. But now and again I have met a person who has claimed that religion has nothing to offer. "Why should I go to church," someone once said to me, "when I have no religious needs?" I had the audacity to reply, "Because Christianity's true." That may seem foolhardy when we live in a pluralistic world with any number of different views of reality and apparently no rational means of telling which view is most likely to be true, and when it is said that all views are historically relative and mere reflections of social structures. Even scientific laws and theories are to be held tentatively. How can any educated person who is not simply dogmatic claim that a religion is true?

Nonetheless, I find myself driven to make this claim. The needs religion fills are relevant to an assessment of its truth, as we shall see, but were it merely a matter of finding religion to be helpful, then a religious commitment would not be essentially different from a personal preference. We would rightly say that just as some people prefer chocolate to other flavors of ice cream, some people prefer to be Christian rather than something else or nothing at all merely as a matter of taste. But when something is said to be true, we have a different situation, especially when it is said of a religion. Christian, as well as other religious claims, are so serious and so demanding personally that adherence to them cannot be properly described as merely a matter of personal taste.

Many people today find they cannot ignore their religion's claim to be true, and yet they are aware of various difficulties in affirming its truth. The modern world has driven a wedge between the mind and the heart, forcing Christians to lead a double life. On the one hand, there are more Christians in the world today and they are more widely distributed geographically than ever before. In spite of immense increases in the world's population during the past five centuries, the percentage of Christians has increased from about 19 percent in 1500 to more than 34

1

percent in 1900. Since 1900 the world population has tripled, and the
number of Christians has virtually tripled as well, keeping up with the
population explosion. You must combine the number of Muslims (17.1
percent), Hindus (13.5 percent), and Buddhists (6.2 percent) to surpass
the number of Christians in the world in 1985. Such growth reflects
immense vitality.[1] In addition, of all the religions of the world none has
been exposed to as intense and persistent critical examination as
Christianity.

On the other hand, in spite of these accomplishments, Christianity has
been on the defensive intellectually. On the basis of physics, biology, philosophy, psychology, sociology, and anthropology, people have claimed
again and again that its day is over. The attitude toward Christianity that
has increasingly dominated the intellectual culture in modern times was
nicely captured in a comment made in 1878 by Max Müller, a distinguished anthropologist:

Every day, every week, every month, every quarter, the most widely read jour-
nals seem just now to vie with each other in telling us that the time for religion
is past, that faith is a hallucination or an infantile disease, that the gods have at
last been found out and exploded.[2]

The situation from the point of view of Christianity, however, is not
as dire as it may seem. On the contrary, our situation is now far better
than it has been in modern times because our intellectual culture is at a
major turning point. A massive intellectual revolution is taking place
that is perhaps as great as that which marked off the modern world from
the Middle Ages. The foundations of the modern world are collapsing,
and we are entering a postmodern world. The principles forged during
the Enlightenment (c. 1600–1780), which formed the foundations of
the modern mentality, are crumbling.

We do not yet know what the future holds, but it is clear that a fundamental reevaluation of the Christian faith—free of the assumptions
of the modern mentality that are generally hostile to a religious outlook—is called for. No longer can Christianity be put on the defensive,
as it has been for the last three hundred years or so, because of the
narrow view of reason and the reliance on classical science that are characteristic of the modern mentality. In fact, in the reevaluation of the
intellectual viability of Christianity which is undertaken in this book, we
shall see that not only are the barriers to Christian belief erected by the
modern mentality collapsing, but that philosophy and science, once
used to undermine belief in God, are now seen in some respects as actually pointing toward God.

The breakdown of the modern mentality is evident in at least four areas. First, it has been taken for granted in the intellectual world that the idea of God is superfluous. We do not need God to account for anything. Subject after subject is studied in our universities without reference to God, so that anyone educated outside church schools or colleges, is given the impression that religious questions are not among the fundamental questions which any person who uses his or her head has to confront sooner or later. It is not merely a matter of the separation of church and state, because the same thing exists in many countries of Europe and in Canada where there is no such doctrine of separation.

But today there are fundamental developments in philosophy and cosmology that actually point toward God. It can no longer be claimed that philosophy and science have established that we live in a self-contained universe. Hume's and Kant's philosophical arguments that it is pointless to ask whether the universe has an external cause have recently been seriously revised in secular philosophical circles, as we shall see in detail in Chapters Three and Four.[3] This radical change has been independently reinforced by recent developments in science, especially in cosmology, which we shall also examine in Chapters Three and Four. In both fields the questions arise, Why does the universe have this particular order, rather than another possible one? and Why does the universe exist? These questions point toward God as an answer. As we shall see, it is beyond the capacity of those fields of inquiry to make a positive pronouncement on the matter. All they can say is that the order and existence of the universe pose real questions that they cannot answer and recognize that God is the sort of reality that would answer them.

This is a complete about-face. Both science and philosophy have been used for several centuries to exclude even the possibility of God. On strictly intellectual grounds, this can no longer rightly be done. This is a fundamentally different cultural situation.

Once the embargo on the possibility of God is lifted, it is easy to show that the issue of divine existence is intellectually inescapable and important. For example, human beings are goal-seeking. Our goals are numerous and in some instances conflicting. To be rational we must order them into some priority. This is true of us as individuals as well as members of various social and political groups.

To order our goals rationally, we must make a match between our needs, interests, and desires, on the one hand, and what the physical and social environments permit us reasonably to hope we can achieve, on the other hand. Our estimate is greatly affected by whether we think this universe is ultimate or not. An estimate based on the conviction that the universe is ultimate is significantly different from an estimate based on the view that it is not. So the need to direct and order our lives as individuals and as societies is a reason to pursue the question of the status of our universe. Our goal-seeking behavior renders the question of what is ultimate inescapable for rational agents.

Furthermore, our needs, aspirations, and desires are far greater than can be satisfied should this universe be all that there is. If the universe is ultimate, then we must greatly reduce our aspirations and suffer the frustration of many of our needs and desires. To assume that we must pay this price is rational and sensible only if we have examined the status of the universe, and indeed examined it seriously and carefully. If people are sensible, they would want to know, earnestly want to know, whether this universe is ultimate or not.

Christians, therefore, need not continue to be defensive. We, just as Socrates in ancient Greece, have a mission: to challenge the supposition that the status of the universe and our place in it have already been thoroughly settled by scientific and philosophic developments. On strictly scientific and philosophical grounds, we will show that science and philosophy do not explain everything. They do not establish what the status of our universe is nor our place in it. Both individuals and institutions, such as schools and universities, ought to consider and study anything that promises to shed light on our situation. We have the opportunity and task of turning people into seekers, as did Socrates.

The second breakdown of the modern mentality is the failure to find a basis for morality and society. A major project of the Enlightenment was to base traditional morality and society on reason and not on religion. It sought to show by reason[4] alone that some things are wrong in nearly all circumstances, that to become a moral person is of supreme importance for an individual and society, and that moral behavior is objective and not a matter of individual choice nor relative to society. The deepest of all our traditional moral convictions is that every person has intrinsic value. But it has been argued recently that all attempts to give morality and society a secular basis are bankrupt.[5]

When as individuals and as a society we chose a traditional morality, heavily influenced by the best in Greek culture and Christianity, the failure in secular philosophy did not matter for practical purposes. But today traditional morality is being discarded, and we find ourselves unable to reach a consensus for action or even a basis for rational discussion on such matters as war, armaments, the distribution of wealth, medical ethics, and criminal justice. We find ourselves increasingly in the time of the Judges, in which each does what is right in his or her own eyes.

The third pillar of the Enlightenment is belief in inevitable progress. Modern science and technology so improved life that they led to a belief

in progress, and in time to a belief in inevitable progress. People came
to believe that science coupled with the power of education would free
us from social bondage and vulnerability to nature. We are now faced
with our failure to eradicate such serious social and economic problems
as crime, pollution, poverty, racism, and war. We are becoming uneasy.
We are beginning to feel that we may able to surmount our difficulties,
but it is not inevitable that we shall. The optimism of inevitable progress
has become tarnished. There is an increasing recognition that evil is real
and that it cannot be removed merely by educational and social reform.
These difficulties do not mean that we are not to work and strive, but
they do mean that we shall have to do so without the assurance that we
are bound to succeed.

The fourth Enlightenment belief that is being questioned is the assumption that knowledge is inherently good. For centuries science has
been regarded as unquestionably a force for good. We are indeed immeasurably better off because of it. But our conviction that science is
intrinsically good and scientists inherently benefactors of humanity
arose largely because the morality that was part of the Greek and Christian heritage guided and restrained to some extent the uses to which
scientific knowledge was put.

Today we are becoming increasingly aware that there is no inherent
connection between knowledge and its beneficial use, with genetic engineering just beginning to open new possibilities of abuse, and with the
power of bombs and other destructive forces at hand. Scientists do not
control the uses to which their knowledge is put, and many even resist
taking any responsibility for its uses. Within a moral order which is basically Christian, there is some prospect for controlling the use of scientific knowledge, or at least of restraining its destructive uses. There are
perhaps some things which people impregnated with Christian attitudes
will not do. However, the Christian order has been widely discredited by
the Enlightenment. This has deprived us of one of the great resources
for controlling the use of scientific knowledge.

We now realize that many of the reasons for thinking that Christianity
is intellectually passé are unfounded. Recent work in the history of science has shown the indispensable contributions which Christianity made
to the origins of modern science. We also realize that there is no inevitable conflict between science and religion. Finally, there is an increasing
awareness that science does not explain everything.

In a postmodern world Christianity is intellectually relevant. It is relevant to the fundamental questions, Why does the world exist? and Why
does it have its present order, rather than another? It is relevant to the
discussion of the foundations of morality and society, especially on the

significance of human beings. The recognition that Christianity is relevant to our entire society, and relevant not only to the heart but to the mind as well, is a major change in our cultural situation.[6]

"Postmodern," as I have characterized it, should not be confused with the way the term is used in theology today. Theology before Hume and Kant is "premodern," and the nineteenth-century theological attempts to come to terms with Hume, Kant, and their successors is "modern." "Postmodern" refers to four broad streams in theology, each of which criticizes modern, or as it is sometimes called, liberal theology. First is confessional theology, whose primary debt is to Karl Barth's attacks after the First World War on the liberal theology of the nineteenth century. Second is the existentialist-hermeneutical stream, which is primarily indebted to Heidegger, but whose roots go back to Schleiermacher's reflections on hermeneutics. Third, there is a very recent, small, theological deconstructionist stream, which is indebted to Heidegger and to an extent Jacques Derrida. Fourth, process theology, as derived from A.N. Whitehead and Charles Hartshorne, has recently been characterized as postmodern.[7]

To avoid still another possible confusion, it is necessary to bear in mind the classification of periods used in physics. The main division is between classical science and modern science. "Classical science" (sometimes called "Newtonian science") refers to all science prior to the twentieth century. Modern science is usually said to have begun with Max Planck's discovery that energy is not emitted continuously but in discrete units or quanta. It is the development of *modern* science that has helped to undermine the *modern mentality* and to create the *postmodern* age.

II

Although the intellectual situation today is vastly more favorable than it has been in recent centuries, the dust from the collapse of the modern mentality has not yet settled so that everyone can see clearly that we are in a new situation. In addition, many of the principles of the modern mentality have deeply penetrated Christianity itself. We have incorporated within Christian theology so many of the attitudes and convictions of the modern mentality that we have become incapable of achieving "the full wealth of conviction" that followers of Christ ought to have, according to Paul in his letter to the Colossians (2:2, NEB). Well-educated Christian people today are generally very far from enjoying the *full* wealth of conviction that it is possible for them to enjoy with complete intellectual integrity. Christian theology has yet to become postmodern.

The way the modern mentality continues to affect theology is splendidly captured in an allegory presented by Basil Mitchell in the 1986 Nathaniel Taylor Lectures at Yale University. Mitchell pictures traditional Christian theology as a barge going down a river. On one side of the river are shoals, which represent the works of David Hume and Immanuel Kant which enshrine some of the most serious intellectual barriers to Christian belief in modern times. To avoid these shoals, theologians have either jettisoned some of their cargo (Christian claims) to lighten the barge and sail safely over them, or they have swung sharply to the other bank to remain premodern. That is, they have either become modern by getting rid of lots of traditional Christian claims, sometimes even the claims that God is Creator and Redeemer in Christ, or they retain the language of traditional Christianity but at the price of repudiating in various degrees the need to take into account knowledge from any other domain. For those who remain premodern, Christian doctrines can be affirmed and discussed as if Hume's and Kant's objections simply do not exist. The primary directions of Christian theology have been either to accept the principles and outlook of the modern world and to minimize the distinctive content and basis of Christian doctrines, or to retain Christian doctrines verbally while isolating them from the present day and in effect remaining premodern. Fideism neglects the long historical development of the Bible and of Christian doctrines. Their development has always involved human reasoning. Fideism, often without realizing it, treats some specific interpretation of Scripture or a particular doctrinal formulation as though it sprang directly from the mind of God into human minds, rather than also requiring the use of the best estimates of knowledge that existed in various historical eras. Unless various views of scriptural inspiration, human nature, and conceptions of God in Christian theology are open to critical examination—an examination which includes our best estimates of what we believe to be true in other domains of inquiry—we are unable to determine which among the various views of theologians and churches are the most adequate and best able to guide us today in our lives and our understanding of God.

The way forward is forward. The principles of the modern mentality enshrined in Hume and Kant do not form an impassable barrier which we must either accept or avoid. The actual situation is that the barrier they and others formed has collapsed. Theologians no longer need to labor within the tight, asphyxiating little world of the Enlightenment or to become premodern. But those who continue to jettison Christian doctrines to float the remaining cargo over the shallow waters of modern intellectual culture and those who continue to avoid modern intellectual culture do not realize this. They allow the thought of the modern world to determine the course to be followed by Christian theology. They remain prisoners of the modern mentality.

The situation has been splendidly described by the poet Christopher Fry in the very title of his play, *A Sleep of Prisoners*. We remain captives within a mental framework that has actually been broken. We are like prisoners who could walk out of a prison because all that would enclose us has been burst open, but we remain inside because we are asleep. Christopher Fry, however, tells us that this is the time to wake up:

> The human heart can go to the lengths of God.
> Dark and cold we may be, but this
> Is no winter now. The frozen misery
> Of centuries breaks, cracks, begins to move,
> The thunder is the thunder of the floes,
> The thaw, the flood, the upstart Spring.
> Thank God our time is now when wrong
> Comes up to face us everywhere,
> Never to leave us till we take
> The longest stride of soul men ever took.
> Affairs are now soul size.
> The enterprise
> Is exploration into God.[8]

The nearness of the kingdom of God is evident not because things are getting better and better but because the issues and decisions to be made are becoming clearer and clearer, and therefore harder and harder to evade. This is how the situation becomes "soul size," however vast and daunting the challenges to human survival may be.

Are the Christian churches ready to meet the challenge? They have within their heritage immensely powerful ideas, not to mention a living Lord. But to a large extent the churches with strong theological traditions suffer from theological amnesia because they have either jettisoned so much or they have so isolated Christian theology within a premodern outlook that they have forgotten how to think theologically. With the demise of the modern mentality, however, there is no need to choose between jettisoning basic Christian convictions and retreating into fideism. A culture that is increasingly free of the assumptions of the Enlightenment view of science, religion, morality, and society is a culture that is increasingly free of assumptions that prevent one from coming to an appreciation of the intellectual strength of Christianity. A fresh evaluation, such as I shall make of what science and philosophy today reveal about the natural world, when combined with an account of how each of us may have access to the grace of God, may persuade Christians themselves of the intellectual viability of Christianity. It must, however, not be overlooked in the accounts of what the natural world shows us and how we may have access to God's grace, which make up the bulk of the argument of this book, that it is only when people find themselves actually receiving God's grace and interacting with God that their minds and hearts achieve the full assurance of conviction in the truth of Christianity. It takes not only thinking but also action to achieve conviction.

III

One aspect of current intellectual culture is unfavorable to my project. As we enter a postmodern or post-Enlightenment world many people, including theologians, are becoming distressed by the plurality of worldviews. Many have been driven to relativism by the collapse of the Enlightenment's confidence in the power of reason to provide foundations for our truth-claims and to achieve finality in our search for truth in the various disciplines. Much of the distress concerning pluralism and relativism which is voiced today springs from a crisis in the secular mentality of modern Western culture, not from a crisis within Christianity itself. The Enlightenment had already discarded Christianity and left it outside the main intellectual stream. For some time Christianity has been at best a stepchild in our universities and research centers, irrelevant to their inquiries, and explicitly excluded from them in Marxist countries. But the crisis within Western culture caused by a loss of confidence in the Enlightenment's ideals—a change which enables us better to exhibit Christianity's intellectual strength—has produced an intellectual culture whose preoccupation with pluralism and relativism makes it inattentive to that exhibition. There is such a widespread acquiescence toward pluralism and relativism in the intellectual culture at large that even many church people would be startled by my claim that the ultimate reason to go to church is because Christianity is true.

There are two ways to deal with relativism. One is to examine and refute in detail all the grounds put forward for relativism in our pluralistic situation and thus to show that we can in principle succeed in our search for truth. This would show the possibility of finding truth in various domains, but it would still leave us with the task of showing the grounds for Christian claims. Another way to proceed is actually to give a case for the truth of Christian beliefs without directly examining and refuting the various reasons people have today for becoming relativists.

I shall follow the second course because many people in Western culture continue to evaluate Christianity (and religion in general) with the assumptions of the Enlightenment. Many people both in the West and among the Western-educated in Asia and Africa still do not know of the developments in science and philosophy which render those assumptions untenable. Western culture at large is still in the process of moving away from those assumptions. As we continue to do so, the fact that there is a plurality of worldviews and religions will continue to drive some people toward relativism. But if we can exhibit the intellectual strength of Christianity, we can render a service both to those who are still captives of the assumptions of the Enlightenment and think that belief in God as Creator and Redeemer in Christ is impossible for an educated mind and to those who are free of those assumptions but are now adrift. An exhibition of its intellectual strength can enable us to live in a postmodern world and to hold Christian claims with all our heart and with our mind persuaded of their truth. My case is directed then both to those still troubled in various degrees by the assumptions of the Enlightenment and to those who are disillusioned with them, but who feel defenseless before the plurality of worldviews and religions and thus do not know how to avoid relativism.

The situation for the Christian religion is both better and worse than it is for other subjects, such as physics and mathematics. On the one hand, unlike all other attempts to determine what is true, our religion is anchored in faith. Through faith God gives access and knowledge of Godself which the study of the natural world, history, and human nature do not of themselves yield (even though significant traces of God are to be found in all of these domains).

Religion is neither a theory nor a hypothetical speculation in search of verification but actual interaction with a reality. Faith is above all to consent to the good that God has in store for us. To perceive that good and to say "yes" to it opens us to contact with God. We experience God's presence. With that relation to God we are able to recognize the traces of God in nature, history, and human experience. Neither in physics nor in mathematics, for example, are we invited to receive a good, to commit ourselves to its realization, and in that realization to find our faith confirmed. In physics and mathematics there is no possibility of knowledge through this kind of faith (even though both disciplines make assumptions and so require the exercise of some other kind of faith, as we shall see in Chapter Seven).

On the other hand, because Christianity is a faith, Christian claims are vulnerable. People without faith lack awareness of God and thus misunderstand the grounds for what Christians hold to be true. Because they do not have contact with God, for them faith is mere credulity. Their examination of the ground for Christian claims lacks an essential ingredient and without it they quite naturally conclude from their examination of nature, history, and human nature that Christian claims are not sufficiently warranted by the hints of God they give. A major concern of the book will be to explain the nature of faith and how it affects the way we assess the grounds for Christian claims. This explanation should benefit both believers and nonbelievers.

Those of us educated in a modern university—whether we are believers or nonbelievers—are prone to ignore or dismiss beliefs based on faith. We have been taught that we must not believe what is not warranted by evidence. Through the critical study of various disciplines, our minds become so shaped or formed that this injunction is internalized. We almost automatically ask of any claim, What are its grounds? How good are they? To be told that the ground for a claim is largely faith is the same as to be told that the claim is virtually groundless. To believe it would be to be guilty of credulity. Because they rely so largely on faith, educated Christians often find themselves wondering whether their commitment to the Christian faith without compelling evidence is not after all credulity.

They need to learn more about the relation of faith to evidence in Christianity. This is presented very simply but accurately by Austin Farrer.[9] He tells us that the notion of "God," just like that of "mother," is a loaded term: it contains built-in attitudes. He compares the situation of an orphan considering the possibility that his or her mother is alive to that of one considering the possibility of God.

For the child, to think of a possible mother is to experiment in having a mother; to try filial existence. The experiment takes place in the realms of the imagination, but it is real enough to the heart. And similarly to think of a possible God is to experiment in having God. The attitude of creature to Creator, of doomed mortal to immortal saviour, it built into the very idea. The heart goes out to God, even to a possible God.[10]

Farrer tells us that he does not know whether we should call this attitude faith because it does not represent a commitment, since we realize that the thought of an existing God is a contested notion. He suggests that it should be called "initial faith," and he also refers to it as the "faith-attitude." Although the thought of God is a contested notion, nonetheless it is not like the figure in a dead mythology. Our minds are divided but also engaged:

I say, "There is a God," and a piece of my heart goes with it; I go on "But then . . ." and my attitude swings into the opposite. Which of my thoughts, which of my attitudes, is I, or speaks for me? It is notorious that I may be deceived in thinking myself committed in one direction, when I am really committed in another. But so long as I know very well that I am not committed, I do not think of claiming to have faith. Yet the faith-attitude is there, if it is no more than one posture among several which I try by turns. To have faith in the full sense, I do not need to bring it from somewhere else, and apply it to the idea; all I need to do is to let it have its way, and subdue its rivals.[11]

The way to subdue rivals is by considering nature, history, human nature, and the gospel story. But one has to *appreciate* the notion of deity if the evidence for deity is to be apprehended in nature, history, human nature, and the gospel story. "Without the readiness of [initial] faith, the evidence of God will not be accepted, or will not convince. . . . [Initial] faith is a subjective condition favourable to the reception of the evidence."[12]

Farrer is concerned not only with initial faith but with a full faith and, in his examination of it, he reveals another aspect of his understanding of the relation of faith to evidence. In the short essay "On Credulity"[13] he describes four domains that give access to four kinds of facts or truths. These differ as facts or truths only because our access to them differs. The first domain is that of specialized studies. We limit our inquiry, for example, to the measurable dimensions of physical processes or to the economic aspects of human behavior. When we do this, we recognize that we are dealing with abstractions; but the abstractions give us access to some facts.

In the second domain we deal with actual people and things. There is a difference between interacting with individual persons and dealing with the abstractions of our specializations, which study only aspects of them. All specializations taken together do not have the same impact on us or yield the same knowledge as does interacting with actual individuals.

The third and fourth domains, unlike the first two, include values and valuation. We can engage in abstract study and even interact with actual people and things without raising the question of whether the facts revealed are to be approved or deplored, or whether a person is, let us say, sincere or perverse. The domain of value is treated by a specialization: ethics. Just as in the first domain, here too we think abstractly. But by observing the limitations of abstract thinking we have access to various truths about such things as the nature of obligation and moral rules, or at least we hope to. The fourth area is religion. As in ethics, we are concerned with values and valuation, but not abstractly. We deal with our entire person interacting with real beings. If we are willing to consider Christianity, we may find that

part of our own minds [yields to] the inexorable truth that we are rebellious creatures under the eye of our Creator, and that our Creator has come upon us in Christ. Credulity, here, is the crime of pretending to believe that there is any way out of this situation but one—to reconcile ourselves to the truth of our nature, which demands our submission to the God who made us.[14]

Of this domain Farrer writes,

Now when the New Testament writers said that in Christ they met the truth, they meant that in him they recognized what was demanding admittance through this door [the fourth domain]. It is of no use, of course, for Christians to pretend that on this ground everybody is bound to agree with them straight away, but anyhow on this ground their position is immensely strong and they need fear no antagonist. There is no constraint, no embarrassment here; here we can take on all comers.[15]

Farrer is describing the effects on the individual of encountering Christ. The question is whether an individual person is willing to expose himself or herself to a self-examination in the light of what is said about Christ.

It is very easy to avoid such self-examination. All that a person needs to say is "Why should I examine myself in this light?" with the intention of evading the general category of evaluation. This question has to be answered solely in terms of truths accessible through the first and second domains. One then has excluded from consideration the very domains which give access to the discipline of ethics and the factors that move a person to love Christ and to have faith in him. But it is not difficult to specify a procedure that enables one to experience the impact of Christ on oneself. Anyone can open his or her heart, just as anyone can close it.

We sometimes use the word "heart" to refer to being sensitive to another person's plight. "Have a heart!" we say when we mean, "Be merciful!" Another use of the word is found in Jesus' remark, "Where your treasure is, there will your heart be also" (Matt. 6:21). This use refers to what we value and seek to possess because of the good it will do and be for us. It is related to the human quest for life. The intellect is involved in this quest but what is at stake is our own person: what we are, what we ought to be, what we may become, what we may hope for. It is this use of the term "heart" that I am employing. To open the heart is to allow what is in the domain of value to affect us. With an open heart we may find in Christ and in the promises of God the good that we need and seek. But without an open heart we shall not.

Frequently we use the intellect to solve problems or to seek knowledge without the questions of the heart arising. We quite properly exclude considerations of the heart when we deal with questions of the properties of a physical process or the economic factors in currency exchange rates (truths of the first domain). It is even quite proper to restrain, though not utterly to exclude, questions of the heart when we consider the nature of obligation or the role of moral rules (truths of the third domain). When we interact with people or things (truths of the second domain), we can and do close our hearts. Sometimes this is proper as, for example, in considering whether a person is worthy of trust. Finally, we can also quite easily avoid Christ's impact on us as judge and redeemer by keeping in check the human search for what is valuable and what gives life significance.

Belief, then, is not necessarily a result of credulity and nonbelief necessarily the result of a proper respect for the principle that evidence must warrant truth-claims. A prior question is whether our hearts are open or closed to religious matters. One whose heart is not open might agree that the existence of the universe poses a real question and that it might be a reason to say the world is created. But since it does not compel us to say that it is created, and since religion is irrelevant to scientific progress, the question of why the universe exists is dropped. Nature cannot be a witness to God's existence and goodness to a person with a closed heart. The same is true with everything that contributes to belief. To the closed heart every indication of God in nature, history, and human nature are thought to be insufficient to establish God's existence or irrelevant to scientific progress, and Christ is not given admittance. *How we seek*—with an open or a closed heart—is crucial.

Assuming that we have not only opened our hearts to the impact of Christ but have also become Christians, we look at nature, history, and our own lives for manifestations of God because we do not want to believe what evidence does not warrant. But when we have exposed ourselves to Christ, credulity is the pretense of believing that our lives have validity without God:

Unless our minds in fact function in these two ways: unless we sometimes see God as truth, and evasion of him as credulity, at other times the proved facts of the special sciences as truth, and the outrunning of them as credulity—unless this is so, we are not confronted with the specifically religious problem of truth.[16]

It is because our minds function in *two* ways that a believer investigates scientific and philosophical questions that are relevant to Christian claims.

The believer also considers historical questions, since "we must have no bogus history."[17] But the investigation is done in a particular way. Farrer points out that many historians limit their search to truths of the first and second domains (specialized and without the dimension of value). Such people, he says, are not going to see truths of the fourth domain breaking out through the façade of history because they have discounted them from the start.

But the historian whose mind is open to the fourth type of truth, and who has some awareness of the abyss of divine being which underlies his own existence, may meet a voice and visitant out of that abyss, when he weighs the strange history of the year 30 as it is mirrored in the witness of those who most intimately responded to it.[18]

In less dramatic language, a person who has exposed himself or herself to valuation by Christ and who engages in intellectual work in science, philosophy, or history with a concern for Christian truth is a person with faith seeking understanding. He or she is seeking to relate religious truths to which there is a commitment to truths in other domains. That is a form of gaining confirmation, but it is not to be understood as the search for evidence that will necessarily move anyone regardless of the condition of their heart. Yet Christian commitment is not a matter of the heart only, for a commitment can be given up should the mind not be convinced of the truth of Christianity from an examination of nature, history, human nature, and the gospel.

This understanding of the relation of faith to evidence differs from the usual philosophical examination of the grounds for belief in God. Philosophers of religion (at least in the English-speaking world) examine the grounds for theism. Theism is not an actual religion but an abstraction. It is what Christians, Jews, and Muslims are said to share: belief in one God, who is all-powerful, all-knowing, and good. Even when they marshall a favorable case for the existence of a benevolent God, as has been attempted more frequently in recent years, there is nonetheless a gap between the case for theism and the beliefs of an actual practicing religion.[19] With this approach, it is easy to regard faith as filling the gap between a warranted case for theism and an unwarranted case for Christianity (or Judaism or Islam). Since belief in a benevolent God is warranted, to have faith in the specific claims of an actual religion seems a reasonable act for those who choose to exercise it.[20]

This interpretation of faith is analogous to a comedian's remark, "I have a marvelous gun. It shoots bullets for eight miles and throws rocks the rest of the way." In the typical examination by philosophers of religion of the grounds for religious belief, faith is a pale substitute for evidence. Examining the abstraction theism, rather than an actual religion, makes it easy to characterize faith in this way.

On Farrer's approach, faith is a response to the good promised to us by God, preeminently in Christ. In that response, we interact with God and begin to receive that good. We do not move from the evidence we can muster for theism to an actual religion by a leap of faith, understood as a substitute for evidence. On the contrary, it is with an "initial faith" or with a full faith (each of which usually develops through interaction with a believing community) that we look critically at nature, history, human nature, and Scripture. There is thus no "gap" to be closed by "faith" after we have engaged in critical study.

Faith, then, is an essential but not the only ingredient in making Christian claims. Reason is used, not only to examine the grounds for Christian claims but also to understand them better. Those with faith seek understanding. This ancient formula has been interpreted in various ways, but every interpretation has recognized that we are to relate Christian claims to our best estimate of what we believe to be true of the events of history and to the workings of nature and the human mind. It is from this interaction of "faith and knowledge," as it is called, that Christian theology as a discipline of inquiry emerged in the earliest centuries of the Christian religion. This search for understanding has sometimes led to conflicts between various formulations of Christian theology and what we believe to be true in other areas of inquiry, and it has led to mistakes as well. For example, it was once thought by some theologians that Christianity had a vital stake in the existence of innate truths. That is, they thought that Christianity was committed to the view that some general principles of logic and some moral truths are imprinted in the human mind. When John Locke in his celebrated *An Essay Concerning Human Understanding* (1690) denied the existence of innate truths and claimed that all knowledge was based on experience, Bishop Stillingfleet of Banbury unleashed a series of bitter denunciations. The good bishop was apparently mistaken. Most Christians today read Locke's denial of innate truths without the slightest apprehension.

To relate our faith to knowledge always runs the risk of making mistakes, but it is necessary. Faith is a distinctive way to gain access to God, but it is not completely separable from other ways of knowing. For example, Jesus was a historical person and what he did and said is vital to us. We know enough about the transmission of historical information to know that errors can be made and that we can easily misinterpret documents from earlier periods. We thus need to know how to judge the authenticity of ancient texts and to develop principles for the interpretation of texts. So we employ various disciplines because we do not want any bogus history as part of our faith and because we want to understand the Bible better.

IV

For an increasing number of people today, the chief obstacle to being fully convinced of the truth of Christianity is not a scientific view of the world that has no room at all for religion but the existence of rival religions. It seems to them that because there are so many religions, it is not possible to make exclusive claims about the truth of any religion. To show the intellectual viability of Christianity vis-à-vis the residue of the Enlightenment is not enough to satisfy their minds of its truth. It is therefore necessary to address this question.

My approach is to develop a theology in which the reality of other religions is taken into account, a Christian theology of other faiths. This differs from the discipline of history of religions, in which an understanding of a religion from the inside is sought. Such is certainly useful and necessary. But as a Christian believer one must go further and seek to learn how another religion fits into the economy of God as Christians understand God's nature and activities. A Christian theology of other faiths seeks to understand another faith from a Christian point of view.

This task cannot be completed since we do not know God's providence fully. The apostle Paul could not fully understand the role those people of Israel who did not receive Jesus as the Messiah were to play in God's providence. He believed that it would be manifest some time in the future. So too we must live with at best only partial knowledge. But if it can be shown that significant knowledge of Christ's saving work is accessible to people of various faiths or of no faith at all, we may continue firmly to believe that, on the one hand, Christ is the Savior of the world and, on the other hand, not condemn another faith or person simply because they are not explicitly or fully Christian.

V

Because the argument will proceed in stages and cover a large diversity of material, an overview of its main stages may be useful. We shall begin with a discussion of the Enlightenment view of modern science and the way it pitted science and religion against one another. This outlook was so persuasive that the immense contribution of Christianity to the rise of modern science has only recently been realized and the picture of science and religion as essentially and intrinsically hostile to one another has been shown to be false. This residue of the Enlightenment is so strong that there is a pervasive opinion in our culture that religion is really outdated and that it hangs on merely because of ignorance, human weakness, and the need of comfort. This prejudice must be cleared away before we can consider the recent developments in philosophy and science which raise questions that point us in the direction of God. Philosophy and science today actually show us that whether the universe is dependent or not is philosophically and scientifically an open question. Our best knowledge from these two fields instead of closing off the possibility of God, as the Enlightenment thought, actually shows the possibility of God. (This is done in Chapters One through Four.)

Once the possibility of God's existence has been raised, we may turn to our need for God, so that the question of the status of the universe is seen to be an important and even urgent human question and not a mere speculative issue (Chapter Five).

The possibility of God and even the need for God do not of themselves produce conviction of the reality of God. But they do lead a rational person to seek God. Such a search, because it is honest, requires a consideration of the teachings of the Bible. Its meaning is opaque, however, unless we overcome the barriers to understanding which are caused by our own personality. We take it for granted that we must prepare ourselves to appreciate works of art or to do chemistry, but we all too often fail to realize that to have faith and to know God's presence also requires extensive and diligent preparation. With the proper preparation, it is possible for a person to experience divine grace and to come to faith (Chapter Six).

The Enlightenment's failure to provide a foundation for ethics and society has left us with no way to counter the widespread attitude that values are mere expressions of personal preferences. This is in effect to deny the reality of good and evil. In our examination of the nature of faith, their reality and our need for a Redeemer will become apparent (also in Chapter Six).

The nature of faith has been greatly misrepresented both by Christian theologians, especially since the Reformation, and by nonbelievers. It has frequently been put into opposition with reason, or below reason, instead of above reason. Although its truths cannot be reached by reason alone, nonetheless they illumine the intellect. Otherwise faith would be blind. A narrow view of reason and the failure to realize that faith and naked intellect belong to different contexts (or orders) are largely responsible for these misconceptions. Both the reasonableness of faith and the relation of reason to divine revelation are described at length (Chapters Seven and Eight).

One of the most serious clashes between the modern mentality and Christianity has been over the picture presented by the Bible of God creating and sustaining the universe, and bringing about events in history and individual lives. It has frequently been said that divine agency is inconsistent with the picture of the universe and history presented by science. A careful examination shows that there is no incompatibility between divine agency and a scientific understanding of the universe (Chapter Nine).

With the recovery of some of the riches of the Christian faith, made possible by freedom from the narrow boundaries of the modern mentality, we are able to discern vital ties between Christ as the prime mediator between us and God and other religious faiths. As long as we are constrained by the modern mentality, we will not achieve a sufficiently deep understanding of Christianity to be able to find God, as revealed in Christ, present in other religions. But God is revealed there in surprising ways. A Christian theology of other faiths will in turn increase our confidence in the truth of Christianity by bringing out features of the Christian faith which are not widely known or appreciated, especially by Christians who are confined by the modern mentality or who have returned to the shelter of a premodern mentality (Chapters Ten and Eleven).

In summary, the core of the argument is (1) that the natural world's existence and order point to the possibility of God; (2) that our own needs, unless deliberately restrained, lead us to search for what is ultimate; and (3) that conviction concerning the reality of God comes from the actual experience of divine grace, frequently made possible through the witness of the Bible and a believing community, but that such experience of divine grace is usually easily overlooked.

I would not dare embark on this ambitious project were it not for a comment by Basil Mitchell. When I expressed my admiration for his book on ethics (*Morality: Religious and Secular*) he said, "I don't think of writing a book as if it were the last word on a subject. I seek only to further the discussion." It is in that spirit that this book is offered, sustained, as was Mitchell's book, by a confidence in the intellectual strength of the Christian faith.

PART I

The Book of Nature

Chapter One

The Christian Roots of Modern Science and Christianity's Bad Image

Herbert Butterfield in the preface of his classic work, *The Origins of Modern Science,* states that the rise of science in the late sixteenth and early seventeenth centuries is the most important event in Western history since the rise of Christianity itself. Compared to the rise of science, the Renaissance and Reformation are episodes, mere internal rearrangements within the system of Western Christianity. Science changed the character of our mental operations, even in the conduct of the nonmaterial sciences, transformed the diagram of the physical universe, and now dominates our daily life by its applications. Every area of the world is now deeply affected by the spread of an industrial order made possible by our sciences; the immense destructive power of modern weapons is a dominant factor in national and international politics and economics.[1]

I

For many people science stands for rationality, evidence, knowledge, enlightenment. Religion, in contrast, stands for backwardness, conservism, superstition, authoritarianism, and is regarded as the enemy and rival of science. These are extreme characterizations, but however much the extremes are toned down, the general impression is that some hostility, some incompatibility, some rivalry between religion and science exists.

Starting in 1934 with three seminal articles by Michael B. Foster,[2] and with increasing tempo during the past twenty years, a study of the history of science has radically changed the picture of the relation between Christianity and science. We have begun to realize that for its very birth science owed a great deal to Christianity. Rather than being a rival, Christianity is one of the major contributors to its rise. Yet just the opposite picture has been dominant for more than two hundred years. So let us briefly point out some of the ways Christianity contributed to the rise of science and the deep harmony between them, and then explain how the opposite picture—one of essential incompatibility—developed and why it continues to dominate the public mind, even among the highly educated.

The rise of science is one of the great puzzles of history. We take its existence for granted, yet it is a very recent phenomenon. There have been several great civilizations, with highly organized cities, impressive achievements in poetry, drama and politics, yet nothing that we would call science developed in them. There was technical skill, for example, in metal work, ceramics, and perfume making, but no detailed understanding of the behavior of matter expressed in mathematical terms. There was impressive observation and recording of the stars, but no comprehensive understanding of their motions.

Classical science began to take a clear shape in Europe in the late sixteenth century. The result of the work of many individuals, it is a breathtaking achievement that makes Western civilization unique and has deeply affected every other extant civilization. The vision of the universe and the power it gives us are so startling that historians have been forced to ask, Why did science not arise in ancient India, Egypt, China, or Greece, especially in Greece? After all ancient Greece had many of the ideas we have used in our science, and the contribution of the Greeks was essential to the rise of science. Why did we succeed where they failed? Investigation of this and other questions have changed our estimate of the relation of Christianity and science. The older picture of Christianity as the implacable enemy of science has begun to give way because it has been increasingly recognized that Christianity was a major factor, perhaps an essential ingredient in the rise of science. Many civilizations had some of the ingredients that seem to be necessary for the rise of science. For example, they had sufficient technology to make the apparatus needed for elementary experiments; they had sufficient mathematics for measurement and calculation. But what they did not have was a set of attitudes toward the material world, a set of attitudes which are vital for the development of science. Christianity had those attitudes. Some of those attitudes were native to Christianity itself; some of them Christianity found in the ancient Greeks. But Christianity preserved those insights. More and more it seems that it was these attitudes, which were part of the mental furniture of the people of Christian Europe, including a few geniuses, which enabled western Europe to create what no other culture has ever created—science.

Christianity was the bearer of fundamental attitudes and convictions that helped people unlock the secrets of nature and develop hitherto unprecedented means to new knowledge. First, it is essential to be interested in the material world. Christians have a strong "other worldly" sense, that is, they believe that the entire universe depends for its existence on a perfect being, but they also believe that nature is good, or more specifically that matter is good. This has not always been the case. There is an ambivalent attitude toward matter in much of ancient Greek thought, and the Gnosticism of the early Christian era considered matter to be evil. But Genesis 1 makes it abundantly clear that the creation is good. However much our world is marred by sin, the physical universe is innocent. It is the human will, not the natural world, which is at fault.

Second, Christians believe that nature is orderly; that it behaves in a consistent and rational way. If something measures a certain size one day, it will be the same size the next. If a liquid freezes at a particular temperature, liquid of the same kind will always freeze at that temperature. Nature is orderly because it is created by a good and rational God.

Ancient Greek thought, most of which also stressed that nature is orderly, was significantly modified by Christianity. For Christians nature's order, though regular, does not have to be the way it is. It could have been ordered differently by God. Its actual order is just one possible order out of many. This led to the gradual realization that we could not just think up a rational blueprint and then say that because it is rational nature has to be that way. Because there is more than one possible rational order, we have to examine nature closely to discover what order is actually in operation. Ancient Greek thought assumed that a single rational natural order could be discovered by sheer thought—or at least mostly by thought. Nature must be that way in spite of the fact that it might appear to be different. The Greeks failed to respect observed fact as having authority. Even Aristotle who did respect observed fact, especially in biology, did not recognize the hallmark of modern science, quantitative fact. But Christianity, with its notion of a personal God as Creator, whose wisdom is reflected in the created order but not bounded by it, after much struggle in the Middle Ages to free itself from Greek rationalism, came to emphasize that the order we observe depends on the choice of an intelligence. We have to experiment, measure, observe to determine as best we can what order our universe actually has and to revise our theories in light of observed facts. Christianity with its conviction of a wise and personal God encourages empirical science, and is more harmonious with empirical science than is much of Greek rationalism. The operations of nature resemble the work of an artist more than that of an engineer or a craftsman. We cannot predict what a character in a novel will do because the actions of characters are not necessary, i.e., deducible from previous actions. But a character's actions will not be arbitrary either. Unexpected actions will occur but they will "make sense" in terms of the situations and the various other personalities involved in the story. Likewise, the Christian understanding of God as rational encourages a search for order in nature but an order that is not necessary. Rather, it is contingent, that is, dependent on the action of a wise God who could have created a quite different, yet orderly, universe.

Third, science is only possible if we think that nature can be understood by the human mind. Christians believe that God's creation can be understood to a significant extent. A rational God does not create an irrational universe. So an order is there to be found. In addition, it is part of our God-given vocation to find as much of that order as we can and to praise God for the wonders of creation. Johann Kepler (1571–1630), one of the pioneering giants of modern science, and Francis Bacon (1561–1626), the most influential proponents of the importance and value of science, both stressed this religious motive for doing science. It is our divinely given vocation to render praise to God by achieving a sounder understanding of God's handiwork. This they passionately believed and advocated.

Finally, the results of our investigations are to be shared. Science is above all a communal affair. Christians in the seventeenth century were aflame with the idea that we can serve one another with a better knowledge of nature. The church was the bearer of the truth which led to heaven and proclaimed it to all. A knowledge of nature would enable us to improve human life on earth. For example, Christian laypeople felt it their responsibility to study nature and so improve medicine, thereby reducing pain and saving life. Bacon went so far as to say that it was our task to restore creation to its prefallen state by the application of knowledge.[3] The use of our talents in the study of nature and the application of our knowledge are, Bacon said, involved in the process of our redemption and sanctification.

The presence of these and other attitudes together in one culture is apparently unique. Ancient Greek thought was vital for the development of our science, and in the Middle Ages Christianity was the heir, preserver, and developer of Greek thought. In spite of severe tensions, there was enough harmony for Christianity to receive, modify, and finally absorb much of Greek thought and infuse it with its own native convictions into a workable, consistent outlook. A famous text, frequently quoted in the Middle Ages, symbolizes this receptivity: "But thou hast arranged all things by measure and number and weight" (Wisdom of Solomon 11:20). Christianity was able to absorb the mathematical approach to nature which was favored by the Pythagoreans and Archimedes, thinkers who deeply influenced the great scientific pioneers Kepler and Galileo (1564–1642). Christianity, by absorbing so much of Greek thought, provided the environment in which a few people of genius half-created and half-stumbled onto what we now call classical science.

The positive role played by Christianity in the origins of classical science has only very recently been recognized in the academic community, but even there, eminent scientists can be found who still assert the earlier belief that the effect of Christianity on science was wholly negative.[4] It is still not generally known to most educated people nor to those responsible for educating people nor to many who disseminate ideas. But it is making headway and is increasingly recognized by historians of science. It is now to be found in textbooks such as Ian Barbour's *Issues in Science and Religion* and White and Shapiro's *The Emergence of Liberal Humanism*. One of Michael Foster's pioneering essays in *Mind* (1934) has recently been reprinted in an anthology used by the Open University in Britain, *Science and Religious Belief*, edited by C. A. Russell.

The main point for our purposes is that a major barrier to taking Christianity seriously has been weakened. Christianity has long been discredited on the grounds that it has been injurious to the development of science because of its restrictive and oppressive attitudes toward the discoveries of classical science. But recent historical work has shown Christianity's vital positive contribution to its rise.

II

Nonetheless, we must admit in all honesty that Christianity was also restrictive. And its restrictiveness gives plausibility to the picture of a fundamental antagonism between Christianity and science. Part of the restrictiveness was due to Aristotelianism. Aristotle's view of the heavens and his entire theory of motion stood in the way of the rise of science. Much of Aristotle's thought had become part of Christian thinking. It took some hard thinking on the part of some Christians, such as Galileo and Descartes, to separate what was essential to Christianity from the views of Aristotle. And many Christians were prejudiced against the new science largely because of their Aristotelianism. But this mixture of Christianity and Aristotle does not explain the powerful, deep, and widespread view in Western society that science and religion are foes, nor the widespread view that Christianity is really an outworn creed which opposed the enlightenment offered by science. To explain this we need to turn to the trial of Galileo by a special commission appointed by Pope Urban VIII.

In 1633, after twenty years of increasing tension, Galileo was tried for heresy and forced to recant, and the Copernican or heliocentric hypothesis that the earth goes around the sun was condemned. The condemnation of the Copernican hypothesis did not come about, however, because of an inherent conflict between science and religion. As we shall see, it is impossible to account for the trial of Galileo and the condemnation of the Copernican hypothesis in terms of an inherent clash between religion and science over the heliocentric hypothesis.

It has frequently been said that there was such a clash because the new Copernican theory removed the earth from the center of the universe. As Sir James Jeans, a major physicist, put it in his *Physics and Philosophy* (1936) "his home was not the majestic fixed centre of the universe round which all else had to revolve."[5] The theory seemed to reduce people's importance. But this is untrue, however often it is repeated in textbooks and by eminent people like Jeans. In Aristotle the earth is indeed the center of the universe, but it is also the lowest place in the universe. Everything above the earth is greatly superior, in fact made of a superior kind of matter. To be at the center is no honor. It is to be at the bottom. Yet book after book, even today, says that Copernicus upset Christianity by displacing the earth from the center of the universe.[6]

The problems introduced by the new astronomy, and later by the new mechanistic physics are far more subtle and far-reaching, as we shall see, than this simple-minded approach reveals. I only mention this frequently repeated mistake to suggest that the trial of Galileo was not caused by Copernicus' theory that the sun is the center of the universe. The trial was indeed shameful, as the article on Galileo in *The New Catholic Encyclopedia* freely admits. It brought credit neither to the Catholic Church nor to Galileo. It was a major event at the time; it did, for example, cause Descartes to withhold publication of his new cosmology. Still, it was the way Galileo's trial was used in the next century by the French *philosophes,* or social critics, that stamped it so deeply and firmly in the Western mind as evidence of an inherent conflict between Christianity and science. The *philosophes,* a group which included Voltaire, claimed that the trial was a prime example of Christianity's opposition to reason and of the church's opposition to free inquiry, and an attempt by the church to preserve its privileges. They pictured Christianity as essentially oppressive, authoritarian, and superstitious; science as the unveiler of truth; and Galileo as a humble, honest, noble servant of humanity. This incorrect picture, created in the eighteenth century, has proved to have great endurance in the academic community and among Marxists.[7]

The *philosophes* used the trial for political propaganda against the power and wealth of the ruling classes and the Roman Church in eighteenth century France. They were political reformers, captivated by the idea of creating a heaven on earth. Newtonian mechanics convinced them that because physical nature could be understood, so too could human nature and society. We could discover the laws by which the human mind and society operate. Then, through a scientific education, we could produce a better world—perhaps even utopia. The only things which stood in the way were the tyranny of despotic rulers and their supporters, which included the nobility and the Roman Catholic Church. The church was especially an enemy because of its doctrine of original sin, which seemed to imply that progress was impossible, and because its "superstitions" darkened people's minds. The *philosophes* claimed that the church and the nobility, each with their vast holdings of land, conspired to keep the people in ignorance so that they could be ruled more easily. The trial of Galileo was interpreted to support their opposition to the church. In their hands it was elevated into a symbol of the tyranny of the church—a symbol of Christianity's attempt to suppress the new light dawning through the labors of science. The trial was portrayed as representing the eternal conflict between darkness and light.[8]

The *philosophes'* picture of Christianity as the inherent opponent of progress was adopted in the next century by Karl Marx. He continued the crusade against religion in the name of science. Science for him included not only physics and the new Darwinism, but also his own laws of history and society. Just as Newton had found the laws of motion, and Darwin the laws of biological evolution, Marx had found the scientific laws of history and society. Progress was now seen to be inevitable, and religion was a barrier to and an opponent of scientific and human progress which had to be and would be removed.

What is the truth about the trial of Galileo? Scholars have gone over the data again and again. There are still many unanswered questions, but it does seem clear that there was no fundamental clash between Christianity and the theory that the universe revolves around the sun.

Arthur Koestler in his outstanding popular history of science, *The Sleepwalkers,* admits that he is no more capable than anyone else of writing an objective history of the trial. Before he discusses it, he openly states his biases. "Among my earliest and most vivid impressions of History was the wholesale roasting alive of heretics by the Spanish Inquisition, which could hardly inspire tender feelings towards that establishment."[9] Koestler also admits that he finds the personality of Galileo equally unattractive, partly because of his insufferable behavior toward Kepler, the only major astronomer who at some risk supported him publicly at an important time.

Koestler continues,

It seems to me, then, that insofar as bias enters into this narrative, it is not based on affection for either party in the conflict, but on resentment that the conflict did occur at all ... It is my conviction that the conflict between Church and Galileo (or Copernicus) was not inevitable; that it was not in the nature of a fatal collision between opposite philosophies of existence, which was bound to occur sooner or later, but rather a clash of individual temperaments aggravated by unlucky coincidences. In other words, I believe the idea that Galileo's trial was a kind of Greek tragedy, a showdown between "blind faith" and "enlightened reason," to be naively erroneous.[10]

A series of accidents and incompatible personalities led to a miserable clash—and the stronger party won. But it has been made to appear that Christianity is an opponent of science and that there is an inherent conflict between science and Christianity. This became a cornerstone of modern culture, which still haunts us today and is officially sponsored by Marxist governments.

The relations of Galileo to the Roman Catholic Church are very complex and there is no need to go into them deeply here. But a few of the major points will help substantiate and illuminate the interpretation I have given to the controversy and its significance. Copernicus' book, *On the Revolution of the Celestial Spheres,* was published in 1543 (the year he died). It attracted very little attention, partly because it was unreadable and partly because, as he himself recognized, the orbits he assigned to the planets were hopelessly inadequate, even with the retention of some of Ptolemy's epicycles. But the main reason was that it contained a disclaimer in the preface (added by Osiander) to the effect that he had placed the sun at the center of the universe only for the ease of making mathematical calculations. It was not a claim about the actual position of the sun in relation to the planets and stars. This was no different from the use made of Ptolemy's astronomy itself at that time. Because of the preface, Copernicus did not pose a serious threat, even though he personally believed that the sun was at the center of the universe. Kepler was the first important astronomer to support the heliocentric hypothesis in his *Mysterium Cosmographica* (1597) which appeared fifty-four years after the publication of Copernicus' book and fifteen years before Galileo endorsed in writing the heliocentric hypothesis in 1613. Up to 1616 the Roman Catholic Church encouraged the discussion of the Copernican hypothesis by Jesuit astronomers who were among the most progressive.

Galileo first attracted major public attention in 1610 at the age of 46 when he published *Star Messenger.* It was notable largely because he pointed out that the moon was pockmarked (with craters, as we now know). This broke with the Aristotelian cosmology in which everything above the earthly sphere is held to be perfect. This was not the first astronomical observation which went against Aristotle, but nonetheless it was an important one. Another important discovery that Galileo made was that Jupiter had four moons. This meant that not everything in the heavens went around the earth. Again, although this was startling, it was not unprecedented. Tycho Brahe (1546–1601), a peerless astronomical observer, believed that the planets orbited around the sun and the sun orbited around the earth.

In 1611 Galileo visited Rome in triumph. The Jesuit astronomers had confirmed his observations. They accepted sunspots, the existence of comets beyond the sphere of the moon, and that the moon was pock-marked; in short, that the Aristotelian cosmology was seriously flawed. They themselves were moving away from the geocentric astronomy toward Tycho's system, which was a sort of halfway house between Aristotle and Copernicus. The Roman Catholic Church's position at that time was that Copernicus' system was to be discussed freely and openly as a hypothesis but was not to be put forward as established truth. In fact, it was not established truth until Newton's *Principia Mathematica* was published three-quarters of a century later (1687).

In 1613 Galileo published his *Letter on Sunspots,* which by its claim that the sun decayed, drove another nail into the coffin of Aristotelian cosmology, which held that the heavenly bodies were eternal. This was the first time that Galileo put into print his support for Copernicus. The *Letter on Sunspots* was praised by several cardinals, including the future Pope Urban VIII, who brought Galileo to trial twenty years later! Clearly more than an astronomical theory caused him to move from praise to condemnation. How did the controversy arise that led to condemnation?

Three phases in the controversy must be distinguished. First, Galileo published his *Letter to Castelli* in 1615 (amplified the following year in *Letter to the Grand Duchess Christina*). It was provoked by a pedant who criticized the Copernican hypothesis and was intended to silence theological objections to Copernicus. Galileo gave his views on how Scripture was to be interpreted in those very few passages that implied that the earth did not orbit around the sun. The letter was submitted to the Holy Office, which ruled that it was unguarded in its expressions but otherwise not objectionable. Soon after this, Cardinal Robert Bellarmine (1542–1621) expressed the unofficial but general attitude of theologians toward the new astronomy. The Copernican hypothesis was not established. Scripture was therefore not to be adjusted to a nonliteral sense in order to conform with it. As the fathers of the church had taken the passages literally, the church was to continue to do so until and unless knowledge of nature was such as to require a nonliteral interpretation of the few passages in question. Copernicus' work was to be given, temporarily, the status of a hypothesis.

Bellarmine's position on the interpretation of Scripture actually went considerably further than the fathers.[11] Unfortunately, Friar Tommaso Campanella's eloquent plea for scientific freedom—written shortly after Bellarmine's *Letter to Foscarini*, at the request of Cardinal Boniface Gaetani, and containing the best understanding of the issues at the time—went largely unnoticed.

The second phase was initiated by Pope Paul V, who became impatient with the controversy and in 1616 ordered the Congregation of the Holy Office to look into the Copernican hypothesis. It supported Bellarmine's position but did not mention Galileo himself in any decree. However, the Congregation ordered Galileo to appear before it, and Bellarmine instructed Galileo not to hold or defend the Copernican hypothesis. Galileo promised to comply. The vital question, however, is whether the Congregation itself formally issued an absolute injunction, forbidding Galileo even to discuss Copernican astronomy. The trial in 1633 turns largely on this question; for if there was such an injunction, then Galileo was technically guilty of disobedience.

For several years Galileo stayed out of major public disputes. But in 1623 when Cardinal Barberini, with whom Galileo was on good terms, became Pope Urban VIII, Galileo began to reconsider his situation. In 1624 he had six long audiences with the new pope. Galileo was so encouraged that two years later—without Urban's knowledge—he decided to take the risk of composing a proof of the Copernican system. It took him four years to complete the task. In 1632 he published his *Dialogue of Two Chief World Systems*. It immediately caused a storm.

One of the scientific disadvantages from which Galileo suffered was the fact that there was no observable stellar parallax. That is to say, if the earth were in orbit around the sun, when the earth was at diagonally opposite points of the orbit, the stars should appear at different positions. But no such displacement was then observable. The only two possible explanations were either that the stars were immensely more distant than was thought to be possible or the earth did not move. In place of stellar parallax, Galileo offered a theory about the tides, seeking to explain their rise and fall as caused by the earth's motion around the sun. This theory, of course, proved false. In addition, Urban VIII believed that he had been made to appear a fool because he thought that one of the incompetent speakers in the *Dialogues* was intended to represent him. He felt personally betrayed and insulted by a former friend and, quite apart from the personal embarrassment, he could not ignore what appeared to be a deliberate affront to the office of the papacy. Some public action was mandatory. Galileo was brought to trial for heresy in 1633, technically for having disobeyed the decree of the Congregation of the Index (which in 1616 had stated that the Copernican system was to be treated only as a hypothesis, not an absolute fact), Bellarmine's admonition, and the much-disputed strict injunction (that he was not even to discuss the Copernican system) allegedly issued to Galileo by the Holy Office. After his recantation, Galileo continued his scientific work, and in 1636 he published his masterpiece on terrestrial motion.

Over and above the personalities involved in the dispute with Galileo and the issue of authority, why was the church so concerned with the Copernican hypothesis? Christian theology and indeed the human imagination from Shakespeare to the common people were very strongly engaged by the Aristotelian worldview. The notion that the universe is infinite could virtually paralyze with fear a man as sophisticated as Kepler. It was going to take time for the churches, both Roman Catholic and Protestant, to adjust to a very different world. Anyone who has had responsibility for an organization, even a small one, knows how important time is. An idea may be a good one, but sometimes to insist on its being effected immediately leads to miserable conflict between those with the idea and those with the responsibility for what happens should it be implemented. It must be remembered that Copernicus' idea was not yet known to be true; certainly the details were hopelessly inaccurate. For the church to intervene on a scientific matter at that time did not mean the same as it would today were it to take a position on some scientific theory. Science then did not have the hallowed status it has since been accorded. Nor was there any body of knowledge or procedures supported by an authoritative institution, an academy of science for example, as in our day.

One must also remember that during most of the period when the conflict between Galileo and the Roman Catholic Church was going on, central Europe was involved in a terrible war, with as serious a loss of life and property as has ever been known even to this day. The Thirty Years' War, which began in 1618, was in considerable part a religious war between Protestant and Catholic. Wars are bad enough, but when they have the added fury of religion, it becomes an extremely ugly situation, to put it mildly. The Roman Church was caught up in a battle with perhaps its very existence at stake in parts of Europe. It is hardly to be expected that it would be quick to adopt a revolutionary scientific idea whose truth was not yet known and which had deep and powerfully disturbing implications.

If we keep some of this in mind, then we can avoid some of the self-righteousness that is often displayed when people talk about the trial of Galileo. To expect utterly dispassionate treatment by the authorities in his day is unrealistic. The entire episode fills one with sadness because of its fateful consequences for the Western world to this day. It became the centerpiece of a distorted portrait of the relationship of science and religion. It led to a picture of inevitable conflict when, in fact, as far as the nature of science and Christian doctrine themselves are concerned, the confrontation need never have taken place. Nothing in the ideas involved made it inevitable. No one is forced to make a choice between a life lived according to science or according to religion. Yet that disjunction has troubled the West ever since that infamous trial was interpreted and used by the *philosophes*.

Only today, and still all too slowly, is the distortion being corrected by historical study. That study is also beginning to reveal the essential contribution of Christianity to the origins of science. Instead of being an implacable opponent, Christianity is increasingly being seen as one of the vital contributors to the mentality which created classical science.[12]

Chapter Two

Has Science Replaced God?

Even if it is granted that Christianity was an indispensable ingredient in the rise of classical science, a person still might think that there must be some incompatibility between them because as scientific knowledge has increased it appears that religion has retreated. It seems to be only a matter of time before everything will be explained by science so that nothing will be left for religion to explain. But this is an erroneous impression. What actually happened is that a *natural* religion, in contrast to a *revealed* or biblical religion, was developed by many intellectuals in the seventeenth and early eighteenth centuries. Natural religion was based on a view of nature which was supposedly scientific. But as science progressed and as the basis of natural religion was philosophically examined, natural religion was steadily undermined.

Many intellectuals today do not realize that there is a difference between natural religion and Christianity. They think that the only possible reasons for belief in God's existence and goodness are those used by natural religion. It is widely assumed that since those reasons have been found to be inadequate for natural religion, Christianity is inadequately supported as well. If we are properly to understand the significance of science and philosophy for religion in modern times, we must distinguish natural religion from revealed religion and consider differences as well as similarities in the reasons which have been given for their truth.

I

Judaism is not a natural religion. Belief in God did not arise among the people of ancient Israel from an attempt to explain nature's existence and order. They believed in Yahweh, their God, before they held to a doctrine of creation, even though the Bible now begins with creation stories. Only in time did the one who delivered them from slavery in Egypt become known to them as Creator. This sequence has far-reaching implications for understanding the grounds for Christianity, which grew out of the religion of ancient Israel. For example, all the stories about God as Creator of the heavens and earth, who formed a

35

special people (Israel) and who sent Jesus Christ to redeem the world, emphasize God's relation to people, not God's relation to the natural world. The creation of human beings is the crown of the first creation story, and God's relation to Adam and Eve is the central focus of the second creation story of Genesis. God's intentions are manifest primarily through the events of Israel's history and the life of Christ. This is why there has been a distinction between the two books of God: the book of nature and the book of Scripture. For centuries both were thought to reveal God, but the book of Scripture was held to give us a much more complete and accurate knowledge of God and of divine purposes. This knowledge was held to be greatly superior to the knowledge the book of nature supplied, even though nature was said to support belief in a benevolent and wise God.

With the rise of classical science a radically new conception of nature developed. Nature was viewed as a great machine with universal laws, unlike Aristotle's physics which had different laws of motion for earthly and heavenly bodies. Some people constructed a new religion based primarily on the understanding of nature as a machine. They regarded the book of nature as superior to the book of Scripture as a source of knowledge of God. A major reason for reversing the traditional roles of the two books of God was the claim that what we need to know about God must be available to everyone, not just to Jews and Christians. Unless other people are told about biblical teachings, they remain ignorant of matters that are allegedly vital for their salvation. Such an arrangement would be unreasonable for a wise and good God to make.[1] What we need to know about God, therefore, can be found *solely* from the book of nature because that source of knowledge is accessible to people everywhere. Whatever the Bible teaches about God that agrees with what we learn from the study of nature is to be accepted; what does not is to be rejected.

In time some went so far as to claim that the Bible was not needed at all. It was useful when the human race was in its infancy. But now that we have achieved enlightenment, we can read the book of nature and avoid all the blemishes, distortions, and absurdities that are found in the Bible.[2] In addition, we can avoid the controversies and strife which arise from different interpretations of the Bible and the claims to special status by various churches. This was especially pertinent because of the bitter religious wars of the first half of the seventeenth century.

"Natural" in the phrase "natural religion" meant not only a religion based primarily or even solely on nature, but also natural in contrast to what is artificial and human-made. The very idea that God is a mystery—that is, beyond the power of human reason to comprehend—yet accommodates Godself to our condition so that we can have a limited but adequate grasp of divine purposes through such things as legends, inspired prophecy, and parables was thought to be ignorance and superstition. That Plato, one of the greatest philosophers of all time, thought that the source of all things was beyond the capacity of the human mind to comprehend and to speak of directly suggests that the charge of ignorance and superstition was superficial. Plato, for example, in the *Timaeus* wrote, "The father and maker of all this universe is past finding out, and even if we found him, to tell of him to all men would be impossible" (28c). He resorted to various kinds of myths to describe the source of the order of the world. Early Church Fathers, such as Clement of Alexandria (c. 150– c. 215), cited Plato as an example of a philosopher who shared with Christian theologians a fundamental conviction concerning the source of all things and who employed tales, analogies, and allegories in order to speak of mysteries.[3]

But this became utterly alien to many people in the seventeenth and eighteenth centuries. Anything that could not be described in terms as transparent as the cogs and levers, pushes and pulls of the parts of a machine was considered to be "occult." Even Newton's gravitation force was attacked by some as an occult property.[4] The person most responsible for this view of reason was Descartes (1596–1650). His *Discourse on Method* (1637) and *Meditations on First Philosophy* (1641) deeply impressed upon the intellectual world the importance of attaining the certainty which could be had in mathematics in every field of inquiry. Descartes convinced many people that the certainty of mathematics lay in its clarity. For an account to be in accord with reason it had to have the clarity of a mathematical proof or demonstration. Mechanical accounts of nature were thought to yield such clarity.

Actually the idea that nature is like a machine greatly narrowed the concepts of "reason," "reasonableness," and "rationality." This has become more evident as our sciences have advanced. In the nineteenth century it was found that nature is not capable of being understood as a machine. Electromagnetic fields are not reducible to categories of Newtonian mechanics. In the twentieth century we are still painfully learning that many scientific theories cannot be "imaged" or pictured, much less be as transparent as the connections between parts of a machine. Nonetheless, very serious damage was done to Christianity in the seventeenth and eighteenth centuries because nature was viewed as a machine. Many intellectuals still require that sound religion must have the same transparency as the older mechanical accounts of nature. None of the great religions of the world can be reduced to such "rationality" without essentially misrepresenting what they say. Until the inappro-

priateness of this understanding of rationality is more widely recognized
by the educated public, the nature of both science and Christianity will
continue to be grossly misunderstood. Christianity will not receive a
proper hearing in academic centers, however much our universities
pride themselves on their objectivity and openness to views from any
source.[5]

Even Christians who sought to retain both books of God were frequently deeply affected by this narrow understanding of reason in their
attempts to defend the reasonableness of Christianity.[6] They used the
same proofs or demonstrations of God's existence and benevolence
from the existence and order of nature as were used by the proponents
of natural religion. They added to these proofs from nature arguments
to establish the truth of the Bible, with its specific understanding of God
as trinity and incarnate Savior. That God revealed Godself to the Old
Testament prophets was shown by the fact that their predictions were
fulfilled. The authenticity of the New Testament revelation was proved
by Jesus' supernatural power to perform miracles.

Old Testament prophecies, however, are not predictions. They are
usually explanations of historical and natural events as God's judgment
on Israel for its failure to trust and obey God, calls to repentance, assurances of forgiveness, revelations of God's intentions, and assurances that
God's promises will be realized. In ancient times accuracy in forecasting
was not among the criteria for distinguishing between false prophets,
who were abundant in ancient Israel, and true prophets. The criteria
then were not essentially different from those which enable us today to
distinguish between authentic and spurious accounts of a religion. Dis-
crimination requires intimate knowledge of a religion and usually some
personal experience of the spiritual life. For example, the discussion of
Old Testament prophecies in the New Testament and early church was
often directed toward identifying Jesus as the promised Messiah or
Christ. His crucifixion was a major stumbling block. A fresh interpretation of the prophets was necessary, including a recognition that the Messiah must suffer, before this barrier to belief could be surmounted. The
realization that prophecies are not forecasts undermines the argument
for divine revelation based on prophecies as successful forecasts.

The idea that nature is like a great machine made the apologetic use
of miracles to support the authenticity of biblical revelation problematic.
Some claimed miracles were impossible because the laws of nature were
necessary and incapable of being suspended even by God. Others argued that God designed the world and foresaw its course of history so
that God did not need to intervene in order for it to achieve the divine
purposes. For God to intervene would imply that the initial design was

faulty. Still others argued that miracles were not needed to give credibility to the teachings of the Bible because any teachings which are true can be fully warranted by reason.[7]

As we have seen, the new science, interpreted philosophically, led to the creation of natural religion. Many Christians who sought to retain both books of God frequently shared the same narrow view of reason as the proponents of natural religion, but the predominant Protestant response to the new science was to abandon the book of nature and to rely solely on the book of Scripture.[8] This outlook is nicely summarized in Pascal's remark, What has the God of the philosophers to do with the God of Abraham, Isaac, and Jacob?[9]

There is indeed a significant difference between a cosmic deity and the God revealed through the Bible, as is reflected in the very distinction of *two* books of God. But their utter dissociation by most modern Protestant theologians was a new departure in Christian theology. This response, however, is historically understandable. Nature viewed as a machine and the narrow view of reason and rational grounds which accompanied the mechanistic philosophy, made the book of nature very unattractive to many of those who believed in a biblical God. But a great deal is lost when nature (in contrast to an inadequate view of nature) is abandoned by theology. Even though nature by itself does not establish God's existence and goodness—as so many Christian apologists and philosophers of the seventeenth and eighteenth centuries thought—nature has a valuable role to play. It raises the issues of God's existence and goodness. Recent developments in science and philosophy indicate that the possibility of God arises from a study of the natural world. We shall explore the significance of this later in detail.

In spite of the rejection of revealed religion by some intellectuals in the seventeenth and eighteenth centuries, natural religion was really a revision of historical Christianity. This is obvious in the case of Lord Herbert of Cherbury (Edward Herbert, 1583–1648), the so-called father of English Deism (another name for natural religion). In *De Veritate . . .* , Herbert expounded the chief principles of natural religion. According to Herbert, it can be established by reason that there is one supreme God, who ought to be worshiped, and that the chief part of worship is virtue. We ought to be sorry for our sins and to repent of them. God rewards good and punishes evil deeds both in this life and in the hereafter. But some Deists denied a future life. Still others went even further by denying that God rewards good and punishes evil in this life. For them virtue is its own reward. Voltaire, himself a Deist, feared that if ordinary people learned this, there would be an increase in lawlessness. These revisions were simply the continuation of the "rational" criticism of Christianity, which sought to purge it of all mystery. In time natural religion's own inadequacies were exposed by devastating criticism from Hume and Kant. But in spite of its inadequacies, the Deism of Lord Herbert and others made a significant contribution to religious toleration, and its treatment of the Bible as ordinary history stimulated the development of critical methods for the study of the Bible.

As I have suggested, many Deists did not think of themselves as opposing Christianity but as its benefactors because they were freeing genuine Christianity from alien and irrelevant material. They were part of a much larger body of educated people, including Galileo and Descartes, who believed that the new mechanistic science revealed the true face of nature so that we could now read the book of nature correctly, but who continued to support a biblical Christianity. For them Christianity was needlessly vulnerable to criticism because it was intertwined with the older Aristotelian understanding of nature and with a worldview which was hopelessly inaccurate. They sought in their various ways to free Christianity from this unnecessary entanglement.

The world picture of the late sixteenth and early seventeenth centuries, which the new mechanistic science pushed aside, is too complex to describe in full but a few features are important for us.[10] Ptolemy's astronomy, with its pattern of complex epicycles, was not accepted as an actual description of the movements of heavenly bodies. It was used simply as a calculating device for the observed positions of heavenly bodies. As an actual physical description, Ptolemy's astronomy was hopeless, and virtually everyone who worked in astronomy knew it. But Aristotle's astronomical physics was taken seriously as an actual description of the heavens. According to the corrupted Aristotle, which was current in the Renaissance, the various heavenly bodies are attached to nine solid, concentric, but invisible spheres. The earth is at the center of these concentric spheres. Everything below the sphere of the moon changes, that it, individuals are born, mature, decay, and disintegrate. But above the sphere of the earth, everything is immutable. The very material of the moon, planets, and stars is superior to earthly matter. This is obvious because the motion of the moon, planets and stars is uniform and circular, and thus eternal. Only the earth, with its inferior matter, has change and decay. Beyond the outermost sphere is the realm of the Unmoved Mover, which is the realm of utter perfection in contrast to the near perfection of the eternal heavens. The spheres above the earth are moved in their never-ending circular motion by a longing for that perfection which is beyond them. Creatures on earth share in that longing.

Another stream of Greek thought complicates the picture. Much of it stems from Plotinus (205–70 c.e.), the greatest of the Neoplatonists. Plotinus populates the layers between the spheres with intelligent beings, so that there is a great, unbroken chain of being, as it is called, extending in a hierarchy of descending degrees of excellence from the divine realm, through various ranks of intelligences who guide the heavenly bodies, to the earth. On earth, the chain of being continues from human beings down to earthworms and beyond. Even within the large divisions of animal, vegetable, and inanimate beings there is a hierarchy based on degrees of power and excellence. For example, gold is superior to brass, rubies to topaz, water to dirt. Although human beings are mortal and earthly, they can aspire to the imperishable realm with some hope of success. They are a meeting place of all that is above and below, a microcosm. They have the God-given destiny to belong to the highest realm, and by God's grace in Christ they may rise beyond the spheres to the divine presence and dwell in never-ending bliss.

What is of particular importance is that everything has a proper or natural place. Its place is determined by the value of its being. For some thing or some one to move out of its proper or natural place causes disruption and harmful consequences. This is consonant with Genesis 1–3, in which the world is created good by God's Word, and disorder, decay, and death are introduced by human disobedience. The Aristotelian/Neoplatonic worldview was thus a physical theory that included values as part of the very fabric of the universe.

In addition, that worldview included an epistemological principle (or way to gain knowledge). There are correspondences between the different levels or planes of being, and by comparing them we can make discoveries and find some of our views confirmed. For example, the sun, as the greatest of the heavenly bodies, is compared both to God (who is on a higher plane) and kings (who are on a lower plane) as a sober truth about their respective roles and not as a superficial metaphor. Obligations and rights are not matters of personal opinion nor only sanctioned by custom and enacted legislation; they are confirmed and supported by the physical order of the cosmos itself.

From our contemporary point of view there is an unacceptable side to this world picture. Consider, for example, Shakespeare's play, *The Taming of the Shrew.* The basis for its action is the conviction, shared by the audience, that a woman's role is to be subordinate to her husband. Only so can each of them be happy. Indeed, acceptance by each of his and her natural place is the only way that society at large can be well governed. The legitimate sovereign is to be supported not only from sentiment but on a rational basis. To go against the rightful place given by nature in domestic, social, and political matters leads to disorder sooner or later. This is why imperfections on the moon's surface or sunspots were so upsetting; they suggested that there was decay in the heavenly regions which were supposed to be imperishable. Physical discoveries such as these were thought to threaten the very foundations of the social, political, and moral order.

The new mechanistic picture of the world utterly displaced this older worldview. In the new mechanistic science, matter and the laws of motion are the same throughout the universe. There is no hierarchy or chain of being, with levels of correspondence, so that we can learn truths about one thing by finding similarities to beings on another level. Reasoning is mathematical, not the detection of analogies or similarities between different levels of being. Only the quantitative aspects of things are relevant. Scientific laws are the measurable relations between such things as time, distance, and mass. Values and the human significance of nature are excluded from the formulation of nature's laws. The new mechanistic science was revolutionary long before there was any technological application of it.

In spite of the urgings of devout Christians such as Kepler, Descartes, Bacon, and Boyle, there was enormous resistance to the abandonment of a worldview which had nourished an entire civilization. These pioneers wanted to detach Christianity from an inferior astronomy and physics, even though it meant abandoning its support for the moral, social, and political order. They were willing to venture onto new seas. Eventually their way was followed because the new science was so superior to the older Aristotelian science that there was no alternative. Our modern view of the world was formed, as in time new foundations were laid for politics, morals, law, economics, and even the fine arts. Not only Christianity, but every human activity was affected by the demise of the older world picture.

Perhaps the most radical feature of the new science of nature was the way change or motion was explained. At the core of Aristotle's edifice of a hierarchical universe extending from the earth to the highest sphere of the heavens and beyond was an understanding of change. All change, which includes all motion and growth, was understood to be a transition from potentiality to actuality. In ancient Greek philosophy there were two extreme views concerning observable motion. At one extreme Heraclitus (c. 500 B.C.E.) claimed that everything constantly changed, so that one could not step into the same river twice. At the other extreme was Parmenides (c. 500 B.C.E.) who by means of pure logic demonstrated that motion was impossible, and that there was a radical divergence between reality (what was demonstrated by reason) and appearances (empirically observed motion). Paradoxically, Heraclitus' view that everything is in flux implies that there is no such thing as change. For if everything is in flux, then from one instant to the next everything is succeeded by something new. For there to be change, something must remain the same while something else varies.

Aristotle met the problem by arguing that what now is can become something else because what it is to become now exists potentially. Clay can become brick. They are not the same thing because clay can also become a pot. But both a brick and a pot are things which potentially exist in clay. The change from clay to a brick or to a pot is a change from potency to actuality. There is some continuity in change. This accommodates both Parmenides, who denied change on the ground that if something changes it no longer is, and Heraclitus, who in effect denied change by having everything in flux.

Aristotle's understanding of motion as a transition from potency to act was enormously fruitful. When amplified, it was used to account for every type of change. Aristotle distinguished four kinds of motion: (1) local motion or change of place; (2) alteration, which is a change of qualities such as the color or shape of an object; (3) quantity, as a body grows larger or smaller; and (4) generation, or the natural process of birth, decay, and death. In all change or motion Aristotle distinguishes four causes or kinds of explanation: (1) material, that *out of which* something is made; (2) efficient, that *by which* something is made; (3) formal, that *into which* something is made; and (4) final, that *for the sake of which* something is made. In the case of an artifact, such as a shoe, we may say that it is made out of leather, by a shoemaker, into a shoe, in order to protect the foot. With a natural thing, such as a tomato or a tree, there is an important difference. The formal and final causes are the same: the thing aims, so to speak, at becoming itself. When a tomato ripens to red, the matter is the tomato (its greenness to be exact); the efficient cause is the rays of the sun; redness is the formal and the final causes. We may see the importance of this by looking more closely at natural growth.

In natural change, which includes growth, we have a process. The end or goal of the process is present from the very start of the process. What something is to become, say a tree, is present at the start of the process, but potentially only (as a seed); otherwise there would be no such thing as growth. It also must be there at the start potentially because the seed becomes a tree, rather than, say, a cornstalk. Formal and final causes are distinguished in terms of potency and act. A form is a final end present in potency, not act. Motion is accounted for in terms of a process of going from potency to act, and all natural objects have their end present in them potentially and they strive to realize or actualize it.

The new mechanistic science utterly rejected such an explanation of motion. Matter was considered to have the properties of extension, impenetrability, shape, and to be either stationary or in motion. All sense impressions, such as color, smell, and taste, were said to be sensations in human subjects which are a result of the various motions of matter. Motion is accounted for in terms of time and distance. For projectiles, which had utterly baffled the Aristotelians, Galileo was able to give an exact measure of their acceleration and describe their path as the precise mathematical shape of a parabola. Descartes's notion of the world as a great machine explained why bodies moved. It was not the result of things striving to actualize their form, but of the impact of matter on matter.

In much of ancient philosophy, including the philosophy of Aristotle, the model for explaining change is that of a human being making something, such as a cobbler or carpenter. An artisan seeks to make something which is useful or which has a purpose. Even natural objects, which in Aristotle have no maker, are still viewed as acting purposively as they move from potency to act. Everything in nature imitates the perfect actualization or realization of the unmoved mover, as each thing strives to actualize its potential. In this fashion all change or motion is understood to be purposive or to strive to achieve its good.

The rejection of formal and final causes by the new mechanical science threatened a deeply held conviction about nature. In both Judaism and Christianity the natural world's goodness is thought to reflect God's benevolence toward human beings. Nature is the way it is because of God's good intentions. The new corpuscular philosophy, as the new science was frequently called, made it look "as if matter can stand by itself and mechanism needs no intelligence or spiritual substance" to guide it, as Leibniz put it, because nature works simply by the impact of matter on matter. There is no purposive or goal-seeking activity present in matter at all. It simply operates in a machinelike way.[11]

This was not the dominant view, however. The new picture of nature revealed by science actually strengthened belief in God and divine goodness because the order of nature was so marvelous that it was utterly implausible to think that it was the result of the chance collision of brute matter. The more complex the order of nature, the less and less likely that the order was the result of the chance collision of particles of matter. The argument from design reached its highest peak of popularity among intellectuals in the late seventeenth and early eighteenth centuries. Since there were no natural processes to account for nature's order, and since chance collision of matter was an inadequate explanation, the present order we observe must be imposed from the outside by a designer. But the inadequacies of the argument from design, especially as stated by Hume, undermined natural religion, and in the eyes of many scientists and philosophers to this day, Christianity as well. But before we look at this in the next chapter, we need to examine a very important but misguided expedient to which many educated people resorted and which can still mislead the unwary.

Newton, whose views had great authority because of his achievements in mathematics, optics, and celestial mechanics, was troubled by the way nature was treated as virtually autonomous by the new mechanistic model. Except for the initial moment of creation and God's initial design of nature, it appeared that the cosmos operated of its own accord. As Alexandre Koyré put it, the workaday God was replaced by the God of the Sabbath, that is, once the work of creating the world was complete, God rested because nature, once made, could run itself. Newton resisted this understanding of God's relation to nature. On the basis of the scientific knowledge of his day, he pointed out that God was still needed to sustain nature's order. For example, according to his calculations, there were slight irregularities in the orbits of the planets which would in time cause the solar system to collapse. Unless those irregularities were corrected by divine intervention, the solar system could not continue indefinitely. This was but one of several things which God needed to do to keep the machine in running order.

There are profound biblical objections to such a "God of the gaps," as this understanding of God's relation to the universe has come to be called. By "gaps" it is meant that no member or members of the universe can be found to account for regularly occurring phenomena in nature. God is inserted in the gaps which could be occupied by members of the universe. This is theologically improper because God, as creator of the universe, is not a member of the universe. God can never properly be used in scientific accounts, which are formulated in terms of the relations between the members of the universe, because that would reduce God to the status of a creature. According to a Christian conception of God as creator of a universe that is rational through and through, there are no missing relations between the members of nature. If, in our study of nature, we run into what seems to be an instance of a connection missing between members of nature, the Christian doctrine of creation implies that we should keep looking for one. If planets inexplicably deviate from orbits which would in time cause the solar system to collapse, we are to look for some mass which is exerting force to account for the

46 The Book of Nature

deviations. (In the case of Saturn's orbit, a new planet, Uranus, was discovered; in that of Mercury's orbit, it took Einstein's entirely new theory to account for its eccentricity.) But, according to the doctrine of creation, we are never to postulate God as the *immediate* cause of any *regular* occurrence of nature. In time, a "God of the gaps" was seen to be bad science as well as bad theology. Science now is programatically committed to a view of nature in which there are no gaps between members of the universe.[12]

Newton and others inserted the Deity into what proved to be temporary gaps in scientific accounts because they were afraid that unless God were shown to perform some functions in nature, nature would be thought to be self-sufficient and we would not need God at all. For them a complete scientific account of all phenomena of nature in terms of the relations between the members of the universe would render nature self-sufficient. We will see later that this is not so, but here we can briefly indicate that divine agency and complete scientific explanations of phenomena are compatible.

According to the Christian doctrine of creation, the creation of the universe is not an event in the past which is over and done with, so that once the universe is created, it runs on its own without the need for any divine activity. God's creative activity is continuous. The view of nature as self-sufficient, once it is created, a view that was held by many intellectuals of the seventeenth and eighteenth centuries, is not the Christian view of creation. Our sciences take the existence of the world for granted and study the relations between its members. Should we seek to give an account of the relations between A, B, and C, we might find that C regularly results from the actions of A and B. It would be correct to say that A and B cause C. But it is perfectly compatible with this to say that C is caused by God, because for A and B and C to exist and to be causally related, God's creative agency must be operating. The scientific account of their relations simply takes their existence and nature for granted. Divine creative activity and a complete scientific account of the relations between the members of the universe are compatible. It was a misguided use of God as a gap-filler in the seventeenth and eighteenth centuries that made them appear incompatible as God was replaced by new scientific discoveries in more and more of the gaps God was allegedly filling.

It may well be that God as creator of an orderly universe significantly influenced the development of this conception of science. But it was not the theological impropriety of a "God of the gaps" that decisively convinced people at large of its scientific impropriety. Rather it was the discovery of scientific explanations for previously unexplained phenomena which improperly had been explained as the result of God's immediate agency as a member of the universe, that was decisive. These replacements of a "God of the gaps" by scientific explanations greatly discredited the intellectual respectability of all belief in God in the late eighteenth century. For example, the alleged irregularities in planetary orbits, which so troubled Newton, were found to be periodic, that is, they righted themselves in the long run so that the solar system is inherently stable. This is why Pierre Laplace (1749–1827), the champion of the inherent stability of the world machine, said to Napoleon, who complained that Laplace, in his book on celestial mechanics, had neglected to mention God, "Sire, I have no need of that hypothesis." The removal of God from various alleged gaps with the advance of science led to the erroneous impression, still widely held, that there is an inherent incompatibility between science and religion, and that as science advances, religion retreats. Such a replacement can only happen if God is incorrectly regarded as a member of the universe. But it can never happen with a Christian conception of God as creator.

Whenever we are at the boundaries of scientific knowledge, there is the danger of turning God into a creature by inserting the Deity into a scientific account. This has happened recently with the Big Bang theory. According to the Big Bang theory our universe has not always been in its present form. It began as a very small, highly dense mass, which exploded and which is still expanding. This theory has been given an incorrect theological interpretation by Robert Jastrow, the cosmologist. According to Jastrow, as scientists approached the earliest moments of our universe, hoping to give a final account of it, they found that theologians had already explained it. He compared scientists to mountain climbers who, when they had climbed over the last ledge, found theologians sitting there waiting for them. Jastrow took it that the Big Bang theory supports the theological doctrine of creation, which claims that the universe has a beginning, a belief which some philosophers and scientists had discarded as a childish notion.[13]

It is indeed the case that the theological claim that our universe began no longer looks absurd to those cosmologists who had assumed that our universe has always been here. Jastrow, however, has made several mistakes. The Big Bang theory concerns the beginning of our universe *as presently ordered*. It moves from where we now are back to the time when our universe was a very small, very dense mass. The theory does not assume that there was nothing before that small, dense mass. The Christian doctrine of creation concerns the beginning of *all things*. The beginning of our presently ordered universe in a cosmic explosion may or may not be the beginning of all things. Should we find that something existed before the dense mass which preceded the Big Bang, the Big Bang would not have taken us to the beginning after all. We would not have reached the last ledge on which theologians are allegedly sitting. No matter how far we go back, we do not know that we have reached the beginning. The Christian doctrine of creation was not put forward because it was believed that we could by our inquiries reach a beginning of the universe, as Augustine so brilliantly showed in Book XI of his *Confessions*.

But even if we could identify the beginning of the universe, we would be no closer to the divine creative activity than we are right now. God's creative activity in sustaining the universe is precisely the same at the present moment as it is at every moment of the universe's existence. According to the Christian doctrine of creation, whatever exists, whenever it exists owes its existence to the continuing creative activity of God. To be clear that God is the *source* of all things and that science deals only with the transformations and relations between *existing* things prevents confusions, such as Jastrow's. It is not only scientifically but also *theologically* correct that science is limited to the study of the relations between members of the universe.

As science advances more and more of the relations between the members of the universe are understood. Often it is said that more and more of the mysteries of nature are being solved, implying that with the continuing advance, all mysteries will be solved. But what Christianity calls mysteries remain mysteries because scientific advances do not dispel them in the least. The nature of God's creative activity is a mystery now just as it was from the very earliest days of modern science and will remain so. This is because none of the kinds of causality which exist between members of the universe, such as sexual generation, mechanical impact, chemical reactions, or transformation of energy from one form to another, is the creative relation between God and the entire universe. However many of the causal connections we discover between the members of the universe, we are not even dealing with the distinctive creative relation between God and the entire universe. We use the various kinds of causal relations between members of the universe to get some idea of the nature of divine creative activity. But the relations between members of the universe are at best only analogous to the creative relation between God and the entire universe. The comparison of the various kinds of causal relations between members of the universe to God's distinctive creative activity does not enable us to comprehend the nature of divine causality itself. The mystery of *how* God creates is therefore not removed by advances in our scientific knowledge which steadily push back the frontiers of the unknown, finding more connections between members of the universe and discovering new members as well. We will examine this more fully in a later chapter in which we shall consider the nature of God's agency in nature, history, and human lives. Our main point here has been to make it clear that science does not replace God's activity. It is evident that one of the main reasons this impression has been given in modern times is the expedient used by Newton and others of treating God as a member of the universe out of a misplaced fear that, were scientific explanations of nature complete, nature would seem self-sufficient.

Chapter Three

The Order of the World Points
to the Possibility of God

Natural religion based solely on the book of nature in the seventeenth and early eighteenth centuries relied heavily on the argument from design. In its classic form, which we shall examine shortly, it claims that the marvelous order of nature that is apparent to everyone is obviously designed because it would be absurd to believe that its immense complexity is the result of chance. This argument was undermined by a combination of philosophical objections in the late eighteenth century and by advances in science in the nineteenth century.

The argument from design, however, misrepresents the issue that nature's order poses. Even though it takes some effort and patience, it is very important to understand this issue precisely. Otherwise it will appear that science will eventually explain nature's order and that to speak of God as the ground of its order will become superfluous. It must clearly be understood that the continuing advance of science does not get us closer to an answer to the questions of why the universe is ordered one way, rather than another, or why the universe exists at all. Unless this is clear, it will appear not only that with the advance of science God will be superfluous but that even to speak of God as the Creator of the universe and the source of its order is to be prescientific.

As we pointed out in Chapter One, one of the major differences between modern science and ancient Greek thought is that for modern science nature's order is contingent, not necessary. Nature's order, though regular, does not have to be the way it is. The order nature has, which we are steadily uncovering, could actually have been different. This is charmingly and informally but nonetheless accurately expressed by G. K. Chesterton in his autobiographical remarks about nature's order.

The only words that ever satisfied me as describing Nature are the terms used in the fairy books, "charm," "spell," "enchantment." They express the arbitrariness of the fact and its mystery. A tree grows fruit because it is a *magic* tree. Water runs downhill because it is bewitched. The sun shines because it is bewitched.

I deny that this is fantastic or even mystical. . . . It is the only way I can express in words my clear and definite perception that one thing is quite distinct from another; that there is no logical connection between flying and laying eggs. It is the man who talks about "a law" that he has never seen who is the mystic. . . .

This elementary wonder, however, is not a mere fancy derived from the fairy tales; on the contrary, all the fire of the fairy tales is derived from this. Just as we all like love tales because there is an instinct of sex, we all like astonishing tales because they touch the nerve of the ancient instinct of astonishment. This is proved by the fact that when we are very young children we do not need fairy tales: we only need tales. Mere life is interesting enough. A child of seven is excited by being told that Tommy opened a door and saw a dragon. But a child of three is excited by being told that Tommy opened a door. . . . Nursery tales only echo an almost pre-natal leap of interest and amazement. These tales say that apples were golden only to refresh the forgotten moment when we found that they were green. They make rivers run with wine only to make us remember, for one wild moment, that they run with water.[1]

The contingency of nature's order does not imply that anything might happen the next minute, but it does exclude the idea that whatever happens is necessary and cannot be otherwise. Nature is studied empirically because there is more than one way for things to be rationally connected. We must observe and experiment to discover the way the members of the universe are actually connected. The connections we find only show us the actual order nature has, but not why nature has that order, rather than another possible order. Nor does the order it actually has tell us why we have a world at all. Given a world, and given this particular one, our sciences can discover or hope to discover the actual connections nature has. As William P. Alston puts it,

If our basic datum is a certain configuration of the universe as a whole, science can, by the nature of the case, offer no explanation. Science tries to find regularities in the association of different parts, stages, or aspects within the physical universe. On questions as to why the universe as a whole exists, or exists in one form rather than another, it is silent. Ultimately this is because science is committed to the consideration of questions that can be investigated empirically. One can use observation to determine whether two conditions within the universe are regularly associated (increase of temperature and boiling), but there is no way to observe connections between the physical universe as a whole and something outside it.[2]

When it is said that God is the ground of nature's existence and order, God is not being used to fill a gap in a scientific explanation that concerns the connections between members of the universe. Rather to speak of God as the ground of nature's existence and order is to address questions concerning the existence of the universe itself and why it has the particular set of members and connections it has. Because these questions are about the universe as a whole, they are beyond the limits of scientific explanations.

Both Hume and Kant, however, have claimed that nature's order and existence do not warrant the claim that God is their ground. Their views have been thought to rule out nature as supplying any support for belief in God. In this chapter I shall consider their objections to moving from nature's order to God, and in the next chapter their objections to moving from nature's existence to God. We shall see that their objections, which have been one of the pillars of the modern mentality, can no longer prevent nature from playing an important role in an account of the intellectual foundations of Christianity.

I shall argue that even though nature does not establish God's existence, nature points to the possibility of God. That is, it raises questions which science cannot answer and which philosophy has been unable to answer. The questions nature raises forms a significant part of my case for belief in God.

I

Our modern natural sciences use impersonal explanations, that is, there is no reference to anyone's intentions in the descriptions and explanations of the workings of nature. For example, the displacement of water by a body and the precise ratio between the amount of the displacement and the loss of a body's weight is an impersonal account.

In a famous and influential passage in Plato's *Phaedo*, Socrates is represented as dissatisfied with impersonal accounts of the workings of the natural world, which were current in ancient Greece. The Ionian philosophers or *physikoi* rejected the Homeric account of thunder as caused by Zeus and storms at sea as caused by Poseidon. For them, everything that occurred in nature was the result of the collision, repulsion, and intermingling of various bodies. Although each of them gave different accounts, all of them tried to find impersonal causes for the operations of nature.

Socrates claimed that an explanation solely in terms of muscles and bones of why he remained in prison waiting to be executed, rather than seeking to escape, would be absurd. To explain why he remained in prison, it would be necessary to refer to his intentions, such as his intention to do only what is morally correct and his belief that it is better to accept the judgment of the court than to seek to escape. The push and pull of his muscles and bones are ultimately explicable in terms of his intentions. Likewise, the pushes and pulls of natural things, which the *physikoi* investigate, are ultimately to be understood as the result of the intentions of some Mind.

Leibniz, who was deeply influenced by this passage from the *Phaedo*, gives an excellent illustration that shows the relation between impersonal explanations, as they were understood in the new mechanistic science of the seventeenth and eighteenth centuries, and personal explanations that refer to the intentions of an agent.[3] He points out that the fall of a city to the army of a prince may be explained in terms of cannon balls being expelled under pressure and striking the city walls with a certain amount of kinetic energy. The fall of the city may be explained in terms of the commands of the prince who ordered cannons to be put in a particular position and fired at a particular spot. To explain why the city fell *both* accounts are needed. The prince's intentions would not of themselves cause the city to fall, but his intentions explain why cannons were put into a particular position and fired.

Events brought about by human actions do indeed refer to human intentions, but are we to say the same about the operations of nature? Is the entire order of nature the way it is because someone wants it to be that way, or because it just is that way? To understand what is at issue here we must recall that our natural sciences seek to describe and explain the relations *between* the members of the universe, not their origin. The existence of the universe and its basic constituents are taken for granted by our sciences. Scientific laws and theories concern only the "transformations of everything that now is."[4] A study of the transformations of the members of the universe does not tell us why there are any members to be transformed. In addition, the laws and theories, which have increasingly revealed the order of nature, do not tell us why nature has this particular order, rather than another. The actual ties between the members of the universe do not tell us why we have those ties because the members might have been tied differently. When we consider the whole of nature, the relations we find within nature cannot tell us why the universe exists nor why it is the kind of universe that it is. The continuing increase of scientific knowledge, which discovers the relations that exist within our universe, does not get us closer to an answer to either question.

It is customary to say that science answers "how questions," not "why questions," and that religion answers "why questions," not "how questions." This is basically correct but not accurate enough. Scientific theories actually do explain why various relations between members of the universe hold. For example, the kinetic theory of gases explains why a gas contracts under pressure. Although scientific theories and religious claims both tell us why something is the case, they answer different kinds of "why questions." Scientific theories tell us why there are connections between members of our universe. They do not tell us why we have this particular system of connections, rather than another possible system. Scientific theories do not explain why the entire order of nature is as it is.

The question why we have this order rather than another can be answered in two ways. We may say: "Nature just is the way it is." Or we may say: "Someone intends nature to have this order." From scientific theories we cannot infer or exclude either of these answers. Scientific explanations deal with what is the case. From "Nature's order is thus and so," we cannot infer that "Nature's order just is thus and so," nor exclude, "This order is intended by someone." In other words, scientific explanations cannot be used to rule out the possibility that nature's order is the way it is because it is intended. Increasing enlightenment about the operations of nature does not diminish this possibility in the least. Because physics and chemistry deal with entities which have neither intelligence nor will, accounts of the relations that exist between them are rightly impersonal. But even though these scientific accounts are impersonal, they do not exclude a personal account of the natural order as a whole. This is why Carl Sagan was so misleading in his television series and book *Cosmos* when he so strongly implied that with the rise and advance of science, we no longer need God because there is nothing left for God to explain. But as we have seen there is: the very existence of the universe and its particular order.

There does not have to be a reason why the universe exists or why it has its particular order. It might just be the case that the universe exists and is the way it is. But there also might in fact be a reason for its existence and order. Increasing knowledge of nature's order does not tell us which of these possibilities is true.

II

Why then are some people satisfied with impersonal descriptions of natural processes? What causes other people, who are inclined to say that the order of nature is intended, to hesitate? Primarily it is because of David Hume's criticisms of the argument from design and Charles Darwin's theory of evolution. Let us first consider Hume's criticisms.

In the *Dialogues Concerning Natural Religion,* Hume ostensibly is concerned with natural religion, not revealed religion. In other words, he is concerned with those who rely *solely* on the book of nature to establish the existence of a benevolent God. Cleanthes, one of his characters in the *Dialogues,* represents natural religion. Unlike earlier Deists, Cleanthes has no confidence in speculative reasoning because it goes beyond the bounds of experience, and therefore he has no use for the views of Demea, another character who relies on a version of the cosmological argument in which the contingent existence of all beings is said to entail the existence of a necessary being. Cleanthes prefers to rely on what is plainly before us all: the marvelous order of nature. He claims that the order of nature is obviously designed because it would be absurd to believe that its immense complexity could result from the chance collision of particles of matter. The notion of design springs naturally to our minds. It is not the result of abstract reasoning, nor has it been taught to us by the clergy whose self-interest should make us suspicious of anything they teach.

Hume's third character, Philo, never denies that we naturally react to nature's order with the thought that it is designed because chance is indeed far too unlikely a possibility to take seriously. He does, however, point out that there is another alternative. There may be principles within natural processes, which make nature orderly, so that its order is the result neither of chance nor design. But since Philo (and Hume) know of no such principles, the only alternative explanation of nature's order is design. It is this ignorance of any natural processes that explain nature's order which make it *appear* that the issue presented by nature's order is that the order is the result either of design or of the chance combination and separation of colliding bits of matter. Since it is very unlikely that nature's order is the result of chance, Philo seeks to undermine natural religion by showing that nature's order tells us so little about its source that it is useless to serve as a foundation for any religion or moral system.

Cleanthes proposes a form of the argument from design in which nature is compared to a machine. The great machine of nature subdivides into a vast number of lesser machines, each adapted to play a role in the larger whole, and with the most minute parts adjusted to each other with an accuracy that evokes admiration as more and more is learned about nature's organization. Nature resembles, on a vastly larger scale, the products of human design. As the effects are similar, their causes must be similar.

This argument is not a strong one. Machines and houses are very dissimilar to the world. Machines need lubrication and fuel to run, and houses have walls, windows, and foundations. Philo undermines Cleanthes' argument by suggesting that the world is similar to a vegetable or an animal. We do not know the cause of their order, so we do not know the cause of the world's order. Cleanthes protests that the world is very different from a vegetable or an animal. It receives no nutrition and has no sense organs. Philo immediately agrees. The world is very unlike a vegetable or an animal, but it resembles a vegetable or an animal as much as it resembles a machine or a house, which is to say that it does not resemble any of them very much. The strength of the argument from similar effects to similar causes is directly proportional to the likeness of the effects. Cleanthes has been forced to admit that the effects are very dissimilar, so he must admit that the causes are very dissimilar.

Philo continues his criticism by pointing out that the only things which we know by experience to be caused by intelligent design are artifacts, such as machines and houses. These are only a small fraction of the entire universe. It is not a wise practice to make inferences concerning the whole from a very small sample. Indeed, arguments from effects to causes are sound only because experience has shown us that when we have constant and repeated association between two things, they are causally related. But in the case of the entire universe we have no experience of an entire universe being caused by something. We have a singular instance of an ordered world, with no experience of world orders being produced. It is thus not proper to use the causal principle, which has arisen from the experience of repeated sequences of events, in a case of such singularity as the cause of the world's order.

Even were the world significantly like an object of human contrivance, so that the world could be said to be designed, the argument does not yield *God's* existence. Any cause whose existence we infer from an effect is known to be no greater than is required to account for the effect. The effect we are concerned to account for is the world's order. Since this is a finite effect, we may not infer an infinite power as its cause. In addition because we do not know that the world is perfectly designed, we cannot infer that its designer is perfectly wise. We cannot even infer that the cause of nature's order is benevolent. Human and animal suffering prevent us from inferring from nature's order that the source of nature is concerned with their welfare. If we consider only the pleasant and unpleasant effects of nature's operations, then we should infer that its source or sources is neither well-disposed nor hostile toward us, but is simply indifferent or unconcerned.

In spite of all these criticisms of the argument from design, it continued to be widely accepted because the only alternative explanation for nature's order, namely chance, was even weaker. John Ray (1628–1705), the great Cambridge naturalist, in *The Wisdom of God Manifested in the Works of Creation* (1691), cited the complexity of creatures and their suitability to their environment as evidence of divine design and benevolence. He moved directly from present-day life forms to a wise and benevolent designer. Natural history continued to be carried out in this manner right through Hume's lifetime and well beyond. Hume's effort to close off the book of nature, even when endorsed by Kant's criticism of the argument from design,[5] did not prevent its widespread use in the early half of the nineteenth century. In fact, natural history became even more popular after Hume's *Dialogues*. As Lynn Barber declared in *The Heyday of Natural History, 1820–70*, "Every Victorian young lady, it seemed, could reel off the names of twenty different kinds of fern or fungus, and every Victorian clergyman nurtured a secret ambition to publish a natural history."[6] The religious significance of natural history was well known, for natural history was also natural theology, which "enabled one to look 'through Nature up to Nature's God.'"[7]

William Paley's *Natural Theology* (1802) and *View of the Evidences of Christianity* (1794)—which Charles Darwin said was one of the two most important books he read while at university—were widely known throughout the English-speaking world. It was Paley (1743–1805) who made the comparison of a watch with plants and animals famous. Because the parts of a watch are so shaped and put together to produce motion that indicates the hour and minutes of the day, clearly a watch must have a maker. Likewise, whenever we examine a plant or animal, we find that its structure, which enables it to survive and propagate its species, is so arranged that the arrangement cannot be the product of mere chance. Therefore, they must have been designed.[8]

It was the advent of Charles Darwin's theory of evolution by natural selection which made Hume's criticism of the design argument effective. Until Darwin, Hume's objections could be passed over because he had no explanation to offer for nature's order. Without any connections between creatures to account for nature's particular life forms, the only alternative to chance was design. Darwin argued in his theory of evolution by natural selection that present-day complex life forms had their origin in earlier, much simpler forms of life. Even though fossil records indicated that there were earlier forms of life than those now extant, a search for connections between them and present-day life forms was greatly hindered by the continuing Aristotelian view that species are fixed and do not change. (Aristotle's physics was displaced by mechanistic physics in the seventeenth century, but his prestige in biology continued into the nineteenth century, and he was understood to have held that species are fixed.[9]) Darwin's theory was the first well-documented alternative to either sheer chance or design. Darwin supplied what Hume lacked: an account of present-day life forms as arising by natural processes from earlier ones. The argument for a designer, which moves directly from present-day life forms to a designer, can no longer be employed because the only alternative to chance is not design.

At first (and even for a few people today) it seemed that a choice was necessary between a designer for present-day forms of life and Darwin's theory of evolution by natural selection. This was largely because people in the English-speaking world had been immersed in a form of natural history or natural theology which moved directly from the present order of nature to a designer, as though present-day forms were created directly by God, without any relations between the members of the universe being involved. The creation stories of Genesis 1 and 2 were widely understood this way, even though such an interpretation was explicitly rejected by leading Reformation theologians such as Martin Luther and John Calvin.[10]

Darwin did not claim to explain the origins of life but to account for how present-day forms of life evolved from earlier ones. And his theory of evolution had some very serious scientific deficiencies. Until it was supplemented late in the nineteenth century by Gregor Mendel's work on genetics, its account of the origin of species was seriously incomplete. It could be said with a show of scientific plausibility that Darwinian science had not explained the origin of present-day life forms. This allowed a rear guard defense of the older teleological argument which moves directly from present-day life forms to a designer. This pitted science and religion against each other in a needless way, for it made it appear that God could be the source of nature's order only if present-day species did not evolve through natural processes from earlier life forms. This made belief in God as the source of nature's order turn on the presence or absence of a natural process, such as natural selection, to account for present-day life forms.

One of the great benefits of Darwin's work is that it enables us to see more accurately the issue nature's order poses. The main points of Darwin's theory of evolution are as follows. Every life form produces far more offspring than the environment can support, which results in a struggle to survive. There are small differences between members of the same species that give some individuals advantages in the struggle for survival. Because these individuals tend to live longer, they tend to have more offspring than other individuals. The population with their characteristics will tend to become more numerous and, over a long period of time, be a step toward a new form of life. Darwin compared the origin of present-day species to the process of selective breeding for domestic animals, such as cattle, to favor certain traits. In the case of nature there is no breeder making the selection; the process operates naturally, hence there is "natural selection."

From this we may see firstly that nature's order does not pose for us a choice between sheer chance and design. There is a natural process that allows new life forms to emerge from older ones. The disjunction between sheer chance and design is the result of the seventeenth and eighteenth century view of matter as utterly inert and acting only by mechanical impact. Once free of this view of matter, science rightly sought (and continues to seek) to account for present-day life forms in terms of laws that hold between members of the universe. Christianity rightly endorses the search for such accounts on the ground that the source of the universe is rational and so there are connections to be found between its members.

Secondly, Christianity is not committed to the Aristotelian view that species are fixed. If Christianity claimed that species are fixed, it would be committed to the view that present-day life forms were given *directly* by God. Christianity would then be forced to oppose not only Darwin's theory but any scientific attempt to find connections between present life forms and earlier members of nature. But the Christian conviction that God is the Creator is the claim that nature's order is intended by God, not the claim that present-day life forms arose directly from God's action.

The creation stories in Genesis 1 and 2 are to be understood as we understand Jesus' parables. The framework of a parable is not identical with its teaching. For example, the framework of the parable of the talents is the story of a rich landowner who entrusts several servants with various talents of gold and leaves them for a time to go to a far country. The parable teaches us that whatever we have, including our lives, belongs to God and that God holds us responsible for how we live. Likewise, we should not take the framework of the creation stories, which apparently treats present-day life forms as issuing directly from God, as the teaching of the stories. If we do, we needlessly pit any scientific account of the relation between earlier and present-day life forms against the claim that the order of the universe is intended by God. This makes belief in God as the source of nature's order depend on the view that there are no principles in the members of the universe which are responsible in any way for nature's order. This is contrary to the Christian conviction that a rational God creates a universe with members that are coherently connected. Rather than defending Christianity against science, it contradicts a fundamental Christian conviction.

Thirdly, the complexity of nature, which natural theology so stressed by citing example after example of the complexity of various organisms, is irrelevant to the fundamental question nature's order poses. It is the fact that nature as a whole has one order rather than another, which raises the possibility that it is intended. The complexity of nature, which requires us to study it empirically, has led to an awareness of the specificity of the constants of nature. This may lead to an awareness of the fundamental issue nature's order poses, as we shall see in Section III. But merely to cite example after example of complexity in nature, with the claim that such complexity could not arise from chance, does not lead to an awareness of the contingency of nature's order.

Fourthly, the fundamental issue nature's order poses is whether it is intended, not whether it is designed. Design applies to human artifacts, such as machines, watches, houses. It is not necessary that nature's order resemble an artifact for us to ask whether it is intended. The contingency of nature warrants raising the question.

Fifth, whether or not nature's order is intended cannot be settled by Darwin's theory and other evolutionary theories in biology to which Darwin's pioneering effort has led. A study of the relations between the members of the universe can only discover what the order is. It cannot tell us whether it just is what it is or whether it is intended.

III

Some recent discoveries about nature's order are presently being used to support belief in God, as in the seventeenth, eighteenth, and first half of the nineteenth centuries, rather than to undermine it.

One of the most important results of twentieth-century physics has been the gradual realization that there exist invariant properties of the natural world and its elementary components which render the gross size and structure of virtually all its constituents quite inevitable. . . . The intrinsic strengths of these controlling forces of Nature are determined by a mysterious collection of pure numbers that we call the *constants of Nature.*[11]

Obviously for life and human life in particular to develop, the natural world must be such as to allow life to arise and to develop into different forms. Various formulations that seek to find the connections between the gross structure of the universe and the conditions necessary for human life to arise are called "anthropic principles."

What is surprising about developments in recent cosmology is that the constants of nature, which have enabled our observable universe to reach its present state, are quite specific. Were they only slightly different, human life could not have arisen.

For example, if the relative strengths of the nuclear and electromagnetic forces were to be slightly different then carbon atoms could not exist in Nature and human physicists would not have evolved. Likewise, many of the global properties of the Universe, for instance the ratio of the number of photons to protons, must be found to lie within a very narrow range if cosmic conditions are to allow carbon-based life to arise.[12]

Because the slightest difference in the constants of nature would have made the existence of life as we know it impossible, one is tempted to infer that they have been selected in order to permit life, and human life in particular, to exist. We must, however, be very careful here. That the necessary conditions for life to arise and for human life to evolve are quite specific must not be confused with the idea that the existence of such specific conditions is extremely improbable. If these ideas are equated, then the significance of the specificity of nature's constants, a significance quite independent of the issue of their probability, is easily overlooked.

It is very easy to equate them because the discovery that the necessary conditions for the evolution of life are so highly specific is surprising. What is presently surprising, however, may not turn out to be improbable. For example, at one time the largeness of the universe seemed to be superfluous for the development of life on the planet Earth. We now realize that in an expanding universe, size is connected to age, and age with the development of life.

In order to create the building blocks of life—carbon, nitrogen, oxygen and phosphorus—the simple elements of hydrogen and helium which were synthesized in the primordial inferno of the Big Bang must be cooked at a more moderate temperature and for a much longer time than is available in the early universe. The furnaces that are available are the interiors of stars. There, hydrogen and helium are burnt into the heavier life-supporting elements by exothermic nuclear reactions. When stars die, the resulting explosions which we see as supernovae, can disperse these elements through space and they become incorporated into planets and, ultimately, into ourselves. This stellar alchemy takes over ten billion years to complete. Hence, for there to be enough time to construct the constituents of living beings, the Universe must be at least ten billion years old and therefore, as a consequence of its expansion, at least ten billion light years in extent. We should not be surprised to observe that the Universe is so large. No astronomer could exist in one that was significantly smaller. The Universe needs to be as big as it is in order to evolve just a single carbon-based life-form.[13]

Just as the size of the universe is no longer thought to be superfluous to the existence of life because we now understand that its size is connected to its age, so too through new scientific theories and discoveries, the values of the constants which are necessary conditions for life may cease to be surprising. This would undermine an argument to the effect that there must be a designer because the values of the constants of nature are highly improbable.

But whether nature's order is intended by someone does not depend on the degree of probability of nature's order. Its very specificity, being a particular order, is enough to raise the question of whether it is intended. The present observable universe did not start in a highly disorganized state and then gradually reach its present condition. The sizes of stars and planets, and even people, are neither random nor the result of any Darwin-like selection process, but can be explained by some highly specific values of the constants of nature. The specific value of nature's constants and its specific initial state pose the question, Why do we have this universe rather than another possible one?

It is important to be clear that the fundamental question nature's order poses does not turn on whether its order is improbable. Otherwise, the question can be dismissed by relying on our past experience in which what was once thought to be improbable concerning the order of the universe turns out not to be so. This happened at the 1985 annual meeting of the Royal Society of Canada, which had as its topic, "The Origin and Evolution of the Universe: Evidence for Design?" Although the papers were given by eminent scientists and philosophers, neither in the papers nor in the discussion was it made clear that the issue of design does not turn on whether the order of nature is improbable.[14]

We shall have more to say about nature's order later because nature does not seem to be arranged in such a way as invariably to promote human welfare. This raises the question, How is it that a benevolent, all-powerful, and all-wise God made a world in which the operations of nature cause so much suffering? We shall see that although suffering at the hands of nature prevents some people from coming to believe in God and even causes others to abandon belief in God, coming to terms with the indifference of nature to our welfare leads still others to a mature belief in God. As Simone Weil put it, nature's indifference, which is a barrier at first, can become a passageway for God.[15]

From this review of intellectual history in both this and earlier chapters we have shown that it has been thought that science and religion are incompatible and that with the advance of science, religion has been forced to retreat. In fact, the fundamental questions which nature's order and existence pose are not treated by science. It takes the existence of the universe for granted, and studies the relations between its members. It cannot tell us why nature has its particular order, rather than another. People who continued to believe in the truth of Christianity in contrast to natural religion during the modern period were not being foolish. The fundamental questions nature poses point to the possibility of God.

The strongest reasons to reject the possibility of God arise from philosophical, not scientific, objections. For nearly two hundred years philosophy has considered it virtual orthodoxy that nature does not even point to the possibility of God. Hume and Kant have been thought to raise such difficulties with the fundamental questions—why does the world exist and why this one—that nature can play no role whatsoever as part of the reason for belief in God. In the next chapter, in which our primary attention will be on the existence, rather than the order of nature, we shall examine their objections and see how they have been undermined in recent years. Then we shall mount a positive case for the belief that God is the source of nature's order and existence.

Chapter Four

The Existence of the World Points to the Possibility of God

Many religious people, without any particular philosophical or scientific knowledge, believe in God because they believe that the world had to come from somewhere. They do not realize that if they tried to formulate an argument which moves from the existence of the world to God, it would probably be vulnerable to Hume's and Kant's objections to the cosmological argument. One of the main pillars of the modern mentality is that Hume and Kant cut off all routes from the natural world to God, not just that of the cosmological argument.

One of the signs that the modern secular outlook is collapsing is that Hume's and Kant's criticisms of the cosmological argument have been found to be both philosophically misguided and scientifically outdated. The removal of Hume's and Kant's embargo is just beginning to be realized in our university centers. In the future more faculty and students will encounter the question, Is the universe ultimate or not? They will see that on strictly intellectual grounds this is a real question and not the result of fallacious reasoning. The limitations of our scientific and philosophic methods to deal with this fundamental question will also become apparent and become a fixture of our intellectual culture. This will replace the pervasive attitude in our educational system that there is no significant intellectual basis for religious belief and that religious belief expresses only an emotional, personal preference, which does not have to be taken seriously by a rational person. The impetus for this new attitude came from scientists as well as philosophical theologians.

As we shall see, the fact that nature's existence is unexplained by our sciences and philosophy should lead a thinking, inquiring person, actively to consider the possibility that there is a God. From that consideration, a person may begin to be affected by God to such an extent that the conviction arises that there is indeed a God. If, however, Hume's and Kant's objections to the cosmological argument were sound, as they have been thought to be until recently, this route to God, along with that of the cosmological argument, would be blocked. Let us turn to Hume's and Kant's embargo and see how it has been lifted by recent developments.

I

Hume treats the cosmological argument in Part IX of his *Dialogues Concerning Natural Religion*. His criticisms have an importance out of all proportion to their brevity. His character Demea presents a cosmological argument, which scholars have identified as the one formulated at the beginning of the eighteenth century by Samuel Clarke (1675–1729), Sir Isaac Newton's close friend and occasional collaborator. Clarke's argument, like all cosmological arguments, relies on the principle of sufficient reason, namely that whatever exists must have a reason for its existence. We shall examine the significance of this reliance on the principle of sufficient reason after we have considered Hume's and Kant's objections, because were those objections sound, then the question, Why does the universe exist? would not even arise as a question to be answered. Once it is shown that Hume's and Kant's objections do not scuttle the question, Why does the universe exist? we shall consider the controversial issue of whether whatever exists must have a reason for its existence. We shall see that Christianity is not committed to the principle of sufficient reason because Christianity does not claim that the universe must have a reason for its existence but only that it in fact does have a reason for its existence.

Clarke's argument is as follows. A contingent being is a being which depends on some other being for its existence. It is impossible for there to be only contingent beings. If the universe consisted of an infinite succession of contingent beings, each dependent for its existence on previous members of the succession, we can indeed explain why each contingent being exists by reference to another contingent being. But if we take the entire chain or succession of contingent beings together as a whole, it is clear that the universe taken as a whole requires a reason for its existence, just as each individual contingent being does. We may ask not only, Why does this particular succession of contingent beings exist and not another? (as we saw in the previous chapter), but also, Why does any succession of contingent beings exist at all, rather than nothing? Clarke (following the principle of sufficient reason, which says that whatever exists must have a reason for its existence) claims that the reason cannot be chance nor can it be that the universe "just is" with no explanation of its existence at all. The only possible explanation is that there is a necessary being, that is a being which carries the reason for its existence in itself.

Hume's replies (in the person of Cleanthes) have become classics and, until very recently, thought by most philosophers and Protestant theologians to be conclusive. First Hume claims that "necessary" cannot be properly applied to a being. "Whatever we conceive as existent, we can also conceive as non-existent. There is no Being, therefore, whose non-existence implies a contradiction."[1] That is, we may say of whatever actually exists that it might not have existed. There is no contradiction in thinking that whatever is, might not have been. But there is a contradiction in saying of a necessary being that it might not have existed because it would be self-contradictory to say that a being which exists by necessity does not exist. Therefore, it is impossible for there to be a necessary being. Hume's Cleanthes asserts that this reasoning is conclusive, and he is willing to rest his refutation of the cosmological argument on it alone.

Hume's argument rests on the particular meaning he gives to "necessary being." For Hume the concept of "necessary being" implies that such a being actually exists because logically it would be self-contradictory to say that a being which exists by necessity does not exist. For him, "necessary being" means necessarily to exist.

In recent years, however, it has been pointed out that there is another sense of "necessary being" which does not imply that such a being necessarily exists.[2] In Christianity God is a necessary being in the sense of a being that has no beginning and no end because God is not dependent on anything in order to exist. It is indeed true that God, if God actually exists, is not a being that might not have existed. This is not true of the members of the universe, such as people. People actually exist, but they might not have, and they might cease to be. That is, they are "contingent beings," beings whose existence is dependent on other things. In contrast to the being or existence of the members of the universe, God's being is that of a necessary being in the sense that it does not depend on anything. To say that God is a necessary being in this sense does not imply that God necessarily exists. Hume's "conclusive" objection to the cosmological argument is effective against Clarke's version of the argument because Clarke thinks of a necessary being as a logically necessary being (one that necessarily exists), but it is not effective against Thomas Aquinas' version of the argument (the "Third Way," as it is called) because Thomas has a Christian understanding of necessary being.[3] Hume, because he takes it that "necessary being" means "logically necessary" (one that necessarily exists) has not shown that a necessary being in the Christian sense is impossible.

II

Hume, however, has another major objection. It is of more significance for my purposes than his first one because my interest is not with a rehabilitation of the cosmological argument but with the question of whether the very existence of the universe poses a question. Through the voice of Cleanthes, Hume claims that it does not. Let us see his reason for this.

Both Cleanthes and Demea agree: (1) that the world consists of contingent or dependent beings, that is, beings that actually exist but that might not have existed; (2) that the succession of contingent beings has no beginning, but is infinitely long; and (3) that each particular contingent being's existence can be explained by reference to previously existing contingent members of the succession.

Demea, however, claims that the infinite succession of contingent beings taken as a whole needs to have its existence explained. Even though each member of the succession of contingent beings stretching back to infinity can be explained in terms of other members of the succession, why there is this succession of dependent beings or any succession of dependent beings at all has not been explained.

Cleanthes, on the contrary, claims that this is absurd. The existence of an infinite succession of contingent or dependent beings poses no question at all. In an eternal succession of objects

each part is caused by that which preceded it, and causes that which succeeds it. Where then is the difficulty? But the WHOLE you say, wants a cause. . . . Did I show you the particular causes of each individual in a collection of twenty particles of matter, I should think it very unreasonable, should you afterwards ask me, what was the cause of the whole twenty. This is sufficiently explained in explaining the cause of the parts.[4]

In other words, if the existence of each member of an infinite succession of contingent or dependent beings is explained by a previous member of the succession, then there is nothing left to be explained. The existence of a succession of dependent beings has been explained with the explanation of the existence of each member of the succession. The existence of the universe, therefore, poses no question.

But the adequacy of this reasoning is no longer accepted even in the analytic philosophic community, which, on the whole, has been aggressively antagonistic toward theism and a champion of Hume's attacks on metaphysics in general and natural religion in particular. William L. Rowe has most effectively shown the failure of Hume's reasoning.[5]

Rowe uses the analogy of a set or collection of men, M. The set is assumed to have an infinite number of members, each member owing its existence to some other member which generated it. He grants that to explain the existence of a given man it is sufficient to note that he was begotten by some other man. So every member of the set M has an explanation of its existence. But

. . . if *all* we know is that there always have been men and that every man's existence is explained by the causal efficacy of some other man, we do not know *why*
there always have been men rather than none at all. If I ask why M has the
members it does rather than none, it is no answer to say that M always had
members.[6]

With the substitution of "contingent or dependent beings" for "men,"
the same argument applies to an infinite succession of dependent
beings, each of which is caused by other dependent beings.

III

Although Hume's objections to the cosmological argument have been
shown to fail, Kant raised an additional one, which is quite formidable.
Since Kant's objection is formulated within the framework of his own
philosophy, in which causality is a category of the human understanding, it is preferable to examine Bertrand Russell's formulation because
it presents its essence independently of Kant's framework. In a BBC
debate with Father Copleston, Russell said,

I can illustrate what seems to me your fallacy. Every man who exists has a
mother, and it seems to me your argument is that therefore the human race
must have a mother, but obviously the human race hasn't a mother—that's a
different logical sphere.[7]

Improperly to apply a property to the whole of a collection because it
applies to each member of the collection is technically called "the fallacy
of composition." For example, it is incorrect to infer from the fact that
each part of a machine is light that the entire machine is light. But Russell claims that more than this is involved because "the human race" is
an abstraction and each person, who is a member of the human race, is
a concrete being.

Russell claims that it is a mistake to ascribe a property—having a cause
or explanation—to the infinite collection of dependent beings that make
up our world because it is applicable only to the members of the collection. It is fallacious to infer from the fact that every member of the
infinite collection of beings that make up our world has a reason for its
existence that the infinite collection itself has an explanation for its existence. It is a mistake to think that the world has a reason for its existence simply because each of its members does.

Rowe very effectively responds to the charge that these fallacies have
been committed. First, he shows that sometimes a collection has a property which each member also has. He suggests: "Suppose we are holding
in our hands a collection of ten marbles. Not only would each marble

have a definite weight but the collection itself would have a weight."[8] Rowe then asks, Is "the universe" understood as a collection of dependent beings an abstraction or a concrete entity?

> Think, for example, of a collection whose members are the largest prehistoric beast, Socrates, and the Empire State Building. By any stretch of the imagination can we view this collection as itself a concrete thing? Clearly we cannot. Such a collection must be construed as an *abstract* entity, a class or set. . . . Our knowledge of things (both past and present) comprising the universe and their interrelations would have to be much greater than it presently is before we would be entitled to view the *sum* of concrete things, past and present, as itself something *concrete*.[9]

Nonetheless, Rowe argues that even though the universe is an abstract entity, this does not render the question, Why does the world exist? vulnerable to Russell's criticism.

> Suppose that every being that is or ever was is dependent. Suppose further that the number of such beings is infinite. Let A be the set consisting of these beings. Thus no being exists or ever existed which is not a member of A. Does it make *sense* to ask for an explanation of A's existence? We do, of course, ask questions about sets which are equivalent to questions about their members. For example, "Is set X included in set Y?" is equivalent to the question "Is every member of X a member of Y?" I suggest that the question, "Why does A exist?" be taken to mean "Why does A have the members that it does rather than some other members or none at all?" . . . In asking why A exists we are not asking for an explanation of the existence of an abstract entity; we are asking why A has the members it has rather than some other members or none at all.[10]

By a shift from asking about the existence of a set as an abstract entity to asking about the membership of a set, Rowe avoids the category mistake Russell says is committed when one asks for an explanation of the totality of things. In asking for an explanation of the universe's existence one is not saying "because every member of the universe has a reason for its existence, the world must have a reason for its existence." This would be to attribute a property to an abstract entity because it applies to members of that abstraction. Nor in asking why the universe exists is one asking of an abstraction why it exists. Rather one is taking the world as an abstract entity and asking why that abstract entity has the membership it has rather than other members, or even no members at all.

Once we see that the question, Why does the universe exist? is not attributing a property to an abstract entity because it applies to the members of that abstraction, and once we see that the question is not about the existence of the abstraction itself but its membership, we see that no fallacy has been committed in asking the question. The very existence of the universe does indeed pose a question, a fundamental one. The unsophisticated perception that the universe's existence is unexplained is a sound one, even though it takes quite sophisticated reasoning to meet Hume's and Kant's claims that it is unsound.

IV

In asking the question, Why does the universe exist? the "universe" has sometimes been treated as a concrete entity. In his celebrated "Third Way," in which he moved from contingent beings to a necessary being, Thomas Aquinas apparently assumed that the world was a concrete entity, a sort of great big thing. In modern philosophy this assumption has been thought to be highly implausible, as we saw reflected in Rowe's remark that by any stretch of the imagination, it is not possible to view the largest prehistoric animal, Socrates, and the Empire State Building as a concrete thing.

Recent developments in cosmology, however, indicate that to speak of the universe as a concrete entity is coherent. Einstein's general theory of relativity provided for the first time in the history of science an account of the totality of gravitationally interacting matter free of contradiction. This made the field of cosmology—the study of the physical universe as a whole—possible.[11]

Then the detection of the red shift in light from heavenly bodies led to the realization that the universe is rapidly expanding. By a process of extrapolation, it appears that our universe, just before the Big Bang, was an extremely dense mass. The present visible universe is the result of the expansion of that mass and the various transformations of energy since that initial explosion. It makes sense to speak of the physical universe as a concrete entity since present-day cosmology does so and does so intelligibly. The question, Why does the universe exist? arises as a result of recent scientific developments.

We do not need to rely on this development in cosmology. We have seen that even if the universe is not a concrete entity but only a collection or aggregate of beings, the question, Why does the universe exist? is a legitimate question. Kant, however, raised a serious objection to considering the world as a whole, whether the world is regarded as a concrete entity or as a collection of beings. He claimed that to treat the world as a whole leads to contradictions. Although these arguments have not been as widely accepted as his criticisms of the cosmological argument, we need to consider the section of his *Critique of Pure Reason* which he called "The Antinomy of Pure Reason" (in the international pagination, A406/B433 to A567/B595).

In the first antinomy, Kant argues that the world had a beginning and that the world had no beginning; that it is spatially finite and that it is spatially infinite. In the second antinomy, Kant argues that there must be a smallest particle of matter and that there cannot be a smallest particle. In the third, we are forced to assert that there is freedom and also to assert that there is causal determinism. In the fourth, we are forced to admit both that there is and that there is not a necessary being.

Kant claims that these antinomies prove that what we experience is phenomena (or the way things appear) and that our experience tells us nothing about noumena (the way things are in themselves). The basic concepts or categories of our understanding are properly employed only to organize appearances. We can steadily increase our knowledge of the phenomenal world by moving step by step in our empirical inquiries concerning sensible objects. The contradictions of rational cosmology, as he calls the treatment of the universe as a whole, arise only when we seek to go beyond all possible sense experience by asking about the extent of the universe as a whole in space and time, about the ultimate constituents of material objects, whether freedom is possible, and whether there is more than contingent beings. This is to use the fundamental categories of the understanding *without* any empirical data. Kant claims that it is evident from the contradictions we encounter in rational cosmology that this is a mistake. These contradictions show that the categories of our understanding are properly used only for the organization of the data supplied by the senses. If we recognize that the categories of the understanding are to be employed solely to organize sense experience, we will thereby recognize that our reason has no power to go beyond all possible experience to the ultimate ground of experience (or the universe as we know it).

If Kant is correct, we cannot ask questions of the universe as a whole because it is an appearance only and cannot be the basis of any claim about its ground. But, as a matter of fact, the arguments of the first antinomy concerning the extent of the world in space fail. On the one hand, Kant argues that the universe cannot be finite. If it were, then we would come to a boundary, and there would be something on the other side of the boundary. This has been undermined by Einstein's theory of relativity in which one possible form the universe might have is one that is limited but unbounded. Kant's argument assumes that space is absolute (not relative) and that Euclidean geometry is the description of the properties of space (whereas in Einstein's theory space is curved). Whether Einstein's theory is or is not a correct account of space, the very existence of a coherent theory of space that is not absolute and Euclidean undermines Kant's assumptions in his argument that it is logically impossible for space to be finite. On the other hand, Kant's argument for the opposite view, that the universe cannot be infinite, is fallacious. Kant argued that if space were infinite, we could not know it. But that we cannot know that space is infinite does not show that it cannot in fact be infinite.

Kant's antinomy concerning time, even though it assumes that time is absolute, has more merit. On the one hand, Kant argues that if time is infinite in duration, then to reach the present moment, an infinite amount of time must have elapsed. This is impossible. On the other hand, if time is of finite duration, then it began. But this is impossible because there would be a time before time began.

Augustine wrestled with this dilemma in Book XI of his *Confessions*. His solution is of continuing philosophical and theological interest. In brief, he proposed that time, like the rest of the universe, is created. There is never a time before the world existed because the world and time are created together; and on the other hand, because time is created, it is not infinite. The antinomy is solved should the world and time in fact be creatures and not ultimate realities.[12] Kant has not demonstrated that to ask about the duration of time inevitably leads to an antinomy.

Because we may speak of the universe as a whole without falling into contradictions, we may indeed ask, Why does the universe exist? We are not forced to conclude that the universe as a whole is an appearance, resulting from the structure of human reason and sensibility and incapable of revealing anything about reality itself. It can be granted that we know things only as they interact with us, so that our knowledge of them is limited by the structure of our reason and the nature of our sense organs. This is far from granting that what we know are appearances that provide no basis whatsoever for saying anything about the universe itself.

V

Independently of the antinomies, Kant argues that the category of causality is a relation between members of the universe only and not between members of the universe and what is beyond the universe (A609/B637). Kant says that according to the cosmological argument, "everything contingent has a cause, which, if itself contingent, must likewise have a cause, till the series of subordinate causes ends with an absolutely necessary cause, without which it [the series of subordinate causes] would have no completeness" (A605/B633). In other words, the succession of causes and effects cannot go on to infinity but must have a beginning or first cause.

Kant claims that the cosmological argument fails because, were we to move back in time from each member in a causal succession of beings, we would ask of whatever we encounter, Why does it exist? We would never reach or come across a being which is without a cause. If we insist that there must be a being at the start of the series of caused beings which does not itself have a cause, we violate the principle of causality. The only way any member of the succession could be a necessary being is for it to be an exception to the causal principle that everything has a cause. If we are willing to violate the principle of causality, we cannot say that the necessary being whose existence we infer is God or a perfect being. By violating or suspending the principle of causality, anything for all we know might be a being without a cause, that is a necessary being. From the sheer concept of a "necessary being" we can say nothing about what it is, except that it is without a cause (A585/B613ff. and A606/B634ff.). To say that the necessary being posited at the start of the series is God or a perfect being is to beg the question.

In addition, to say that by "necessary being" we mean a being whose perfection is the reason it exists assumes the validity of the ontological argument. That is, if the concepts of a "necessary being" and a "perfect being" were identical, from the concept of "a perfect being" we may infer that such a being exists because it is necessary. With a valid ontological argument, the cosmological argument is superfluous. Without a valid ontological argument, in which necessary being means perfect being, the cosmological argument cannot establish the existence of God.

In the seventeenth and eighteenth centuries the cosmological argument was often cast in the form: there must be a necessary being *in the causal succession* of beings. It differs from Clarke's cosmological argument in which the succession of contingent beings is infinite, and the reason or cause of the existence of the succession is *not itself a member* of the succession.

Kant's criticisms apply to both formulations of the cosmological argument. On the one hand, if a necessary being stands at the start of the succession of contingent beings, then the causal relation between a necessary being and the rest of the succession is the same kind of causality as holds between contingent beings. This is why this version of the cosmological argument is vulnerable to the charge that it violates or suspends the causal principle when it infers the existence of a necessary being. The only way any member of the succession could be a necessary being is for it to be an exception to the causal principle that everything has a cause, as we just saw. On the other hand, if a necessary being does not stand at the start of the succession of contingent beings, as in Clarke's formulation of the cosmological argument, its causal relation to the members of the succession of contingent beings is a different kind of causality from that which holds between the members. We cannot, therefore, use the causal principle that applies to members of the succession as a premise in an argument to infer the existence of a being that is outside the succession. The existence of a succession of contingent beings may indeed raise a question, but we cannot infer on the basis of the kind of causality that exists between the members of the succession that the succession as a whole has a cause.

The refutation of the cosmological argument is extremely useful for exhibiting an important aspect of the theological claim that God is the Creator of the universe. The causal relation between God and the universe is not the same as the relations that exist between the members of the universe. Rather than being detrimental, Kant's basis for refuting both forms of the cosmological argument concurs with a fundamental theological principle. It has been held from the earliest days of Christian theology that God is not a member of the universe, and therefore God's relation as Creator to the members of the universe is not the same as any of the relations that exist between its members. For example, members of the universe are causally related by such things as generation (offspring result from sexual intercourse and pollination), impact, and gravitational force. God does not produce the universe by any process of generation, nor is divine creative causality impact or gravitational force. Because God is the Creator of every kind of relation between the members of the universe, the relations between members of the universe differ from the creative relation between God and the universe.

This is the reason God cannot be reached by scientific investigations that study the relations between members of the universe. To posit God's existence because, let us say, the universe began with a highly dense mass that exploded, commits a serious mistake. It is to infer the existence of God in order to complete the succession of caused beings by having God at the start of the succession. But the causal relations between the members of the universe which allow us to extrapolate from the present back to a Big Bang and a highly dense mass just before it are not like the causal relation between God and the universe, so that we may with one more step extrapolate to God. On the basis of the causal relations science uses, we cannot infer that the highly dense mass was created by God. Nor on the same basis can we deny that the universe was created by God. God is not the final member of the succession of beings studied in cosmology or in any of the sciences any more than God was the top story of Aristotle's hierarchical universe, the unmoved mover. There is a discontinuity between God and our scientific explanations because God's relation to the universe is that of Creator and our sciences study the relations between the members of the universe.

Even though God's creative activity is different from the causality which exists between members of the universe, we can conceive of God as the cause or Creator of the universe. Kant explicitly rejects Hume's argument to the contrary in the *Dialogues Concerning Natural Religion*.[13] According to Hume we must either speak of God anthropomorphically or say that God is so different from anything else that we cannot attribute to God any characteristic whatsoever. Neither is satisfactory.

Frequently philosophers and theologians have incorrectly attributed Hume's position to Kant on the ground that Kant claims that all that we experience is phenomenal and not noumenal and that our categories of the understanding prevent us from thinking anything noumenal. But Kant explicitly says in the *Critique of Pure Reason* that although we cannot infer from our phenomenal experience that each of us is a noumenal self (because the same ego may underlie all of us), nonetheless the idea of each of us as a noumenal self is a coherent notion. We simply cannot establish its existence by pure reason (A339/B397 to A405/B432). Likewise, the idea or concept of God, that is, of an uncaused being that is the ultimate condition of everything else, is coherent. Such a being *may* exist. It is simply that we are not able to determine by sense experience nor by inference whether such a being does or does not exist.

In addition, Kant explicitly argues in his *Prolegomena to Any Future Metaphysics* (356–60), written and published between the first and second editions of the *Critique of Pure Reason*, that we may characterize or describe God's nature and relation to the universe analogically. God's creative relation to the universe is analogous to the causality between its members. Kant's account, though briefer, concurs in essentials with that of Thomas Aquinas.[14]

VI

We have now seen that the existence of the universe poses a question. It is one thing, however, to have a question that makes sense, and another for us to be able to answer it. Those who relied on a version of the cosmological argument such as Clarke used, knew that the causal relation between God and the universe is not the kind of causality that exists between members of the universe. They did not rely on that kind of causality to infer that there is a necessary being outside the infinite succession of contingent beings, but on the principle of sufficient reason.

Although this principle can be formulated in several ways, the essential idea is that whatever exists has a reason or cause for its existence, though the precise nature of the dependency is not specified by the principle.

According to the principle of sufficient reason, an infinite succession of contingent beings must have a reason for its existence. The penalty for denying the principle is to have an unintelligible universe. That is, on the one hand, we would seek for an explanation of the existence of every member of the succession of dependent beings in terms of previous members of the series but, on the other hand, there would be no reason for the existence of the succession itself. Of the existence of the world itself we would simply say, "It just is." We must hold either to the view that everything is intelligible or to the view that the existence of the universe is a brute fact.

Those who advocated the cosmological argument in the more sophisticated form that Clarke employed were convinced that the universe had the intelligibility our minds seek and demand. They were convinced of the power of human reason to move from the sheer existence of the world to a necessary being. This is one of the reasons the cosmological argument fell out of favor early in the eighteenth century. There was a growing skepticism concerning the power of reason to go beyond the bounds of experience in the fashion of the cosmological argument well before Hume and Kant formulated their specific objections to speculative metaphysics and to the cosmological argument in particular. Hume's famous remark that any book which does not consist of mathematical reasoning or reasoning based on experience is to be consigned to the flames because "it can contain nothing but sophistry and illusion"[15] was a reflection, not a source, of a widespread attitude toward speculative metaphysics in the eighteenth century. He knew he could rely on the approval of many intellectuals when he had Cleanthes, in the *Dialogues Concerning Natural Religion,* extol the order of nature—because it is a matter of experience—as the basis for belief in God and dismiss with disdain Demea's argument from nature's existence to a being infinite in power, wisdom, and goodness. Kant, unlike Hume, influenced his contemporaries, as well as posterity. His *Critique of Pure Reason* made such a powerful case for the limitations of reason that no philosopher has been able to ignore it.

In addition to Hume's and Kant's claims about the limitations of reason, we today have become very leery of trusting "what seems reasonable to the human mind" because we have learned from our experience in the sciences that nature sometimes surprises our expectations and shatters our previous views of its laws. "That whatever exists has a reason for its existence" may seem eminently reasonable but that does not mean that the principle is true. Uneasiness over the power of reason is so extensive that the principle of sufficient reason is generally not endorsed by philosophers outside Roman Catholic circles. Without that principle one cannot *infer* from the contingency of the world's existence that there is a necessary being.

VII

We have now completed our investigation of Hume's and Kant's objections to the cosmological argument. Until the last few years their objections were thought by virtually everyone outside Roman Catholic circles to block any move from the existence of the universe to the existence of God. The fact that they are not decisive creates a new intellectual situation in Western culture because it means that the existence of the universe does after all pose a legitimate question. We may not be able to answer it philosophically—that is, infer from the world's existence that it is, or is not, caused by God—because the cosmological argument depends on the truth of the principle of sufficient reason. We do not know whether the principle that whatever exists must have a reason for its existence is true or false. A person may legitimately respond to the question, "Why does the universe exist?" by saying "Why should it have a reason for its existence? What makes you think that it must?" To reply, "But everything must have a reason for its existence" is simply to repeat the very principle at issue. No one has yet been able to show that everything must have a reason for its existence in a way that has won the approval of the philosophical community at large.[16] Nonetheless, the impossibility of deducing God's existence from the world's existence does not mean that the existence of the world raises no question. We do not know either scientifically or philosophically that the world "just is." There might be a reason for its existence, and God might be the reason. God is a possible answer to the question posed by nature's existence.

It is widely believed in the philosophical community that people believe in God because they implicitly or explicitly rely on some form of the principle of sufficient reason. This would make the validity of belief in God a question of the soundness of that principle. Consider, for example, Milton K. Munitz's opening remarks in *The Mystery of Existence:*[17]

Why need we vacillate, or be under tension, between choosing either a "Greek" way of looking at the world, as something to be understood in itself, or a "Hebraic" way of looking at the world, as something made by a Power that transcends it? Both modes of thought are trying, each in its own way, to satisfy the human drive for rationality and intelligibility. Both operate with some form of a Principle of Sufficient Reason.

We are not sure why the ancient Hebrews believed in God, and in a Creator God, but on the basis of historical study of the Old Testament, it appears that Munitz is far from the mark. Gerhard von Rad in his widely respected *Old Testament Theology* argues that the oldest creedal statements of ancient Israel do not contain a reference to creation. They begin with the call of Abraham.[18] When, later in their development, the Jews confess such a belief, it is apparently in order to affirm the universal sovereignty of their God, Yahweh, who is not only their God but the God of all peoples and Lord over nature itself. The mode of this affirmation is creation stories. There is no evidence to suggest that they were motivated to explain the existence of the world by the drive for rationality and intelligibility and employed some version of the principle of sufficient reason. They did not begin with creation (belief in God as Creator) and then move to belief in a Redeemer. Rather they believed in a Redeemer God and then moved to belief that their God was responsible for the order and existence of the world.

Belief that the world is dependent on a transcendent reality apparently does not turn on the issue of the principle of sufficient reason. Yet the large amount of attention given to the traditional proofs of God's existence by philosophers of religion has given the impression that the truth of the major theistic religions—Judaism, Christianity and Islam—turns on the truth or falsity of the principle of sufficient reason. This is a far more significant matter than it may seem at first, for it affects the tendency in modern times to reduce religious beliefs to nonreligious contexts and make them part of our scientific or philosophical inquiries, as if God were the top story of the universe, instead of its creative source.

Perhaps we can make the difference in context clear by pointing out the difference between an *answer* and an *explanation*. Our sciences seek to find repeated and repeatable patterns in the interactions between the members of the universe and to formulate them into laws. These laws are explained by being subsumed under theories. To say that God created the universe does not imply that God is a theory under which we subsume and explain creative activity. Nor was God's existence initially posited by the Jews, as we have just noted, because the universe's existence is unexplained and they sought complete intelligibility. God does, however, answer the question, Why does the universe exist? It exists because someone created it.

The Genesis accounts of the beginning of the world identify *who* intended its existence and do not merely claim that it is intended by someone. That is, the question is answered in such a way that not only is our "whence" addressed but also our "whither." We are told our significance and our goal. God, the one who called Abraham and Sarah and later brought the children of Israel out of slavery in Egypt, intends us to enjoy life with God. (Paradise is where God is present; paradise for us is to be with God.) But we are not where we ought to be. We are responsible for this situation, and we resist our restoration. We are informed by the rest of the Bible that God's intention for us to inhabit God's "garden" is more fundamental than our pride and folly. (This is the foundation of the Christian doctrine of justification by grace; the doctrine of sanctification concerns the path of our actual restoration or our pilgrimage from where we are to where we ought to be.) The significance of our lives is to be understood with God's intentions as the beginning of all things and as their finality. We do not know what God's intentions are, except for ourselves, and even in our case, not fully. Still we seek to understand our lives within the context or setting of God's intentions for us insofar as we can understand them.[19]

The Septuagint translation of the Old Testament, which was used in ancient times by Jews who read Greek but not Hebrew, has the Greek word *arche* for "beginning" in the opening verse of Genesis. *Arche* nicely suggests the duality of God's creative intentions, the "whence" and "whither" we have described. *Arche* means not only beginning in the sense of a temporal start, but also "beginning" in the sense of a story to be narrated. It also means "beginning" in the sense of a "principle" from which other things are derived, as we use the word in such phrases as "principles of geometry," or "principles of physics." God as our beginning is an answer to the question, Why does the universe exist? but that beginning is the beginning of a story *with an end.* That beginning contains the principle of our being or nature, the being that we are intended to become. As T. S. Eliot put it in his *Four Quartets,* "In my beginning is my end" (our goal is intended from the very origination of our being), and "In my end is my beginning" (the realization that we have a goal or end is the beginning of our attempt to become what we are intended to be).

Even though belief in the Christian God does not arise initially because we think that the universe must be intelligible, such a belief does answer the question, Why does the universe exist? To a believer the universe is intelligible. But the situation seems to be even more complex than simply which comes first, belief in God or belief in the intelligibility of the universe, important as that is. The Greeks believed in the intelligibility of nature but never asked, Why does the universe exist? This omission may not be an oversight, because the very question has a religious and theological source. Once there is the conviction that the universe is created by God, on strictly philosophical grounds we can see that the members of the universe do not explain why we have this universe rather than another or any universe at all. But the question was not raised by any philosophical reasoning among the ancient Greeks nor apparently by anyone else.[20]

This further suggests that the grounds of the principle of sufficient reason are religious and theological. Rather than the principle being the route to God, on the ground that without God the existence and order of the universe are unintelligible, it is the conviction that there is a good and wise Creator that leads to the conviction that the universe has an intelligible order and that its existence is not just a brute fact. Once the book of Scripture spread the idea that the universe is created by a wise and good God, both Christian and non-Christian can perceive that nature's order and existence pose questions about their source. But only those with a conviction that the universe is intelligible because of a belief in God the Creator are intellectually distressed with the notion that the mind can properly rest content with a universe whose order and existence are to be accepted as brute facts.

The way the questions nature poses have been resisted by Hume and Kant and the following they have had, even though their reasoning was faulty, suggest that once the contents of the book of Scripture become known in a culture, the only way one can be intellectually content with the idea that the universe "just is" is by resisting an active consideration of the possibility of God. Just to argue that the principle of sufficient reason has not been established on philosophical grounds and therefore there is no warrant for saying that the universe must have a source smacks of evasion.

God as the reason for the existence of all things surrounds scientific explanations about the relations between the members of the cosmos with a "whence" and a "whither," informing us that we are to live our lives with God, that our present state is our responsibility, and that so much of our activity is to be understood as a resistance to the realization of divine intentions. This answer is compatible with the scientific evolutionary account of the origin of human beings (arising from other members of the universe) because every human being is a member of the universe (a natural being made of the clay of the earth). But our very existence, like that of every other member of the universe, is dependent on the continuing creative activity of God. That creative activity, as we shall see later in detail, makes active creatures that are capable of development and capable of causing other beings.

We may summarize the distinctions between scientific, philosophic, and theological contexts by contrasting the way each treats both the order and the existence of the universe, drawing upon this and the previous chapter. Scientists study the relations between the members of the universe. In science the question, Why is the universe ordered as it is? means, Is the universe or some feature of it so complex that it suggests that it was designed?

In philosophy, the question is, Why does nature have this order rather than another possible order? This question arises because of the contingency of nature's laws (they do not have to be the way they are). It arose among medieval philosophers such as William of Ockham (c. 1300–49), that is, before scientists propounded the mechanistic view of the universe and before we realized how complex the universe is.

Christianity does not claim that the order of the universe is such that we ought to infer that nature is designed. However great or little its complexity, nature's order is intended by God. Since Darwin's theory of natural selection more or less explained how very complex forms of life arise from much simpler forms, we have not been inclined to move toward the idea of design, however great the complexity is. But scientific procedures and assumptions which do not regard nature's order as intended, do not contradict the Christian claim that the order of the universe is intended by God. It is the Lordship of God over nature, not nature's complexity, which is the basis of the claim. God as the source of nature's order gives us no specific information about the relation between its members. But, as we pointed out in Chapter One, an important ingredient in the attitude that led to the creation of classical science was the conviction that a wise and good God created the universe. In addition, it was the conviction that God was Lord over nature that led medieval Christian thinkers to realize that nature's laws are contingent, not the contingency of the laws that led to God.

Science takes the existence of the universe for granted in its study of the relations between its members. As we have just seen, philosophic discussions have greatly refined the formulation of the question, Why does the universe exist? and made it clear that we are able to infer an answer only by use of the principle of sufficient reason.

In Christianity there is no commitment to the principle of sufficient reason. It does not claim that there must be a reason for the order and existence of the world. Nor is God posited to satisfy an alleged human drive for rationality and intelligibility. Rather, when Christianity speaks of creation, it is talking about the Lordship over nature of the one who called Abraham and Sarah, and it is claiming that our beginning includes our finality so that our life has a purpose to be realized.

To affirm God's existence is not an issue of "science versus religion," that is, Is the universe so complex in its order that we are to infer that it is designed? with science taking one side and theology taking the other. Nor is it an issue of "philosophy versus theology," that is, Are we to say that there *must* be a reason for the order and existence of the world? with whatever philosophy determines about the principle of sufficient reason being decisive for theology. Rather the controversy is between a theological view and a rival theological view, that is, between saying, "God is the reason we have a universe" and saying, "The universe just is." Each side of this controversy is a theological position because we do not know from our sciences or our philosophy that the universe "just is." To be an atheist or an agnostic is to hold a theological position, albeit a negative or undecided one, not a scientific or philosophical position. An understanding of the particular contexts of science, philosophy, and theology on the issue of the status of the natural world should make this clear. In addition, the fact that the universe's order and existence do not establish God's existence is not a good reason for being an atheist or agnostic. This is not the role nature plays in leading to belief in God.

A genuine conflict has occurred in modern times, not over our origins but over our future or our prospects. As we pointed out in the Introduction, one of the pillars of the modern mentality is that human progress is inevitable, a conviction allegedly supported by science. This conviction fails to recognize our limitations, especially our inability to eradicate evil and to establish a utopia. This conflict between Christianity and the modern mentality is not between theology and science but between Christianity and an unrealistic estimate of what we are able to achieve through our science and other forms of knowledge. Later we will have much more to say about the reality of evil. We have broached it here because the theological answer to the question, Why does the universe exist? simultaneously addresses our origin and our future.

VIII

Even though theological and philosophical contexts are different, philosophical discussions of the question, Why does the world exist? are relevant to Christianity. If we could explain the existence of the universe solely by reference to its members, or if the question, Why does the world exist? were the result of logical fallacies, it would be incorrect to affirm that there is a Creator God, regardless of the context of that affirmation. The universe must be something that might have a reason for its existence and whose reason has not been supplied by its own members. The ancient Hebrews seemed to have had a belief in a divine power before they believed in the creation of the universe. For the contemporary Christian the sole or primary reason for belief in God may not be that God accounts for the universe's existence. Nevertheless, one could not believe in a creator were there not a question which a creator answers. This is a necessary condition for belief in a Creator God. We would know that the world did not have a creator were it incorrect to ask, Why does the universe exist?

Another value of philosophical reflection is that it shows that the question, Why does the universe exist? does not depend on an experience of awe and wonder at its existence, such as Wittgenstein and Tillich describe. Consider this account from Wittgenstein:

. . . what have all of us who, like myself, are still tempted to use such expressions as "absolute good," "absolute value," etc., what have we in mind and what do we try to express? . . . In my case, it always happens that the idea of one particular experience presents itself to me which therefore is, in a sense, my experience *par excellence.* . . . I believe the best way of describing it is to say that when I have it *I wonder at the existence of the world.* And I am then inclined to use such phrases as "how extraordinary that anything should exist" or "how extraordinary that the world should exist."[21]

Wittgenstein goes on to say that the verbal expressions he is driven to utter because of this experience are nonsense because our words express only "facts" and this experience concerns "values." Tillich, who describes this same kind of experience as an "ontological shock" or the "shock of being," also says that verbally the question, Why does the universe exist? is nonsense, even though he believes that the intuition is sound and he builds a great deal of his theology on it.[22]

Both men's reference to the "nonsense" of the question reflects the Humean-Kantian embargo on it, which was still in place in their day. What is important here is that, even though the existence of the universe causes some people to have an experience of awe and wonder, we may recognize that the universe's existence poses a question without such an experience. This is the value of Rowe's formulation. The question can be plainly stated with precision as, Why does the collection of caused beings have any members at all? This is important because many people are adverse to whatever smacks of mysticism and they may dismiss the question the existence of the universe poses on the ground that it relies on such an experience. In addition, even though the experience of awe and wonder does not itself show that the formulation of the question, Why does the universe exist? is free of fallacious reasoning, nor that the universe's existence poses no question that has not already been answered, nor that it is untrue that that the world "just is," the experience can be a powerful motive to investigate the question, Is there a reason for the existence of the universe? The motive provided by a sense of wonder at the world's existence is a sound one on which to act because the world may indeed have a reason for its existence.

The questions the order and the existence of the universe pose may vary in intensity from person to person, from a quite mild acknowledgment of the fact that we indeed do not know that the world "just is" to an intense degree of wonder, as suggested by Tillich's expression "ontological shock." But how can an answer be sought if scientific study of the relation between the members of the universe gets us no closer, and we make no use of the principle of sufficient reason?

In the next chapter we shall consider the role the order and existence of the universe may play as part of the basis for a present-day belief in the existence and goodness of God. As we shall see, the fact that nature's existence is unexplained by our sciences and philosophy should lead a thinking, inquiring person actively to consider the possibility that there is an answer to the question and indeed that God may be the answer. From this consideration a person may begin to be affected by God, that is to interact with God (even though one is only considering the possibility of God), and from that interaction come to be affected to such an extent that the conviction arises that there is a God. Philosophers have treated the moves from nature's order and existence to God primarily as an inference (the teleological and the cosmological arguments), not as a move because of the interaction between beings, God and humans.

Chapter Five

The Need for God and the Book of Nature

As we have seen, nature points to the possibility of God because the order and existence of the universe are not explained by its members. The God described in the book of Scripture is possibly the reason why the world exists and has its order, but such a God is not pointed to *explicitly* by the book of nature. Why then speak of God? Because human needs lead us to call the world's existence and worth as the highest and best reality into question, we turn to an active consideration of the possibility of God. This can lead to an appreciation of what the book of Scripture tells us about ourselves and God. From that appreciation, the response of faith may arise, a response that is wholly reasonable.

A study of the natural world today usually fails to lead to an active consideration and an appreciation of the book of Scripture because the linchpin of human needs is missing in our thinking. As we saw in Chapter Two, with the rise of modern science all values were excluded from scientific laws and theories. Even though human beings are purposive agents, seeking to satisfy their needs, their purposive activity and the study of the physical universe were kept apart. Our intellectual history created a conflict between our hearts and our heads, between "religion and science," and between "religion and philosophy." An appreciation of the relevance of God to human needs—what Austin Farrer called "initial faith"—often leads nowhere because it is thought that, however attractive the Christian vision may be and however drawn we may be to the notion of a benevolent deity, we ought to resist the impulse of our hearts in order to be intellectually honest.

The account we have given in the previous chapters of the book of nature in postmodern times, however, shows us that there is no longer any reason to think that there is an essential conflict between the heart and head. Our science and philosophy, which once seemed to have banished God from the intellectual sphere, now enable us to see that nature's order and existence point to the possibility of God. We may therefore examine human needs in relation to the possibility of God with perfect intellectual integrity. As a matter of fact, we shall see that not to do so would be to act unreasonably.

In this chapter we shall specify four human needs which lead us to ask the question, Does the universe have a source? These four reasons to call into question the universe's existence and worth as the highest and best reality[1] enable nature to become a witness to God, and not just to point toward a possible source. We are brought face to face with a rationally inescapable and vital question: Are we actively to seek God?

We shall then describe in the following chapters how a response of faith may reasonably follow from what the book of Scripture tells us about ourselves and God. If we do respond with faith, this is not the end of intellectual inquiry but the start of an intellectual and spiritual inquiry traditionally called "faith seeking understanding." Let us begin with those human needs which bring us face to face with the question, Are we actively to seek God? Although "witness" is a theological term, the argument that follows is philosophic.

I

The first reason to call into question the universe's existence and worth as the highest and best reality, as we mentioned in the Introduction, is that we must make choices. Human beings are goal-seeking and, because our goals are numerous and in some instances conflicting, we must attempt to order them into some rational priority. This is true for us both as individuals and as members of various groups.

To order our goals rationally, we must estimate what our natural and social environments allow us to pursue with some chance of success. This estimation is greatly affected by whether the universe is ultimate or not, for an estimate based on this world as ultimate is significantly different from an estimate based on the view that it is not. So the need to direct and order our lives is a reason to ask whether or not the universe has a source. This need renders the question concerning the status of the universe inescapable for rational agents.

The second reason to ask about the status of the universe is closely related to the first one. Not only are human beings goal-seeking, but the magnitude of human aspirations, needs, and desires seems to be greater than the world can satisfy. This is a far more forceful reason for asking whether the universe is ultimate. The need to direct and order our lives because of the number of goals and the irreconcilability of some of them makes the issue inescapable; this need makes it an important and even pressing issue. We have to decide whether to reduce our aspirations and deny some of our needs and desires because the world cannot satisfy them. Such measures are rational only if we have examined the status of the universe and indeed examined it seriously and carefully, since our aspirations, needs, and desires are very important to us. Their reduction or denial is not easily accomplished. If we find that the universe is *not* the highest and best reality, perhaps many of them can be met. It is rational to try to find out whether there is more than this world and, should there be reason to think there is, to try to find out what it is.

Human aspirations, needs, and desires are so extensive that it would be a prodigious task to set them out and defend the soundness of a particular account. But I think I can briefly indicate that our aspirations, needs, and desires are of such a nature that it is unlikely that they can be satisfied if this world is indeed all that there is.

Spinoza in his essay, "On the Improvement of the Understanding" tells us that as a young man he decided to forego comforts, the pursuit of wealth, sensual enjoyment, and fame in order to seek our true end and good. In his *Ethics* he claims to have found it. He argues that, although nature is indifferent to many of our aspirations and desires, a knowledge of nature and a contemplation of that knowledge will give us happiness. But it is important to note that with Spinoza's conviction that the universe is all that there is, one must accept death as final, accept that most people are not able to gain a knowledge of the universe such as he claims leads to happiness, and accept that the desire to be unconditionally loved is not included as part of human fulfillment.[2]

It is, of course, possible to accept death as final and to accept that the route to fulfillment is limited to people of sufficient intelligence and education to follow it. But that it takes strenuous effort to come to terms with one's own death and the death of others indicates that we do in fact aspire to continue to live, if not forever, certainly for longer than we do. That a particular kind of knowledge of the universe gives happiness but only to those few endowed with the capacity to acquire it means that if this universe is all that there is, most people will not find their fulfillment.

Spinoza is not a pessimist. He is optimistic about the possibility of some human beings finding fulfillment, even if the world is ultimate. It should be noted, however, that the element of elevated joy which Spinoza evinces comes from the exercise of the intellect. There is a renunciation of nonintellectual needs and desires, including the need to be loved unconditionally. After such renunciation, contentment may result. But contentment is not the positive joy which comes from fulfillment.

Marxists are also optimistic. They claim that people in capitalist economies are alienated, especially from their labor. People should find fulfillment in work and in the products of their work. People in capitalist societies, however, work at enforced tasks and the product of their labor is money. This and other forms of alienation can be corrected by a new social order.

For an orthodox Marxist, death is final. Most of those who live before the new social order is established have no hope of fullness of life. In addition, there exists no truly socialist society, so that we cannot determine empirically what is the case. There is, however, an easily recognizable phenomenon which bears directly on the point.

As human beings we seek to satisfy our desires. No matter how much we get or whatever it is that we get, sooner or later we want more or something different. As Plato put it in his dialogue, the *Gorgias,* we are like leaky jars (493b-d). It is as if we were containers into which things are always being poured but which never get filled because there is a hole in each container and something is always leaking out. We often think and feel that if only we had more, we would be satisfied, or if we had or did something different, our potential would be realized, our happiness assured, our fullness achieved. Yet we are at peace for such short periods, and it only takes the news that someone else has attained some recognition, some honor, some praise, for us to feel a pang of envy or discontent.

This phenomenon is easy to recognize, but it takes courage to keep it before one's attention and to admit what it shows about us. One of Jean-Paul Sartre's merits is the persistence with which he calls it to our attention, brilliantly analyzing the tenacity with which we deceive ourselves about it. It is extremely painful to face squarely and to retain fully as part of our outlook the truth about our incapacity to find fullness in anything that is part of the universe. Each thoughtful person's reflections on his or her own experience and observations of other people supply ample reason to be skeptical of the Marxist's claim about a future social order.

It may, of course, be impossible for human beings to find fulfillment, whether this world is self-contained or not. The nature of human fulfillment is so difficult to determine that the very notion of it may be incoherent. But this does not affect the fact that human beings seek to be happy, that they are like leaky vessels, and that death is a very serious barrier, to say the least, to the possibility of fulfillment. These facts show that we have aspirations which we cannot even hope to have fulfilled should the world be self-contained.

It may be that usually only people who are either highly successful or unusually unsuccessful in attaining their goals and in satisfying their needs and desires wonder persistently about whether this world is all that there is. The successful ponder because they have gained so much and still are dissatisfied, the unsuccessful because they have so little hope unless there is more than this world. For both of them, if fullness of life is to be found, it is not going to be found in this world. The issue of the status of the universe may be a pressing one only for such people, but it is an important one for all thoughtful people who have recognized the magnitude of their aspirations, precisely because what we want is important to us and the examination of the fit between what we want and what is possible is a rational activity.

The next two reasons we are to examine explicitly deal with the particular character of the universe. The order of the universe is beautiful, especially to our vision and intellect; but the very same order which delights us also causes us to suffer. Both of these facts can lead us to ask about the status of the universe.

The order of nature produces an experience of beauty by means of our eyes and brains. This effect can be called "subjective" in the sense that it is the result of the action of objects and light upon our sense organs and brains. But this does not mean that the beauty we perceive is subjective in the sense of a delusion (there is nothing abnormal about us), nor in the sense of an illusion (as in the case of the appearance of a bent stick in water). Given our perceptual nature and the nature of light and the objects of our world, we correctly perceive the world as beautiful.

The fact that sensuous beauty is the result of relations between our brains, sense organs, light, and the natural world makes the beauty we perceive all the more noteworthy. Things are so ordered that we receive the effects of immense beauty from many perspectives, and at various levels of magnification by microscopes and telescopes, even though the appearance of the objects we perceive changes drastically through perspective and magnification. Parts of our planet seen from mountaintops and also in photographs taken from various distances in space are radiantly beautiful to us. That such beauty is the result of the relations between our organs, light, and the natural order, all of which could have been different, renders the situation all the more remarkable. Such experiences of beauty seem to add nothing to the biological evolution of the race. That we are bathed, so to speak, in beauty from so many perspectives and magnifications by the relations between our organs, light, and the natural world renders the negative connotations of the word "subjective" inappropriate.

The experience of sensuous beauty has its counterpart in the experience of beauty by the intellect. The order of nature, which causes an experience of sensuous beauty, is studied in such fields as chemistry, physics, and biology. Many people who understand these subjects well not only gain pleasure from understanding nature from these points of view but also find the order of nature intellectually admirable, and they speak of the beauty of its order with exhilaration. It is the same natural order responded to in different ways—by our senses and by our intellect. It affects us through both these means with a sense of joy and pleasure.[3]

Although the enjoyment of the beauty of the world can be an end in itself, this experience can also suggest to us that there may be something beyond this world and lead us to ask whether there is. For if we attend to an experience of the beauty of nature, we may find that it suggests to us some finality, some completeness, some wholeness of immense value and importance. What the finality or completeness is always eludes us, and we cannot clearly say what it is. It is as if the world promises to give us some unspecified fulfillment, and this fills us with expectancy of something to come; yet it never comes. Beauty reveals to us that the magnitude of our aspirations is even greater than we have so far noted by the facts that we are goal-seeking and like leaky jars. Beauty enables us to recognize even more profoundly that what we seek is not here but, if it is at all, is beyond the universe. The beauty of the world, by suggesting some finality, completeness, and fulfillment which it itself does not give, gently points us beyond itself.[4]

Simone Weil claims that the beauty of the world can suggest to us not only that nature has a source, but also something of what it may be like. She does this in the course of her criticism of the seventeenth and eighteenth century version of the teleological argument. As we saw, it is based on using a machine as an analogue for the world. It is argued that the world's order is similar to that of a machine. Just as a machine has an intelligent designer, so too by analogy of like effect like cause, the world's order is the product of intelligent design.

Weil rejects this argument, as do many others, but from a novel perspective. She says that the analogue of a machine, or more specifically a watch (made infamous by William Paley), is not a proper image because it does not take love to make a watch nor does the examination of a watch awaken love in a person for its maker.[5] The world is more appropriately compared to a great work of art. She claims (as do Dorothy Sayers and Iris Murdoch) that great art requires renunciation on the part of its creator. This is more evident perhaps in those arts in which the object has a personality, so to speak, as in literature, sculpture, and the dance. An artist must renounce some of his or her own personality in order to create personalities with genuine independence and quite distinct from himself or herself, rather than mere projections of himself or herself. Such a creative act of renunciation requires a respect and reverence for what is not oneself. Furthermore, the appreciation of a great work of art often causes one to love its creator and to have a sense of gratitude, respect, and even reverence, without anything being known about its creator, except the work of art itself. So too does the beauty of the world. It not only suggests to us the possibility that there is something else besides the world but leads us to admire, respect, and even reverence its source.[6]

It is important to note that Weil does not say that since we feel a certain way about human art works, and the world is beautiful, then we ought to feel the same way about the world's beauty. Rather, she claims that the world's beauty can and does produce certain effects. She then notes that they are like the effects produced by great works of art, and so those who use the teleological argument with a machine as an analogue are far wide of the mark. She does not suggest that we reformulate the teleological argument with a new analogue. She does not argue that since the effects on us of the world's beauty and a great work of art are similar, therefore there must be a source of the world's order just as there is a source of a work of art.

The world's beauty, then, gives us a reason to ask, Does the world have a source? The experience of beauty can make us aware of some finality, completeness, and fulfillment, which we cannot specify, yet which points us beyond this world since our expectations are not met by the world itself. This experience leads the mind to inquire about the status of the world. Moreover, the world's beauty gives us some intimation of what might be beyond, and, in the admiration, respect, and reverence the world's beauty causes us to feel, it even gives us an intimation of our relation to what may be beyond. The elevated joy of admiration, respect, and reverence might even be a hint of what fulfillment for us would be like.

The main point, however, is that the natural beauty of the world, perceived both visually and intellectually as the order of nature, can lead us to ask whether nature has a source. Even this point is not essential to the argument I am preparing to give. I myself think the experience of beauty is an important reason to ask about the status of the world and extremely suggestive concerning what its source may be and our relation to that source. Hume in his *Dialogues Concerning Natural Religion* completely ignored the beauty of the world. Even without natural beauty as a reason to examine the status of the world, we have already given two others which show it is an inescapable, important, and even pressing issue for rational agents. This is all that is essential for the case I am to present. Furthermore, the intimation of what that which is beyond the world may be like can also come to us through suffering, which we shall now examine.

The order of nature which results in the experience of beauty is the very same order which causes storms, disease, and accidents. These evils

are usually called "natural evils," and they frequently are used as coun-
terevidence to a theistic worldview, as we mentioned briefly when we
cited Weil's claim that nature's indifference to our well-being is at first a
barrier to belief in divine benevolence but that it can become a passage
for God's goodness to reach us. This is an important stage in the development of a mature Christian faith and will be examined in the next
chapter. Here I am concerned to show how affliction, a specific form of
intense suffering, can lead one to raise the question, Is the world ultimate? with a particular urgency.[7] Each of us is vulnerable to the possibility of affliction, so what we say here is not limited to those relatively
few who have actually been afflicted.

The substance of my analysis of affliction is dependent on Simone
Weil's essay, "The Love of God and Affliction."[8] In this essay Weil deline-
ates the nature of affliction as a specific form of suffering. It can be
caused by physical suffering, if it is very prolonged or frequent; and it
has physical effects, for example, difficulty in breathing at the news of
the death of a beloved person. But the source of affliction is primarily
social. Weil seems to have had in mind the condition of the refugees of
whom she herself was one during the Second World War. A refugee is
uprooted from the fabric of social relations, so that he or she no longer
counts for anything. There is social degradation, or at least fear of it.
Even more horrible, the afflicted person inwardly feels the contempt
and disgust which others express toward one who is socially of no account. It is reported that some even feel guilt and defilement.

Affliction poses a problem because, unlike other kinds of suffering,
no purpose can be found for it. For example, when we consider nature's
indifference, we will see that suffering can break our egocentric and
anthropomorphic outlook. Also, in many instances people develop and
exhibit admirable character in response to suffering. A Stoic, such as
Epictetus (c. 50– c. 130), who was lame and for a time a slave, went so
far as to say that a person can bear whatever comes, even death, without
degradation.[9] But affliction is an exception. It degrades. It fills a person
with self-contempt and disgust, as we see in the case of lepers as reported in the New Testament and today with victims of rape. What could
be the point of affliction? Weil claims that this is the question that a
person suffering affliction asks with persistence. "So soon as a man falls
into affliction the question takes hold and goes on repeating itself inces-
santly. Why? Why? Why?"[10]

The afflicted man naïvely seeks an answer, from men, from things, from God,
even if he disbelieves in him, from anything or everything. Why is it necessary
precisely that he should have nothing to eat, or be worn out with fatigue and
brutal treatment, or be about to be executed, or be ill, or be in prison? If one

explained to him the causes which have produced his present situation, . . . it will not seem to him to be the answer. For his question "Why?" does not mean "By what cause?" but "For what purpose?"[11]

The workings of nature only specify causes of the affliction without giving the victim any purpose for it.

There can be no answer to the "Why?" of the afflicted, because the world is necessity and not purpose. If there were finality in the world, the place of the good would not be in the other world. Whenever we look for final causes in this world it refuses them. But to know that it refuses, one has to ask.[12]

If then affliction has a purpose, and not just a cause, this purpose must reside outside the universe.

Beauty and affliction are two aspects of the natural world. One is lovely; the other is horrible. Yet each leads one to look for a finality or a good which the universe itself does not have. One who is greatly moved by beauty or who suffers affliction is open to receive an answer. But the answer is not sought in terms of the satisfaction of a mere intellectual interest. It is a craving for a good as a fulfillment of a longing or as a relief from misery. That is the kind of answer which is sought to the question, Does this universe have a source?

There are, then, five reasons to ask whether the universe is ultimate. Together they make the question a desire not merely for a reason for the sheer existence and order of the world but also for guidance as to which among our many goals to pursue, so that we might order our lives and determine whether our aspirations are realistic. They show that the issue of the status of the world is an inescapable, important, and even pressing one for rational agents. To treat the issue as though it were raised simply because the world's existence and order are not explained by its members and thus as a desire simply to satisfy our curiosity, is to isolate it artificially from other concerns we have as rational agents. Its context is quite naturally and appropriately that of a pilgrimage. It is as though human beings are on a journey and must look for guidance in their search for a full and significant life. The depth of our aspirations or longing is evident for those who are particularly sensitive to nature's beauty, and the passionate intensity and urgency of this quest are especially evident in the case of intense suffering. Our next step will be to see how, given the recognition of the proper context, we may satisfactorily answer this inescapable, important, pressing, and even urgent question concerning the status of the world.

II

I shall first argue that the five reasons we have for pursuing the question, Does nature have a source? enable us to view nature as a witness, and then that it opens us to the possibility of receiving another witness, that of the Christian community, which looks to the book of Scripture.

In Christianity "witness" has at least three elements. First, a witness is something which reveals a fork, indicating at least two possible directions to follow. Second, a witness makes it incumbent on a person to act: either to follow or not to follow a particular direction. This may be done consciously or unconsciously. Our practice indicates the nature of our decision. Third, a witness is often expressed verbally. In the Old Testament, prophets frequently chastised the people of Israel for some specific evils, and called upon them to return to the ways of God.

The existence and the order of nature do not address us verbally. But this does not disqualify them from being a witness. Consider, for example:

> The heavens are telling the glory of God;
>   and the firmament proclaims his handiwork.
> Day to day pours forth speech,
>   and night to night declares knowledge.
> There is no speech, nor are there words;
>   their voice is not heard;
> yet their voice goes out through all the earth,
>   and their words to the end of the world.
>
>   (Ps. 19:1–4)

It is my claim that nature meets the requirements for being a witness. The world's existence and order are unexplained by its members. It thus places before us two possibilities: either nature has a source or it does not. But this can easily be dismissed as unimportant. The fact that the world's existence and order are unexplained by its members is insignificant to one who considers only what we need in order to do science, and to one who thinks the issue of the status of the universe turns only on the principle of sufficient reason. Nature then fails to act as a witness.

But nature becomes a witness when we note that rational agents need to decide how to satisfy their needs and desires, and what to do about aspirations which are greater than a self-contained universe can satisfy. To a person who seeks to order his or her goals rationally, the issue of the status of nature is inescapable. And because our aspirations are so great, it is an important and even pressing issue. We are faced with what William James calls "a forced and live option."[13]

The other two reasons to ask whether or not nature is ultimate, though not essential, reinforce my claim. Some people may recognize the witness of nature through beauty or through affliction, whether their own or others'. The recognition that if there is a good that gives us fulfillment and relief from distress, it is beyond this world shows that nature has functioned as a witness. An alternative has been seen and, once it is seen, a choice must be made; for a craving has been awakened and we must seek either to satisfy it or deny it.

As we have said, although the concept of "witness" is a theological one, my argument is a philosophic one. It relies on a reasoned account that the status of the world is unknown to us; that the world may have a reason for its existence and order; and that because people are goal-seeking, with great aspirations, in a world whose beauty is suggestive and whose order causes affliction, alternatives are posed for a rational agent. A rational agent is faced with the necessity of making an important decision. The criteria for something to be a witness are satisfied by nature's existence and order.

But how, in the face of such a witness, is a decision between alternatives to be made rationally? What reasons can be given for responding one way rather than another? The situation is analogous to that of Christian in John Bunyan's *Pilgrim's Progress*. He sees that a decision must be made, but only part of the distance toward the goal is indicated.

"Do you see yonder wicket-gate?" The man said, "No." Then said the other, "Do you see yonder shining light?" He said, "I think I do." Then said Evangelist, "Keep that light in your eye, and go directly thereto. So shalt thou see the gate; at which, when thou knockest, it shall be told thee what thou shalt do."[14]

To see the existence of the universe is unexplained by its members, and then to ask persistently, Does nature have a source? because one sees that the issue is inescapable, important, and even urgent, is actually to be following one of the alternatives, as far as it presently can be followed. The reasons to ask the question are the reasons to follow the path. One can have moved onto that path and have reasons to do so, without being able to see one's way very clearly or to see one's final destination, any more than Christian could when he set out on his journey. One follows it, however, not as one committed to the reality of a source of this world, but as one exploring that path. One has what Farrer called "initial faith."

Sound reasons, then, to explore one alternative are available. As rational agents, we need not wait for grounds which establish that Christianity is true before we become seekers. On the contrary, if we are not moved by the existence and order of nature and our needs as rational agents to become seekers, we shall not find the grounds which convince us that Christianity is true. The gate which leads to God is the book of Scripture and the community which incarnates its understanding of human life, nature, and nature's source. But we will never get to that gate any more than Christian could reach the gate which was beyond his vision unless we follow the path which we can see. In our case, it is the path nature's witness indicates. We are to venture on it as a seeker, not as a disinterested party considering pros and cons for theistic belief. If we do not venture as a seeker, moved by vital human needs, then we shall not find those things which convince us of the reality of God. Most modern philosophic discussion is kept on a disinterested basis, as if allowing the human significance of the question to intrude would be unphilosophic. This is an artificial isolation of the question because human beings are not just thinkers but also rational agents, that is, people who must act and who act to secure their well-being. The rational and thus proper way to discuss the question of the possibility of a source of nature is as a seeker exploring a vital question.

Although it has been usual to try to go directly from nature to God, we shall present another route. It is based on the fact that we are not only rational agents, who need guidance, have aspirations, and suffer, in contrast merely to being thinkers, but we are also rational agents in communities. This has two relevant aspects. First, most of us are in contact with a living religion. We do not seek to answer the question about the status of the world in the first instance by studying philosophical theology but by responding to the witness of a living religion. If the need for guidance, the pressure of our aspirations, and the reality of suffering have turned us into seekers, then to be on the path that is exploring the possibility of God means we sincerely desire to have more of that path illumined. We want to be shown how to progress further than the hints we have gained from our needs and nature's beauty. We are in a condition in which we can consider appreciatively the witness of the book of Scripture and the Christian community and not just the witness of nature. Second, we are related not only to nature but also to history and a particular society with various institutions such as towns, schools, churches, clubs, families. Our outlook is deeply influenced by our social environment. Therefore, in the next chapter we shall consider the book of Scripture and the Christian community and show how an appreciation of their witness enables us to respond with faith and to experience the reality of God.

PART II

The Book of Scripture

Chapter Six

The Experience of God's Grace: Faith and the Book of Scripture

Walker Percy, the novelist, once said that the most important difference between people is between those for whom life is a quest and those for whom it is not. We have given several reasons why we ought actively to seek our own well-being. We should not thoughtlessly gratify our immediate needs and desires and neglect our aspirations. Nor should we merely accept what is taught directly and indirectly in our schools and colleges, in our families, and by our friends. We ought carefully and critically to consider in what ways we may find our well-being or happiness.

The Christian church is only one of many institutions in our society, but it differs from nearly all the others in that it claims that our well-being is to be found in obedience to God. As we have seen, a rational person ought to take this seriously because the members of the universe do not explain why we have a universe, and the possibility of God very much affects what we can hope for out of life. But how is a connection to be made between actively seeking our well-being and the claim that it is to be found in obedience to God? It is to be made with faith.

Faith is usually thought to be utterly irrelevant to an examination of the rational grounds for holding to the truth of anything, including the truth of Christianity. But toward the end of Chapter Five, we pointed out that the book of nature, combined with our needs, ought to make any rational person a seeker. Since all Christian churches teach that to find both God and the good God intends us to have require faith, a genuine seeker who behaves rationally must consider the nature of faith. We shall, therefore, examine the nature of faith and show how those who genuinely seek God may indeed find God through faith. Then in the next two chapters we will show why it is reasonable to believe that God's intentions are revealed through ancient Israel and Jesus Christ. The view of faith I shall present applies in its essentials to all the major branches of Christianity: Eastern Orthodoxy, Roman Catholicism, and Protestantism.[1]

Faith is not a particular feeling or emotion, so that one might conduct a search to determine whether one has had such a feeling or experience.

One may, for example, have been "born again" and experienced an immense thrill. I personally have known such a thrill, but to experience such a thrill is not essential to having faith because some people have never had such an experience and yet they have faith. In Christianity, faith involves the recognition and acceptance of God's saving work in Jesus Christ. To recognize the good that God intends for us to receive is to have experienced God's grace; faith is our consent to receive that good. To understand the nature of faith we must examine what is involved in our recognition and consent to receive the good God intends us to have, a good that is to be received both now and in the future.

Faith has at least four major features. (1) We must be changed in order to receive the good God intends us to have. (2) We learn more fully the nature of the good God intends us to have when we submit ourselves to God's judgment. To affirm God's judgment is to consent to become what God intends us to become, namely, people who love justice or righteousness and who are full of divine love. God's judgment always has within it a positive aspect because it assures us that with God's help we shall become what God intends us to be. (3) Faith is to endure the suffering which, in spite of all we can do, results from the operations of the natural world and to endure the suffering caused by social and political injustices that we have been unable at any given time to eradicate. By enduring suffering properly we are able to shift from our egocentric and anthropocentric perspectives. This enables us to realize that our well-being is to be found in the good that is God. (4) To have faith is to seek to overcome barriers between people because our well-being is found in a community in which love of neighbor is practiced.

In the rest of this chapter we shall examine each of these four aspects of faith in detail because they describe our interaction with God. Only through interaction are we able to discern or recognize God's intentions and actually begin to receive the good God intends us to have. As we shall see, it is a great misunderstanding to treat faith as the absence of reasons to make affirmations. Rather, it is precisely in faith, understood as an interaction, that we become convinced of God's reality. Christian claims are not only to be thought about. They call upon us to do some specific things: to consent to being changed; to submit to judgment; to accept inevitable suffering; to seek reconciliation with all people. It is in doing these things that conviction is found.

After we have examined these four aspects of faith, we shall, as we have said, show why it is reasonable to have faith, even though what is affirmed by faith is beyond what can be established by reason alone, that is, by reasoning conducted without a consideration of the contents of the book of Scripture (Chapter Seven), and then we shall examine the relation of reason to the contents of the book of Scripture (Chapter Eight). This will complete the case for my claim that Christianity is true.

In the examination of the nature of faith that follows, everything that is said is within the realm of reason. Even though we are talking about faith and the contents of the Bible, what we say is philosophical, that is, we are making an examination by means of reason. This must be emphasized because in philosophy of religion today the nature of faith and the specific contents of the Bible are usually ignored. It is because the nature of faith is ignored or misunderstood that the relevance of faith to an evaluation of the intellectual basis for Christian claims is not generally realized. What follows, including the emphasis on the volitional element in faith, namely consent, is intended to be as much a reasoned analysis as any to be found in the philosophy of religion.

I

The claim that God seeks our well-being is easily misunderstood. Many people are initially attracted by Christianity because it promises wonderful things: help in our daily struggle to earn a living and raise a family, guidance when we are unsure what course of action to follow, forgiveness for failures, protection from harm, cure for illnesses, and life beyond death.

Other people, particularly philosophers, are prone to discuss the existence of God without taking into consideration the attractiveness of the picture of living in a world in which there is such a God. They either are unattracted or ignore what Farrer calls "initial faith." Even when they do take it into account, they sometimes suspect, as did Freud, that precisely because this picture is so attractive, faith is merely the result of wishful thinking.

Such a criticism may be valid in particular instances. But for "initial faith" to be genuine we must not only respond to the attractiveness of the good things promised but be willing to be changed. Consider, for example, the great blessing of forgiveness that is promised. Critics often point out that it is very convenient being a Christian because when Christians do something wrong, they know that they will be forgiven. Even though we are threatened with severe punishment should we break God's commandments, if we confess our wrongdoing, God will forgive us. From this it appears that Christians do not have to become moral people. Some Christians have indeed thought themselves superior to non-Christians of great moral integrity. "Being right with God," it was said, "is what counts."

But this is to abuse the good that God would do us. God does indeed offer to forgive us, but to receive that forgiveness is to desire to become a better person. We cannot receive anything from God, much less God's forgiveness, by remaining the same or by desiring to remain the same. Many of us would like to be famous, say as a ballplayer, pianist, or scientist. But even if we have the talent, it takes a great deal of effort and sacrifice to develop a talent. Likewise with the good that God would do us. We cannot remain the same and also receive the good that God would give us. As Jesus put it in a parable, we are like a man who found a pearl of great price. To find the money to buy that pearl, he had to sell all his other pearls. There is a price to be paid if we are to receive the good that God seeks to bestow. The price is that we must be changed.

An initial attraction when it misperceives the good which God would do us does not grow into a mature faith. Even should one make the transition from initial faith to a commitment, a mature faith may never develop. This is evident in Jesus' parable of the sower (Matt. 13:1–23). In the parable, some seeds fell along a path where it was eaten by birds. Other seeds fell on rocky ground. Although the plants grew quickly, because the soil lacked sufficient depth, they withered from the heat of the sun. Other seeds fell among thorns which choked them. Only the seeds which fell on good soil developed into mature plants and yielded a crop at harvest time. Jesus told his disciples that the seeds sown on rocky ground represent the faith of people who respond gladly to the word of the kingdom of God but in whom it is not rooted. When difficulties arise because living according to God's way runs counter to the practices of society, they fall away. The seeds sown among thorns represent the faith of those people who care more for wealth. The promises of God are unable to hold such people when it comes to a choice between God and their desire to be prosperous.

The way that the good God intends for us is understood depends on the condition of the person who hears of it. This is why it is so easy to abuse the teachings of Christianity and to have a faith which is not genuine. Many of these abuses are the result of belonging to what Pascal calls "the order of the body." The Bible refers to the order of the body as "the flesh" or "the world." Those wishes, wants, and desires—including our thoughts—that seek earthly goods belong to the order of the body. Whatever can be gratified by earthly goods belongs to the order of the body. Pascal says that it is the order of kings, captains, and rich people. That is, whatever can be gained by the use of force or be bought belongs to the order of the body. A person who is dominated by a concern for these things is one who belongs to the order of the body. Such son is completely blind to any other order. Pascal writes,

The greatness of intellectual people is not visible to kings, rich men, captains, who are all great in a carnal sense.

Great geniuses have their power, their splendour, their greatness, their victory and their lustre, and do not need carnal greatness. . . . They are recognized not with the eyes but with the mind, and that is enough. (308)[2]

We may illustrate this blindness with the story of Ptolemy, the former general of Alexander the Great, who called upon Euclid, the great geometrician. He asked Euclid to teach him geometry but to do it quickly because he planned to lead his army on a campaign. Euclid replied, "Sire, there is no royal road to learning." Mathematics is beyond the reach of power or force. It belongs to a different order.

This blindness leads to a reduction of what belongs to a higher order to the terms of a lower one. For example, visitors to Princeton often ask its residents the way to 112 Mercer Street, where Albert Einstein once lived. Most people want to see his house because Einstein was famous, not because they appreciate the greatness of his scientific achievements. This is evident from the lack of interest in the homes of other great physcists who lived in Princeton, because, unlike Einstein, they were not "number 1." The greatness of the achievements of the mind are understood in terms of the greatness of the order of the body, namely in terms of fame, and not in terms of the greatness inherent in intellectual achievement itself.

The reduction can sometimes be humorous, as we find in a story told about Edmund Gibbon, the author of *The Decline and Fall of the Roman Empire*. Subjects of the king of England are honored for their achievements by being received at the court. When Gibbon presented the king with the most recent volume of his great study, the king remarked, "Ah, Mr. Gibbon, another big, thick book. Scribble, scribble, scribble, eh, Mr. Gibbon?" In this instance the reduction is amusing, but often the reduction is painful to those who belong to the order of the mind. People in America are generally anti-intellectual and make fun of eggheads.

Just as those who belong to the order of the body are blind to the greatness of the order of the intellect, those who belong to the order of the intellect may themselves be blind to the greatness of the order of the heart. The heart is a metaphor to indicate the fact that we seek and respond to what is valuable and lovable. All of us seek what is valuable or what we think is good for us. The question is whether what we seek at the level of the body or at the level of the intellect will be able to satisfy us or give us well-being. Let us here consider the order of the body.

Is what can be obtained by power or money able to satisfy us? We have many resources to draw upon to help us in our reflections. For example, earlier we cited Spinoza's autobiographical remarks and the ancient image of a leaky vessel that Plato believed would enable us to recognize from our own experience ample reason to give a negative reply. Jeremiah 1 and 2 uses the image of "broken cisterns," which is similar to Plato's, but the prophet applies it to an entire society. Jeremiah asserts that the people of Israel have dug cisterns so that they will have a supply of water independently of God, the fountain of living water. The prophet declares that these cisterns are broken cisterns and will not hold water.

Our ultimate dissatisfaction with all the pleasures and joys of the world, both bodily and intellectual, is the theme of Goethe's great poem, *Faust*. Faust abandons his studies and makes a bargain with the devil. He may have anything he pleases, but the moment he becomes bored, his life is forfeited to the devil. In time Faust becomes bored. The poem is virtually a commentary on Jesus' remark, "For what does it profit a man, to gain the whole world and forfeit his life?" (Mark 8:36). The world does not contain that which can fulfill us. We can easily learn this for ourselves, if we reflect on our own search for satisfaction. These thoughtful remarks can help us persevere in our reflections on our own experience and help us resolve to make this truth about ourselves a part of our character.

For the heart to find complete satisfaction it is necessary for it to be purified because most of our wants and desires belong to the order of the body and the order of the intellect. They so occupy our attention that we cannot even perceive the good which would satisfy us and which God seeks to give us. This is reflected in Jesus' remark, "Blessed are the pure in heart, for they shall see God" (Matt. 5:8). Unless the heart attains some degree of purity, so much of what Jesus says remains paradoxical and beyond the reach of our own experience. For example, consider his remark, "Whoever drinks of the water that I shall give him will never thirst" (John 4:14a). Our experience tells us that no matter what we drink, we will always get thirsty again because our bodies use up moisture. To speak of water that will permanently quench our thirst is a contradiction on the level of everyday—earthly or bodily—understanding. His teachings remain paradoxes until our hearts are so purified that we see that our true good is beyond the goods that are obtainable by power, money, and intellectual endeavor.[3] Jesus tells us how the condition of the heart can be gauged: "Where your treasure is, there will your heart be also" (Matt. 6:21).

In addition, unless their hearts are sufficiently purified, the benefits God promises us are abused by people who are attracted to Christianity. Such so-called "religious people" seek to gain through God the things that can be gained by power and wealth and also protection from the dangers to which even the powerful and rich are vulnerable. Some people are so repelled by this abuse that they never examine Christianity sufficiently to come to an appreciation of the nature of the good God seeks us to have.

How can the heart be purified? How can we come to recognize or appreciate the greatness of the order of the heart? This brings us to the second aspect of faith: submission to judgment.

II

In the Introduction we noted that Austin Farrer characterized our situation as one in which "we are rebellious creatures under the eye of our Creator."[4] We can recognize this, Farrer claims, if we are willing to examine ourselves by the standards set by Christ. I pointed out that it is very easy to avoid such self-examination. Here we need to show why we ought to submit to such a self-examination because of our awareness of our own evil.

The failure in modern times to give morality a nonreligious basis is becoming increasingly recognized. It is widely held today that we determine what is called "good" and "evil," and because it is we who make the designations, they lack objective character. Our "value judgments" are not the recognition of the value of things and people; rather we confer on them whatever value they have for us ourselves. We are not wholly consistent in this, but it is the prevalent way we talk in public discussions about good and evil, right and wrong, because neither any religion nor any ethical or political theory is thought to have sufficiently good grounds to determine what anyone is to value.

However, there is a way to recognize the reality of good and its authority over us. This is a way that must be followed, not an argument whose validity establishes a conclusion for us without our having to do anything. To experience and thereby recognize good, we must perform a good act. To experience and thereby recognize evil, we must either refrain from an evil act or having performed an evil act repent afterward.[5] Arguments that seek to show the objective reality of good and evil are unavailing, because we are blind. We must act before the arguments, inferences, and distinctions that are used in ethical and political philosophy can be morally fruitful. We must make an examination of our actions at a fundamental level before the very categories of good and evil as dealing with realities, not human preferences, come into play.

It may seem perverse to say that we discover the reality of good and evil by doing good and refusing to do evil or repenting of it, when it seems obvious to us that a person who does not do evil is sheltered from its reality and so is an innocent, unsophisticated person. A young person is sometimes tempted into evil by an older more sophisticated person who says, "Come on, you don't know what you're missing."

But at a fundamental level, prior to the designation of which actions and things are good and which are evil, there are characteristics of good and evil which enable us to experience their objective reality: good limits us and evil does not (at least not at first). The attraction of evil is that at first it imposes no check on our wishes, wants, and desires. We can get our own way. It is thrilling to get our own way, to feel the ease of transition from desire to attainment, to glide along without any impediment. But good acts as a check to our wishes, wants, and desires. To refuse to do evil is to limit ourselves because we recognize another reality that is not ourselves, which we must make room for, and refuse to violate by getting our own way at its expense. Good breaks our egocentric perspective which puts everything in orbit around ourselves, as if we are the center of reality and the value of everything is determined by how it suits our wishes, wants, desires. Our existence is more real to us than the existence of anything else because the existence of everything else is evaluated in terms of its usefulness and attractiveness to our purposes. Everything is subordinate to our will. To do evil is to attempt to retain that perspective and relation to others. To refuse to do evil is to recognize that we are not at the center and that all things are not to be judged with ourselves at the center. It is voluntarily to relinquish that perspective, or at least to recognize that the perspective is illusory and to repent of the reduction of others to our unimpeded will. To do good is to act in accord with the limitations caused by the existence of other realities.

At first good is hateful to us because to frustrate our wishes, wants, and desires is painful. We resent the need to exercise self-limitation. But it is in doing good that we actually find our good; for it is not good to live alone. We are not self-sufficient. To find a full life we need to be in community. The fundamental requirement for community life is the recognition of the reality of others. A price has to be paid. But after it has been paid we can find a good that cannot be achieved in living from an egocentric, illusory perspective.

At first doing evil is attractive because we do not have to check our wishes and desires because of others. It is only after we are well into evil that we start to experience the horrors of life without the benefits of community. We can go so far into evil that even the partial community life which once was possible for us becomes increasingly inaccessible.

This examination of the reality of good and evil is based on the story of the Garden of Eden. That story is not a description of a historic event in which human beings first committed evil. The story is about "the beginning" in the sense of the *arche,* or the principle of our being, which is God's intention for us to live in community and our resistance to God's intention. The story insists that God has not abandoned that intention in spite of the fact that we are unable fully to realize the goodness of community life.

The story implies that to find our well-being, we are not to follow the way of those captains, kings, and rich people who seek to get their own way by force and money. The great temptation of power and wealth is to override whatever limits our desires and wishes because they frequently give us the means to do so. We can easily fail to pay sufficient attention to the reality of others and to rationalize our actions for the untroubled enjoyment of getting our own way. Power and wealth can be exercised properly only by those who recognize a level of good that is above what the unbridled use of power and wealth can attain.

The intellect has a vital role to play because it is from thinking about our actions that we can recognize the reality of good and evil at a fundamental level. But to experience the reality of good and evil, one must act. Their reality is recognized as objective, by the force they exercise: good by the pressure on us to limit ourselves for the sake of others and the joy of a more adequate relation to others, evil by the bondage which limits our participation in communal life. Without any experience of the reality of good and evil, we are hard pressed to resist arguments for moral relativism and subjectivism, which are so prevalent in our culture and which philosophical theories of ethics and society have been unable to counter by showing on the level of the arguments alone the reality of good and evil. But one who exercises some degree of self-limitation because of the reality of others and who enjoys the benefits of community, however limited and fragmented a community it may be, knows from experience the reality of good and evil, even though it is very difficult to formulate a full account of their nature and the nature of a genuine community life and how it may be realized.

The Old Testament is a testimony of the tenacious effort of the Jewish people to create a genuine community among themselves and with their neighbors. To a considerable extent, the Old Testament is an account of how difficult it is to achieve genuine community or even fully to conceive of its nature. That tenacious attempt continues to be a source of strife among Jews and between Jews and others. Yet once the illusion of an egocentric perspective is penetrated by the reality of good and evil and God's intention that we find our good in communal life is recognized, the struggle to realize a just community, in which we shall be in love and charity with our neighbors, cannot be abandoned. One of the reasons to trust the integrity of the Old Testament witness to God's intention for us is the frankness with which the Jews present their failures in their sacred Scriptures. Newer insights and deeper understandings of God's intention and ways to achieve that intention do not cause them to delete or suppress previous insights which are now recognized by them to be inferior, limited, or even serious misunderstandings.

When our egocentric perspectives have been pierced and our character significantly shaped by the fact that we are but one reality among many, we find ourselves, sooner or later, in a quandary. We desire to be more justly or properly related to others. We desire to respond more appropriately or fairly to the reality of others and to have others respond appropriately or fairly to us. We come more and more to desire a true community. But we do not yet love justice with all our heart.

When we are treated fairly or recognized properly, we do not love justice itself because we find such treatment pleasant. Our attention is so occupied by the pleasure that we do not attend to the goodness of justice itself. When we are treated unfairly, we are indirectly aware of the goodness of justice. We realize that justice matters because of the harm we suffer from injustice. But we do not yet love justice itself. To love justice is to desire to become perfectly just, that is, to become like or assimilated to what we love. A way to test whether we do love justice itself is to heartily desire that the consequences of the evil we do fall directly and solely on ourselves. That would be to love justice itself. To perform this test honestly on ourselves makes us aware of the fact that we also desire to be saved *from* justice. We do not want the consequences of the evil we do to fall directly on ourselves and on no one else. We become caught in such a contradiction—loving justice and yet fearful of it. We are then in a condition from which we can respond to a supernatural remedy.

Many Christians are prone to accept *too* quickly Christ as the bearer of our sins and evil. That is, we may not yet have reached the place in our development in which we are in the condition described above and by Christ in the sermon on the mount, "Blessed are those who hunger and thirst for righteousness, for they shall be satisfied" (Matt. 5:6). The Greek word translated as "righteousness" can equally well be translated as "justice," as do Plato's translators and the translators of a French version of the New Testament. For us to grasp more fully what Christ meant by "righteousness," we need to realize that it involves a passionate desire for justice. But if we have that passion, then in consistency we must desire that the consequences of all the evil we do may fall directly and solely on ourselves. But when we do judge ourselves justly, we find it too horrible to bear. Nonetheless to keep returning in our thoughts to this inability fully to desire that justice be exercised on ourselves gives us access to a path that leads us to the cross of Christ as the act by which God enables us to love justice with all our heart and not to shrink from its judgment on ourselves.

As Wittgenstein noted, "*Nobody can truthfully say of himself that he is filth. Because if I do say it, though it can be true in a sense, this is not a truth by which I myself can be penetrated: otherwise I should either have to go mad or change myself.*"[6] Is "filth" too strong? Is it a just evaluation? Does it not fail to take into account our moral achievements, our merits, our greatness, our reality as human beings which must be respected? Those assessments are all compatible with a self-evaluation that issues in such words as "filth," because to love justice passionately leads to such expressions, as any glance at the words used by saintly people about themselves would show.

We can truthfully say it of ourselves, however, if we are loved by one who loves us in spite of our failures to be just. This love enables us to speak truthfully about ourselves because it is the love of one who is wholly just, who innocently suffers the consequences of other people's injustices, and who as the creative Word of God has the power and authority to identify itself with every victim of injustice and, as the one who suffers at our hands, grant us absolution for our evil. In our self-evaluation we may truly believe that we are filth because we believe that we can be changed and in fact are being changed.

To love justice itself so that we ask that our evil fall solely and directly on ourselves and yet to shrink in horror from it is the way we are assimilated to God. Justice puts us into a contradictory situation; it leads us to look to a reality which is on a higher level for relief. To have faith is to believe that to love God incarnate who is wholly righteous or just makes us just because we can become like what we love. To have faith is to believe that a love of justice itself brings us nearer to it, that those who hunger and thirst for it shall find satisfaction because they shall find their relief in the love of God.[7]

Perhaps we can now better appreciate the greatness of the order of the heart. Pascal characterizes it as follows:

Jesus without wealth or any outward show of knowledge has his own order of holiness. He made no discoveries; he did not reign, but he was humble, patient, thrice holy to God, terrible to devils, and without sin. With what great pomp and marvellously magnificent array he came in the eyes of the heart which perceive wisdom! (308).

Jesus does not have the greatness of the order of the body, as does Alexander the Great, nor the greatness of the order of the intellect, as does Einstein. According to Pascal, Jesus' greatness is his humility. He did not measure himself by the cultural standards of his day, as did some others, who scoffed at the fact that he was a carpenter (Mark 6:3), nor by the greatness of the order of the intellect (his education was that which could be gained at the local synagogue school). Some of the creatures made by the Word of God are greater in these respects than the one who is the Word of God incarnate, and that one is not ashamed of Jesus' inferiority.

Christ is also patient. Christ does not impose God's will on us or seek to win our allegiance by giving us material prosperity, security from danger, nor earthly power—all tempting ways to win followers—but Christ patiently calls us to recognize God's ways of leading us to our well-being. It is because of Jesus' resistance to those three temptations, that Pascal says Jesus is "thrice holy to God."[8]

Pascal says Jesus was terrible to devils. Many in the modern world do not believe in devils. Still, it is worth noticing that in the Gospel stories Jesus has no difficulty with powers which allegedly are terrifying and bent on doing human beings injury. They unwillingly are forced to obey his commands. This is in quite sharp contrast to human beings, who can resist Jesus' commands. If nothing else, this suggests that God does not lack raw power but that God greatly restrains it in dealing with us.

Jesus is without sin and therefore does not use his power independently of God but tells us that "My food is to do the will of [the One] who sent me, and to accomplish [God's] work" (John 4:34). Jesus' utter dependence on God's will and ways leads him to suffer at our hands for our redemption. Unlike us, Jesus is completely orientated toward God.

What is the wisdom which those with hearts may perceive? In the Introduction we mentioned that Austin Farrer characterized it as the truth we receive when we allow ourselves to be evaluated by our Creator, who has come upon us in Christ. We may recognize the magnificence of God's way of realizing God's intentions in spite of our resistance by becoming incarnate and thereby able to suffer as we suffer and seeking to win our love with the greatness of that love. Rather than exterminating us or abandoning the good God intends us to have, God enables us to become just and puts within our reach a way for our evil to be removed.

The removal of our evil can be experienced by anyone. In one of his parables Jesus explicitly claimed that the Son of man was present in every human being. (See the parable of the sheep and the goats, Matt. 25:31–46.) We are not able to perceive Christ in every human being with our sense organs, but we are able to experience the effects of a purity present in each person, in so far as each person bears the image of God (Christ is explicitly said to be the very image of God). For example, I remember seeing a colleague walking past my house one day. He was a colorless person who used to wear outlandish dress in an attempt to make himself interesting. I looked at him with scorn and a sense of superiority, thinking how glad I was not to be like him. Then it occurred to me that we were essentially alike, both creatures, made in God's image. Our essential status was the same. However great our differences, they did not alter that essential status in the least. My scorn and sense of superiority immediately disappeared. Some of my evil—my unjust attitude toward another person—had been taken away by attending to the image of God that each of us bears.

Pascal refers to Jesus as having "his own order of holiness." Holiness is freedom from the burden of evil and the state of being full of charity. Part of Jesus' greatness is his holiness. To pay attention to him either indirectly, by attending to the divine image that we all bear, or directly, by attending to Jesus as portrayed in the Scriptures and by praying, has the effect of relieving some of the burden of evil we carry and enabling our love for others to increase.

Each order has its own major concern. The order of the body is concerned primarily with the gratification of the senses, the order of the mind with the achievements of the intellect, the order of the heart is concerned primarily with the motivation and goals of the will. When purified, it is motivated by divine love and has divine love as its goal. Such a love cannot be produced by either the body or the intellect. Pascal writes,

Out of all bodies together we could not succeed in creating one little thought. It is impossible, and of a different order. Out of all bodies and minds we could not extract one impulse of true charity. It is impossible, and of a different, supernatural order (308).

Charity can be produced only by divine action, by the gracious spirit of God at work in us, or as Pascal puts it, by inspiration.

III

To develop a mature faith we must come to terms with the suffering caused by nature's operations. In the seventeenth and eighteenth centuries, the book of nature was used to argue for the existence of a designer and even for the existence of a benevolent designer. In Chapter Three, it was mentioned in passing that Hume attacked not only the inference from nature's order to a designer of nature but also the inference from nature's order to a benevolent designer. In his *Dialogues Concerning Natural Religion*, Parts X and XI, Hume argued that because of the immensity of human and animal suffering it is improbable that the alleged designer of nature is concerned with their welfare. Not everything is injurious to them, but from a mixture of good and evil we cannot infer that the alleged designer of nature is either purely benevolently or purely malevolently disposed toward them. If we consider only the pleasant and unpleasant effects of nature's operations, then it is more likely that its alleged designer is unconcerned with or indifferent to their welfare. It has been a pillar of the modern mentality that nature is indifferent to our well-being, and it has been thought that its indifference is an insuperable barrier to a rational belief in the goodness of God.

Actually a major part of having faith is to come to terms with the suffering caused by the operations of the natural world and indeed the suffering caused by the injustices of society. By enduring what we cannot or have not been able as yet to change, we can learn more about the good God seeks to give us. Suffering helps break our egocentric and anthropocentric perspectives and enables us to realize that our well-being is to be found in the good that is God.

In modern times there has been a marked tendency in Christian theology to ignore nature's indifference and, in much of popular piety, to assume that if we are good Christians, God will protect us from all harm and give us success and material prosperity. This is widespread, even though Jesus said that the Father "makes [the] sun rise on the evil and on the good, and sends rain on the just and on the unjust" (Matt. 5:45b). In this passage and elsewhere in the New Testament, Jesus frequently combated an Old Testament view that all blessings and misfortunes experienced by individuals and nations are the result of God's rewarding those who obey and punishing those who disobey.[9]

Jesus' example of the indifference of the operations of the sun and rain to our moral or spiritual condition is in line with the book of Job, in which an utterly upright person suffers terrible misfortunes. It is also harmonious with Isaiah's teaching about a servant who innocently suffers for the benefit of others. These examples show that even in the Old Testament it is not uniformly taught that there is an invariable connection between our moral and religious conditions and our earthly prosperity and misfortune. One of the reasons many people's faith fails to grow into a mature faith is that they never realize that God does not give us immunity from suffering, or if they are told that this is Christian teaching, they refuse to give it their consent.

We will now see how faith in the goodness of God can grow into a mature faith by drawing upon the thought of Simone Weil. She explains how nature's indifference, instead of being an impassable barrier to an inference by our intellect to God's goodness, can become a passageway for God's goodness to reach us. It can lead to the realization that God's goodness is superior to and incommensurate with the goodness of created things.

For this to happen, we must rise above our egocentric and anthropocentric point of view. This means to accept the indifference of nature and the unavoidable injury it does to human beings and to us personally. It must be emphasized that we are to do all we can to mitigate the negative effects of nature on us, but no matter what we do, we cannot avoid some suffering at the hands of nature, if no more than the fact that we all grow older and eventually die. This is a bitter truth to accept because nature destroys so much that is precious to us. But to come to terms with our vulnerability to nature is to come to terms with the truth about ourselves: we are natural beings and, like all natural beings, we are mortal and vulnerable to disease, accidents, and natural catastrophes. Were it not for the beauty of the universe, which is the effect of the operations of its laws, we could not love it. But in loving nature as a whole, and not just those aspects which are favorable to us personally or to human beings generally, we are drawn out of our egocentricity and anthropocentricity.[10] We are purified through our attentiveness to the beauty of the world because by attending to the overall harmony of its relations, we come into contact with God. Then "each sensation is like communion, that of pain included."[11]

To understand this more fully we must consider Weil's idea that contradiction on one level can enable us to reach a higher, supernatural level that makes sense of the opposition. There is no *logical* contradiction between God's benevolence and our suffering, as Hume admits in his *Dialogues* (Part XI) and as Alvin Plantinga has argued against some important twentieth century philosophers.[12] But the various attempts to reconcile God's benevolence with our suffering all seem hollow to people who are in duress because they focus on the causes of suffering, such as the improper use of freedom, not the purposes of our suffering, which so often are not available. Also, as Hume argued in Part XI of his *Dialogues Concerning Natural Religion,* these attempts should not lead a person to belief in the goodness of God. At best they only enable a person, who already has a belief in God's goodness to retain it.[13]

To get beyond this situation, we must move to a higher plane or to a supernatural level. In *Gravity and Grace* Weil writes, "The word good has not the same meaning when it is a term of the correlation good-evil as when it describes the very being of God."[14] Necessity or compulsion, which nature exercises on our bodies, is the very opposite of that good which is God. But we do not experience that good through nature until we recognize that nature's operations produce both goods and evils. The order of nature causes both sunshine and rain, good health and illness, growth and decay, life and death. Its operations give us both members of the pair "good-evil." As long as nature gives us good things (for example, good health), we do not notice that we are as much subject to compulsion as we are in those instances in which bad things happen to us. We notice nature's compulsion only in those things that are bad for us.

If we notice nature's compulsion only in what is injurious, we do not have even a notion of God's goodness and that it is not the same as the good in the pair "good-evil" that flows from nature's operations. This is why Antony Flew, for example, argued that to say that God is good and not to mean pretty much the same as we mean by good in our daily life is a fatal equivocation. When attributed to God, "goodness," "justice," and "love" are meaningless.[15] Only when we face the fact that nature operates by regular laws, that it is indifferent to our welfare and causes both good and evil, and allow it to break our egocentric and anthropo-centric perspective, can we even conceive of the possibility of one whose goodness is beyond the pair "good-evil." When we face the truth of na-ture's indifference and accept our vulnerability to its operations, we know in our very bones that the happiness or well-being we crave is not to be found in this world.

When we look beyond the goods and evils that result from the oper-ations of nature, we come into contact with that good which orders na-ture into a harmonious system of regular laws. As long as our hearts are set on the goods which have evils as their counterparts, we are not open to contact with God through nature. God does not give an order to na-ture which produces an earthly paradise for human beings. Nature is ordered to lead us to God by the recognition that we are under nature's compulsion and that nature does not provide for our well-being.

In their treatment of the problem of evil many modern philosophers follow Hume's classic argument that, because it is easy to conceive of a better ordered world than our own, no intelligent person who did not already believe in God would conclude from an examination of human and animal suffering that a benevolent intelligence designed the uni-verse. But what is meant by "a better ordered world?" For Hume and his followers it would be a world in which there are far more goods and fewer evils of the pair "good-evil" flowing from nature's operations. It is assumed that a verdict on the goodness of God is to be rendered on the basis of the prevalence of one member of the pair over the other.

Weil, however, says the very indifference of nature is a way to experi-ence the goodness of God. By facing nature's indifference we can be-come the kind of person that makes contact with God. If we humbly accept the truth that we are subject to the compulsion of nature's operations, our egocentric and anthropocentric illusions are broken and we are in contact with reality. To be in contact with reality puts us into indirect contact with God, the one who orders nature.

Weil explains what she means by "indirect contact" with the analogy of a cane used by a blind man. A blind man, who guides himself by touching objects with a cane, uses it as an extension of himself. Through the cane he is in contact with objects indirectly. The universe is connected by a system of laws. We use the laws of nature to effect our ends. We may use all the universe—treating it as a whole because of its inner connections—as a blind man uses a cane. If we accept the truth that we are subject to the compulsion of nature's operations, nature becomes an extension of ourselves. It gives us indirect contact with the creator and designer of the world. Nature is between us and God, and we touch each other through the medium of nature. This indirect contact becomes a passage through which God's goodness is experienced.

Weil bases this claim on her own experience of God's goodness. She tells us that it first occurred to her while reciting George Herbert's poem "Love."

Often, at the culminating point of a violent headache, I make myself say it over, concentrating all my attention upon it and clinging with all my soul to the tenderness it enshrines. I used to think I was merely reciting it as a beautiful poem, but without my knowing it the recitation had the virtue of a prayer. It was during one of these recitations that, as I told you, Christ himself came down and took possession of me.

In my arguments about the insolubility of the problem of God I had never foreseen the possibility of that, of a real contact, person to person, here below, between a human being and God.[16]

Many other people have reported that it has been in the *midst* of suffering that they have found God's goodness for the first time or in new ways.[17]

The opposition between nature's indifference and God's benevolence is resolved on a higher plane. But we may reach this resolution only by *action*.[18] We must accept nature's indifference. Nature's indifference levers us upward, so to speak, to a different plane when it breaks our egocentric and anthropocentric perspectives. Only then do ideas such as Weil's become convincing. The fact that we must face the opposition in our own lives and the relevance of such an action for the problem of evil are consistently ignored in philosophical discussion.[19]

It is difficult to consent to the good that God would do us because what God seeks to give us is the good that is Godself. This is evident in the parable of the laborers in the vineyard. A man went to the market place and hired some people to work in a vineyard for the sum of one denarius. At different intervals during the day, he hired still more people to work in the same vineyard. At the end of the day those who had worked only the last hour were paid one denarius. When those who had worked the longest saw this, they were delighted because quite naturally they thought they would get more. When they did not, they complained, "These last worked only one hour, and you have made them equal to us who have borne the burden of the day and the scorching heat" (Matt. 20:12). The owner of the vineyard replied, "Friend, I am doing you no wrong; did you not agree with me for a denarius? . . . Do you begrudge my generosity?" (Matt. 20:13,15b).

There have been many attempts to explain this puzzling parable because it is unfair that all should have been paid the same. It is the same kind of unfairness that we find frequently in the distribution of good health and prosperity. Our bafflement and complaints are voiced in the Old Testament lament, "Why do the righteous suffer and the wicked prosper?"

Simone Weil appears to have found the key to the parable. "He pays only one type of wage because he possesses only one type of wage. He hasn't any change."[20] That is to say, all God has to give us finally is God-self. It is not a distribution of the members of the pair "good-evil" according to some scale of moral or spiritual merit, as both religious and nonreligious people often assume. Every attempt to explain the unfairness of the distribution of the pair "good-evil" in the Old Testament and in various theodicies fails. There seems to be no way to overcome the unfairness, except by the insight that a parable such as that of the laborers in the vineyard discloses of God's intention.

With knowledge of that intention we can believe in God's benevolence in spite of nature's indifference and the injustices of the social and political order. When every effort has been made to mitigate suffering and to achieve social justice, suffering can lead us to a more mature faith because it forces us to look beyond the pair "good-evil" to the good that is God.

After we have faced and more or less come to terms with our vulnerability, we can ask God to guide, assist, and protect us in our daily life because, with God as our good, we can trust divine providence. The nature of that providential care is nicely captured in George Herbert's poem, Colossians 3:3 ("For you have died, and your life is hid with Christ in God").

There is a double motion to the Christian life. Our earthly life goes along a horizontal course, like the printed words of the poem, and like them has a meaning.

My words and thoughts do both expresse this notion,
That *Life* hath with the sun a double motion.
The first *Is* straight, and our diurnall friend,
The other *Hid,* and doth obliquely bend.
One life is wrapt *In* flesh, and tends to earth.
The other winds towards *Him,* whose happie birth
Taught me to live here so, *That* still one eye
Should aim and shoot at that which *Is* on high:
Quitting with daily labor all *My* pleasure,
To gain at harvest an eternal *Treasure.*

But more is taking place in our lives; for as we move through our daily tasks, our hearts are being shaped so that our desire is for Christ, our treasure. This is shown by the diagonal line which connects a word from each horizontal line. It is only by moving along the horizontal as best we can, obeying God, that we acquire the building blocks for the construction of that life which is hid with Christ in God.

This means that we can trust that what we are doing and what happens to us from the operations of the natural world and the social order make a contribution, even when we are not able to see that they do. All moments of dismay and dryness, as well as times of elation, make a contribution to that life which is being formed but which is not visible to us, especially when we are in states of distress. On this view, God does not grant us great faith so that having great faith we will follow. On the contrary, it is in following that our faith grows and becomes mature.

Were it not for the seed of divine love or grace, which gets into us when we relinquish the order of the body, we would not be able to endure severe deprivation and suffering with faith. There are moments of horror in facing the indifference of nature's operations on our bodies. There is an interval in which we feel utterly abandoned by all possibility of good, just as Jesus did for a time on the cross. When its mechanism injures us and those we love, we would not be able to love nature were it not for the beauty of the world and the seed of love which enables us to respond to its beauty. That seed of love will not show up on an X-ray. But it manifests itself in our love of justice, our increasing freedom from the burden of our evil, and our love of nature.

For this reason Weil writes, "the sense of our wretchedness is the sense of reality. For we do not invent our wretchedness. It is true. That is why we have to value it. All the rest is imaginary [to those who are still egocentric and anthropocentric in their outlook]."[21] Likewise she notes, "The tremendous greatness of Christianity comes from the fact that it does not seek a supernatural remedy against suffering, but a supernatural use of suffering."[22] We may use our suffering to lever ourselves to a higher plane. Nature then is not a barrier to belief in God's benevolence but a means through which we experience God's goodness.[23]

To develop a mature faith we must come to terms with Christ's suffering and not just our own. One of the greatest barriers to the recognition that Jesus was the Messiah or the Christ was that he suffered and was crucified. Although the Jewish people often explained their suffering as a punishment for their failures to be faithful to God, they knew that sometimes they suffered unjustly, as reflected in their lament, Why do the righteous suffer and the unrighteous prosper? There was a deep longing for justice. The promised Savior or Messiah was to establish justice and save Israel from unjust suffering. But Jesus failed to do this. Rather than delivering those who suffer unjustly, Jesus himself became a victim. How could a person who was utterly defeated by the power that belongs to the order of the body, free Israel from unjust suffering?

This glaring incompatibility was obvious even to uneducated people. For example, when Jesus asked his disciples, "Who do men say that the Son of man is?" (Matt. 16:13b) they answered, "Some say John the Baptist, others say Elijah, and others Jeremiah or one of the prophets" (Matt. 16:13a–14). That a prophet should suffer would not be surprising. But in reply to the question, "Who do you say that I am?" the apparent contradiction between messiahship and suffering is evident. For Simon Peter, who first confessed that Jesus was the Messiah and was praised warmly by Jesus, was utterly unable to take in Jesus' teaching that the Messiah must suffer, be rejected, and killed. He exclaimed, "God forbid, Lord! This shall never happen to you" (Matt. 16:22b). Jesus had made an elementary blunder, and anyone, even an uneducated fisherman, knew enough to rebuke him.

Perhaps even more explicit is the story of the resurrection appearance on the road to Emmaus. Two of Jesus' disciples met him as they were walking from Jerusalem, but they did not recognize him. They were downcast, they explained, because their hopes that Jesus was the Messiah had proved false. That the Messiah should suffer and be killed in a shameful way was something that they had not been able to take in. Jesus voiced distress at their foolishness and blindness and proceeded to explain the meaning of various passages of the Old Testament which showed that the Messiah must suffer. Only after this explanation and as the stranger broke the bread at mealtime did they recognize the Christ, risen from the dead (Luke 24:13–31).

Unlike these disciples, we are accustomed to the suffering of Christ. Our tendency is to think that because Christ suffered, we do not have to. We need to have our eyes opened to the fact that the good that God would do us is not available apart from suffering but is achieved precisely in and through suffering. Much of our suffering is useless. It springs from our egocentric and anthropocentric illusions and our acts of injustice. The Word of God becomes incarnate and suffers innocently so that we will want to make a distinction between the suffering which results from egocentrism, anthropocentrism, and our own injustices, and that suffering which is the inevitable result of being a creature and a victim of injustice. Because the Messiah is free of egocentrism, anthropocentrism, and injustice, Christ suffers only because Christ too is subject to nature's workings and other people's injustices. If we look to Christ, we will come to desire to be like Christ. We will want to make a distinction between what we suffer because of our egocentrism, anthropocentrism, and the injustices we commit, and what we suffer because we are creatures and are victims of other people's injustices. This distinction can be made in our lives by our acceptance of the inevitable suffering that occurs because we are natural beings, subject to the wear and tear of nature's working, and because we are learning from suffering unjustly to love justice and to work for it.

Faith then is to yield our consent to "distance." There is a "distance" between us and God that is the entire created order. We are subject to its working, but with faith, we live under our Creator's rule and indirectly we are in contact with God. As much as we may want to be free of the consequences of human injustices, we also want all people to turn from their injustice and receive God's mercy. Faith is to endure God's way of seeking to redeem us all.

This process often taxes us severely as we see in Herbert's poem, "The Temper I."

> How should I praise thee, Lord! how should my rymes
>   Gladly engrave thy love in steel,
>   If what my soul doth feel sometimes,
>   My soul might ever feel!
>
> Although there were some fortie heav'ns, or more,
>   Sometimes I peere above them all;
>   Sometimes I hardly reach a score,
>   Sometimes to hell I fall.
>
> Oh rack me not to such a vast extent;
>   Those distances belong to thee:
>   The world's too little for thy tent,
>   A grave too big for me.
>
> Wilt thou meet arms with man, that thou dost stretch
>   A crumme of dust from heav'n to hell?
>   Wilt great God measure with a wretch?
>   Shall he thy stature spell?

Oh let me, when thy roof my soul hath hid,
   Oh let me roost and nestle there:
Then of a sinner thou art rid,
   And I of hope and fear.

Yet take thy way; for sure thy way is best:
   Stretch or contract me thy poore debter:
This is but tuning of my breast,
   To make the musick better.

Whether I flie with angels, fall with dust,
   Thy hands made both, and I am there:
Thy power and love, my love and trust
   Make one place ev'ry where.

Life under God is strenuous but not grim. We have the power to improve things; we may enjoy the beauty of the world; we are to enjoy the glories of life; and we have the light of Christ shed on the negative aspects of life. Without Christ we should simply suffer and not have the encouragement that our suffering may become like Christ's.

IV

Because the good God intends us to have is to be found in community life, to have faith is to seek to overcome the destructive barriers that exist between people. Faith is to believe that we ought to and will be able to love our neighbors.

As we have pointed out, the Old Testament is a record of the tenacity with which the Jews sought to achieve the community which God intends us to have. God's covenant and Law were intended to be a blessing to their common life. But in Jesus' day there were deep divisions within the Jewish people. For example, when Jesus asked a woman to draw him a drink from a well, she asks him, " 'How is it that you, a Jew, ask a drink of me, a woman of Samaria?' For Jews have no dealings with Samaritans" (John 4:9). The theological tenets of the Samaritans did not differ in essentials from those of the Jews, yet they were not considered to be Jews.[24] It is no accident that in the parable of the Good Samaritan (Luke 10:25–37), Jesus had a Samaritan's action demonstrate what it is to love one's neighbor as oneself, a commandment which, according to Jesus, is second only to the commandment that we are to love God with all our heart, soul, strength, and mind.

Not only were the Jews divided into these two communities, but some groups, such as tax collectors, were considered outcasts. This division is reflected in Jesus' parable of two men, a tax collector and a Pharisee, who went to the Temple to pray. Jesus commended the tax collector, who could not bear to raise his eyes toward heaven, but could only beat his breast and plead, "God, be merciful to me a sinner!" rather than the Pharisee, who cited his achievements and thanked God that he was not like others, especially like the tax collector (Luke 18:10–14).

The parable of Lazarus and the rich man reveals another division which Jesus repudiated. Often poverty was thought to be a mark of God's displeasure and wealth a sign of divine favor. But according to this parable, after their deaths, Lazarus is in Abraham's bosom, being comforted, while the rich man is in torment, separated from them by an impassable chasm. Jesus taught that even though Lazarus was poor, he was still part of the covenant community because he was received by Abraham, the father of the entire Jewish people (Luke 16:19–31). By his failure to consider Lazarus part of the community, the rich man actually excluded himself from the community, and after he died that self-exclusion was evident.

Jesus' first disciples found it difficult fully to accept his radical view of community. For a time in the primitive church there was a genuine danger that it might be lost. Paul, however, never faltered in his struggle to overcome the division between Jew and Gentile, and indeed all vicious divisions. "There is neither Jew nor Greek, there is neither slave nor free, there is neither male nor female; for you are all one in Christ Jesus. And if you are Christ's, then you are Abraham's offspring, heirs according to the promise" (Gal. 3:28–29).

Paul's acceptance of the practice that those who had been Jews could continue to observe the Jewish ceremonial Law and that those who had not been Jews were free from such obligations implied that there may be differences between people without them being injurious to the larger community's life. If unity in Christ is paramount, particular traditions enrich and enhance its life.

The Christian church has never been able fully to realize God's intention in its own community life. In spite of the power of God's grace to remove evil and to inspire us to overcome hurtful divisions between us, we still all too often fail to love our neighbors as ourselves. The church's failure indicates that the practical difficulties of creating a true community require great skill and wisdom, but it also shows the immense power of sin.

The source of sin is hidden from us. The story of the Fall in Genesis 3 does not actually tell us its origin. None of the motives in the story of Adam and Eve are sufficient to account for their disobedience. Their susceptibility to the blandishments of the serpent shows that they already had the desire to use their freedom as they wished, and not to use it creatively to realize more fully the incipient community life with God, other creatures, and between themselves. That Adam and Eve looked to the serpent for guidance shows that they were already disobedient before they took fruit from the forbidden tree.

The story shows us something of the nature of sin. Adam and Eve believed that apart from God they themselves could determine what was good for them. In fact, they do not act independently but listen to a serpent. What it tells them to do is simply the opposite of what God has told them. The serpent, in spite of its air of sophistication, is actually like a small child whose only idea of freedom is to say "No!" to parents. The "good" that the serpent holds before them is to be like God. This is not an original idea but an imitation of the good God intends us to have; for God intends that we are to become like God. That is we are to participate in divine life, an eternal one. Neither Adam nor Eve nor the serpent are original. Failure to trust that God seeks their well-being and guides them toward it causes untold harm. This is true of us as well.

By showing the inadequacy of their motives, the story of Adam and Eve shows us the incomprehensibility of sin. Unlike us, they cannot blame their disobedience on a bad environment, for they are in a garden that is a paradise. They cannot blame it on the way their parents raised them, for they have no parents. And, as we have seen, they cannot make the serpent fully responsible, for they only listen to it because they already wish to use their freedom in their own way. This seems to be intentional. The absence of any reason that could account for their resistance to God indicates the incomprehensibility of sin.[25]

Sin is not the name of a motive but a general description of all the ways we fail to be oriented toward God and experience the consequences of that failure. We can use our environment, upbringing, and the influence of other people to explain our failure to look to God for our well-being. But because Adam and Eve are unable to use these as excuses, the story teaches that even were we in optimum conditions as they were, we would still resist God. Because there are so many factors affecting our behavior we can easily avoid admitting the reality of sin. The story of Adam and Eve, by removing all such factors, informs us that the source of our resistance to God is incomprehensible to us. But whatever the origin of our resistance may be, it is an empirical fact that we do resist recognizing that we are creatures of God and that God seeks our well-being. We are responsible for giving our consent to that resistance, that is for continuing to resist all that indicates the reality of God and God's way of leading us to our well-being. The Old and New Testaments illustrate many concrete ways people resist God both as individuals and as communities.

There is an analogy between sin and the force of gravity. Gravity is not the resistance we feel when we try to push a body, but this resistance is an effect of gravity. We describe gravity in terms of this and other effects. At first Newton was accused of having introduced an occult quality with his concept of gravity. It took some time before most philosophers and scientists were at ease with the idea of a force that is conceivable only indirectly through its effects.

In spite of the inexcusability of our continuing resistance, God does not abandon us but continues to show mercy. In the story of Adam and Eve, after their disobedience God gave them clothes to cover their nakedness and continued to be their God, seeking their well-being and that of their children. We learn from the rest of the Bible how God seeks to help us realize our well-being. Rather than waving a magic wand to rid us of our resistance and the harmful consequences of our resistance, God calls us into partnership. With God's help and guidance, we are to strive for a proper community life in which we may begin to find our well-being. The goal cannot be achieved all at once, but with patience we can move toward it.

The opposite of faith is despair, that is, to be without hope that we can move toward the well-being we crave. The creative use of our freedom is to exercise all our ingenuity, knowledge, and good will to work, with God's help and guidance, toward true community. This involves learning from our experience and from the experiences of those in the past who have sought to walk before God.

We may define sin in terms of orientation: it is to look elsewhere than to God for our well-being. This is reflected in the New Testament Greek word for repentance (*metanoia*), which means a change of heart, implying that one has turned around and has a different view of things. The Latin meaning of our word conversion is to turn about. These spatial metaphors for our orientation also help us to distinguish between sin and evil. If sin is to be turned away from God, then evil is to walk away from God. The further we walk, the more deeply we are in evil. To repent or turn toward all that promises to give us well-being is not to be freed from all evil. We must now walk toward God by obeying God's will.

This distinction between sin and evil enables us to understand how agnostics (or atheists) may be morally better than some Christians. The Christian was more deeply into evil than the agnostic when he or she changed direction and has not yet moved sufficiently closer to God to be as morally good as the agnostic. An agnostic may receive God's grace unknowingly, improve morally, and move closer to God, as is suggested in Jesus' parable of the sheep and the goats (Matt. 25:31–46).

Moral improvement is fraught with spiritual danger for both a Christian and an agnostic (or atheist) because it can lead to a sense of self-sufficiency and superiority. This is portrayed in George Herbert's poem, "Humilitie." In the poem animals represent the passions, our beastliness, so to speak. The lion is anger, the hare is fear, the turkey is desire, the fox is craft. The animals are subject to the crow, who represents reason. The anger of the lion becomes gentleness; the fearful hare develops fortitude; the jealous turkey becomes temperate; the crafty fox becomes just. But all the virtues become spoiled because without humility we are defenseless before the appeal of pride.

It has always been a central teaching of Christianity that the greatest danger to us as spiritual beings is pride, not our lusts and passions. They can, of course, destroy us, but they can also be controlled, and we can be undone by our pride at being able to control them. Our intelligence and efficiency lead to self-sufficiency and smugness. We become like the elder brother in the parable of the Prodigal Son or like the Pharisee in the parable of two men who went into the Temple to pray, both of whom thought they were superior.

Humility is not one virtue among many but a necessary condition for our virtues to be virtues rather than the source of a barrier between ourselves and others. Humility is not to pretend that we have no accomplishments, to lie about ourselves, or to degrade ourselves. It is to recognize that our virtues do not elevate us above others. We are unable to change our status as creatures no matter what we have achieved. They do not raise us above other people but move us along a horizontal continuum, on which we have achieved more than some and less than others. Being ahead of others may mislead us into thinking that we are above others and being behind others into thinking that we are below them. To recognize that we are creatures keeps us from allowing earthly distinctions to become a great chasm that separates us from others. Our status can be changed only by God, who elevates us all by divine love and intentions for us. Only when we love our neighbor as ourselves, whether we are explicitly Christians or not, is our essential equality recognized. As long as we seek to find our well-being through our achievements, we are possessed by our ego which keeps us in orbit around it and prevents us from becoming the person God intends us to become.

As we have seen, sin is not to be identified with any specific motive or experience. It manifests itself in any number of experiences, including our resistance to the good God would do us. This is true of various other motives, such as rebellion and pride, and experiences, such as alienation, anxiety, boredom, isolation, lack of self-control, self-pity, guilt, unworthiness, all of which are manifestations of sin. Sin also manifests itself in our failures to achieve a proper community life because these are not merely failures to overcome the many practical difficulties of social life.

The Christian community, in spite of its failures, is particularly relevant today. For nearly three hundred years Western society has been motivated by the idea of inevitable progress. But the concept of progress has been increasingly narrowed to mean mastery of the physical environment, control of human society, and ever-increasing material prosperity. Concern for justice has been limited to the distribution of power and material goods. Improving our life on earth is part of the Christian vision. In ancient times Christianity resisted the rejection of the belief in the goodness of the material universe by Gnostics and others. In modern times it inspired both Francis Bacon and Descartes, who are so largely responsible for encouraging efforts to improve life on earth, as mentioned in the first chapter. Its attacks more recently on materialism have been primarily provoked by the increasingly narrow understanding in Western society of the nature of human well-being. Our culture is failing to inspire a rich and significant community life because life is increasingly understood within the boundaries of the order of the body. Consider, for example, Wittgenstein's autobiographical remarks:

A culture is like a big organization which assigns each of its members a place where he can work in the spirit of the whole; and it is perfectly fair for his power to be measured by the contribution he succeeds in making to the whole enterprise. In an age without culture on the other hand forces become fragmented and the power of an individual man is used up in overcoming opposing forces and frictional resistances; it does not show in the distance he travels but perhaps only in the heat he generates in overcoming friction. But energy is still energy and even if the spectacle which our age affords us is not the formation of a great cultural work, with the best men contributing to the same great end, so much as the unimpressive spectacle of a crowd whose best members work for purely private ends, still we must not forget that the spectacle is not what matters.

I realize then that the disappearance of a culture does not signify the disappearance of human value, but simply of certain means of expressing this value, yet the fact remains that I have no sympathy for the current of European civilization and do not understand its goals, if it has any.[26]

This is a description of alienation. Wittgenstein, like so many others in our century, could not find a public life to which he could make a positive contribution. As Robert Bellah and others have argued, the only good to be realized has increasingly become a private, personal good, not a community good.[27] With the increase of purely private aims, there is a corresponding loss of our sense of personal significance. Today, confidence in material progress is becoming undermined because of two world wars, the cold war, the development of immensely powerful weapons, and ecological damage to the environment.

The Christian church is essentially a philanthropic community, concerned with service to others. In the Eastern church, for example, Jesus is referred to as *philanthropos*, that is, a lover of humanity. To be his follower is to become like him, a lover of humanity. From the very start there has been a concern for the poor, for widows and orphans, for the sick, the mentally ill, and the retarded. Education in the West owes an unparalleled debt to Christianity. Again and again Christianity has inspired efforts for the community good.

Part of the ability of Christianity to inspire community efforts, in spite of several blows from wars, famine, and plagues, is its continuing belief in a future. Neither war nor plague is able to defeat God. An issue that always faces human being in times of crisis is, who or what is in charge? In Christianity there is a sense of peace because of a confidence in God's power and good intentions toward us. In addition, we believe in the nearness of God's kingdom, not because things are necessarily getting better and better, but because we see with increasing clarity the need to give our allegiance to God's purposes. The kingdom of God is at hand when it becomes harder and harder to ignore or evade God's ways. Such convictions enable Christians to continue to work for the common good, to be philanthropic, even in a deteriorating situation. Because of faith in the good God intends us to have, Christian hope can survive even the disintegration of a culture, as it has the destruction of both the ancient and medieval civilizations.

The Christian community is an eschatological one. Eschatology is the doctrine of last things, that is, the realization of God's intentions. As pilgrims, deeply troubled by our resistance to God's intentions and hard pressed with the difficulties of achieving them, we nonetheless live now in the light and presence of our goal. The Christian church lives in light of the crucified and resurrected Lord, and in its worship celebrates Christ's victory over evil, sin, and death. It anticipates the fulfillment of that victory in all of us. At worship, the church is at the intersection of two worlds, the fallen, broken, divided world and the world that is to come. At worship, what is to come enters the present, forgiving our sin, absorbing our evil, inspiring us with divine assistance to continue our efforts to realize God's will in our families, in our friendships, in our work, in our political life, in our recreation. The church is both an earthly institution and the bearer of that which is from God.

Christianity is also particularly relevant today because we have a plurality of communities. No one is any longer a member of a single cultural tradition, whether Western, Middle Eastern, Indian, Asian, or

African. Increasingly these traditions are interacting. We are now required to make room for each other because it is no longer possible for each to be itself and to rely primarily on its own internal developments. The capacity of Christianity to encourage different cultures to make room for each other will be examined in the last two chapters.

The ability of Christianity in modern times to inspire our society has been hampered by a suspicion of tradition. To question every authority in philosophy and science was part of the genesis of modern history. Everything that is handed down from the past is to be tested. Since so much of science is a new departure from the old, there has been a marked tendency to think that what comes later is superior to whatever went before. Yet Christianity lives from and by a past; its hopes and expectations of what the future will be are largely based on the past, above all on the call of Abraham and Sarah and the new covenant in Christ.

Every tradition and past must, indeed, be examined, including the Christian tradition. It is not to be accepted blindly, as some critics think. But one is to accept and practice many things which one does not yet understand or fully understand. One may do this reasonably. As Pascal put it, "One must know when it is right to doubt, to affirm, to submit. Anyone who does otherwise does not understand the force of reason" (*Pensées* 170).

We shall examine this in the next chapter where we shall show the reasonableness of faith.

Chapter Seven

The Reasonableness of Faith

Faith is usually thought to be utterly out of place in philosophy, science, and indeed in all intellectual inquiry. It supposedly undermines the entire enterprise of reasoned inquiry. What is the use of any inquiry, if you are going to end up believing what you choose to believe anyway? Even though some grounds for religious beliefs are available, they are not sufficient to establish their truth. To leap beyond the evidence and to submit to an authoritative revelation is completely unacceptable in any university discipline. From the point of view of intellectual inquiry, theology is not legitimate because it begins with an authoritative revelation that is to be accepted by faith. Those religious people who have made significant contributions to a discipline are often viewed with puzzlement by agnostics and atheists. How can they have such able, critical minds in their academic or scientific work, yet accept religious beliefs by faith? Any educated person ought to recognize that our only reliable guide is our intelligence.

What is dismissed as incompatible with rational inquiry is not Christian faith but faith understood as a blind submission to authority or a "leap" to make up for a gap in the evidence. It assumes that faith and reason are mutually exclusive. Christian faith, however, involves the use of reason and without reason it is not Christian faith. To show this, we must first specify what is meant by reason.

I

There are many different views of the nature of reason, but it is primarily Hume's and Kant's views that have led both philosophers and theologians to think that reason is opposed to faith. The opposition can be indicated economically by recalling Basil Mitchell's analogy in which Christianity is likened to a ship going down a river. Hume and Kant are similar to shoals which prevent the ship from passing. Many theologians have either lightened the ship by jettisoning much of the cargo of Christian beliefs so as to float over the shoals or veered sharply toward the opposite bank of fideism, or a blind faith, in order to slip past the shoals and to continue with unrevised Christian beliefs. An examination of

Hume's and Kant's views of the nature of reason will not only illustrate two different views of reason but will also treat those views which are widely thought to preempt any possible role for reason within faith.

Although we have already examined Hume's *Dialogues Concerning Natural Religion* at some length, we did not explicitly treat the view of reason which Hume attributes to Cleanthes. According to Cleanthes, reason is quite competent to deal with

human affairs and the properties of the surrounding bodies [but] when we carry our speculations into the two eternities, before and after the present state of things; into the creation and formation of the universe; the existence and properties of spirits; the powers and operations of one universal spirit, existing without beginning and without end; omnipotent, omniscient, immutable, infinite, and incomprehensible: We must be far removed from the smallest tendency to scepticism not to be apprehensive, that we have here got quite beyond the reach of our faculties.[1]

Cleanthes believes that natural religion, in contrast to Christianity, is based on the kind of reasoning found in treating human affairs such as in economics, politics, and literature. Natural religion is not concerned with an infinite being that is beyond the power of reason to conceive. Unlike the subtle and refined reasoning of Christian theology, natural religion has the constant check of common sense and experience to guide its arguments, as does reasoning about trade, politics, and literature. But, as we saw, Hume's other characters, Philo and Demea, undermine natural religion itself. They show that even on the basis of Cleanthes' view of reason we are unable to infer from the order of the universe an intelligent and benevolent designer.

In the *Treatise on Human Nature* (1739), Hume endorses a view of reason which is so narrow that it cannot establish even the common sense world that is assumed in our reasoning in economics, politics, and literature. He argues that the only contents of our awareness are sense impressions and ideas. Ideas are based on sense impressions. When Hume tries to trace our ideas of material objects, causality, and our own selves back to their originating sense impressions, he cannot find in sense impressions sufficient warrant for the continuing existence of material objects, for a necessary connection in causal sequences, or for a self that is the subject of sense impressions and ideas and that is more than either. Hume explains how our beliefs in the continuing existence of material objects, necessary connections, and in the self are a product of our unreasoning nature. Even though these common sense beliefs cannot be founded on sense impressions, when we are not reasoning philosophically, we continue to hold them. On this view, not only are the "speculations" of Christianity and the inferences of natural religion beyond the powers of reason, so too are our everyday beliefs about tables and chairs, causal relations, and our own selves.

Kant tells us that Hume "awoke him from his dogmatic slumbers." His upbringing in the rationalistic school of Christian Wolff (1679–1754) had led him to take for granted the power of reason to discover necessary and universal truths. But Hume's analysis of the causal relation deeply disturbed him because he believed that if Hume were correct, the universal laws of Newtonian mechanics had no foundation. Kant agreed with Hume that there is no sense impression of a necessary connection between the members of a causal succession. But he argued that there must be necessary connections in causal succession, otherwise experience as we know it would be impossible. Likewise he argued that there must be substances or enduring objects, otherwise the distinction in our experiences between those sense impressions which are objectively successive (events) and those which are objectively simultaneous (objects) would be impossible. Necessary connections in causal succession show that the principles of Newtonian physics hold throughout the universe; substances show that the amount of matter in the universe is constant, that is, that the principle of the conservation of matter holds.

Kant is able to save Newtonian science but at a very high price. We can know that its principles hold universally only because all our experience is phenomenal (an appearance). The categories of substance and causality (as well as the other ten categories of the understanding) are rules of the mind according to which all that we experience is constructed by reason. According to Kant, reason is powerful, so powerful that we are enclosed within a world that it has constructed.

Actually Kant failed to provide a foundation for Newtonian science. His arguments that causality and substance are categories of the understanding assume that time is absolute. Since Einstein's general and special theories of relativity, this is not a viable view of time. Even if Kant's arguments that there must be necessary connections were sound, his arguments do not specify which scientific laws are necessary. We could not know whether or not the necessary connections that nature must have are Newton's laws of motion.

Kant is, nonetheless, correct in pointing out that science cannot operate within Hume's narrow view of reason. For Hume science is the discovery of correlations between observed phenomena. For modern science such correlations are only the bare beginning of what science does. Modern physics, chemistry, and cosmology rely on theories that employ theoretical entities and properties in order to make discoveries and provide explanations for observed correlations and low level laws.

They use terms which are not straightforwardly derivable by reference to our everyday experience, much less to sense impressions. Hume's conception of science, based on his view of reason, cannot accommodate the greater part of modern physics, chemistry, and cosmology.

In the twentieth century some philosophers, known as logical positivists, tried to revive a Humean philosophical and scientific outlook. Like all positivists, they claimed that the procedures of science specify the nature of rationality. For them physics was the paradigm of rationality. The rationality of all other sciences was judged with physics as the standard.

But the rationality they attributed to physics—a pattern of reasoning according to the rules of formal deductive logic, a feature that distinguished them from other positivists as *logical* positivists—did not actually fit the way physicists conducted their investigations and evaluated their results. When this became apparent, the logical positivists said that they were giving a "rational reconstruction" of physics. The relation of that reconstruction to the rationality of physics was never satisfactorily explained. In addition, like Hume, they were uncomfortable with theoretical entities in science and never found a way to square them with their Humean conviction that only sense impressions exist. Although logical positivism had its origins in German-speaking philosophy, its interpretation of the nature of science and rationality was dominant in English-speaking philosophy from the late 1930s to about 1960.

Logical positivism had ceased to be plausible to many philosophers some time before Thomas Kuhn's *The Structure of Scientific Revolutions*[2] made it known to a larger public that the tide had turned against a positivist's view of the nature of science and rationality. Kuhn distinguishes between normal science, which operates within an accepted paradigm, and revolutionary science, which causes a shift in paradigms. According to Kuhn, some of the reasons for a paradigm shift are not internal to scientific development. At first many philosophers of science thought that Kuhn's views challenged the very rationality of science. In time, several aspects of Kuhn's work were quietly absorbed into the history of science and seen to have long been part of good historical practices in other fields of history. Even though all of Kuhn's thesis has not been found satisfactory, the grip of the positivists' view of reason on the general intellectual public, a view allegedly based on the pattern of scientific reasoning, has been broken.

At the present time, precisely what procedures are used in the various sciences and how they are validated is at the forefront of debate. It is clear, however, that the understandings of science in Hume, Kant, and the logical positivists are far too narrow and simple to do justice to scien-

tific procedures and that no one science ought to set the standards for rationality in all the other sciences. In addition, the kinds of reasoning used in the various sciences do not necessarily exhaust the range of rational procedures.

This has been stressed in particular by a branch of the sociology of knowledge which concentrates on science. It considers the social circumstances in which science is practiced to see how they retard or accelerate scientific development. Religion is among the social forces it considers. The truth or falsity of religion, however, is accorded no more consideration than the truth or falsity of astrology, magic, or alchemy, which are also studied for their effects on scientific development. Martin Rudwick calls this approach "the weak program" because it assumes that the actual contents of a science are derived primarily from the interaction of an external nature with human rationality.[3] In contrast to this, he supports what is called "the strong program" in the sociology of science. It explores the possibility that the social circumstances and aims of a society, as well as the particular makeup and outlook of an individual scientist may affect the actual contents of science.

It is generally agreed that scientific knowledge is not read off nature but is a highly mediated relation to the natural world. Our observations are "theory-laden," that is, they are made possible and are affected by our instruments and mental constructions. In the strong program, our mental constructions, as well as all other aspects of science, are examined to see how they are socially influenced in their formation and acceptance.

The strong program views science as just one of many cultural enterprises that require analysis and evaluation. That a particular scientific view becomes accepted cannot be explained simply by saying that it is true. The questions of why and how it was accepted and why and how other views were rejected by particular scientists at a specific time must be examined from a social point of view. It may be that a particular scientific view was not significantly influenced except by the most general social circumstances. But this cannot be assumed to be true of scientific claims in general. It must be determined by an examination of each particular case. From this point of view, the practices and results of the various sciences are not automatically assumed to set the standards of rationality for all the other disciplines, including religion, nor to exhaust the range of rational procedures to which other disciplines—for example, literary criticism and religion—must conform.

The approach of the strong program does not imply that scientific knowledge is merely a social product. Because nature does not com-

pletely determine our theories, it does not follow that *any* theory may be proposed and accepted regardless of the input of the natural world. The external world places limits and constraints on what procedures may be followed and what theories may be proposed and accepted. More than one interpretation of a play by Shakespeare are viable, but there are some interpretations which are not. Just as the text has a differentiating effect on viable interpretations of a Shakespearean play, the external world, over time, has a differentiating effect on various scientific constructions. We are not reduced to utter relativity because science, like every other human activity, is highly mediated.

It has not been possible to reach an agreement as to precisely what the nature of proper reasoning is even in those areas of inquiry about which we are most confident, namely the "hard sciences." This does not mean that we are not reasoning properly there and in other areas. To learn enough about even one field of inquiry is a very demanding task, and the ability to step back and give a plausible account of the nature of reasoning is a rare talent. It is no wonder that historians and philosophers of science are still hard at work seeking to understand the nature of scientific reasoning in the various branches of science.

We can say with confidence, however, that what is taking place in the sciences does not rule out the possibility of God, as we have shown in earlier chapters. It is also clear that the views of reason found in Hume, Kant, and the logical positivists are so narrow that they cause difficulties not only for theology but for the sciences. To put theology beyond the pale of reason on the basis of their views of reason is to put our sciences beyond the pale of reason as well.

The sociology of knowledge, which has contributed so much to the breakdown of narrow and restrictive views of reason, has led, as we have just seen, to the exaggerated statement that scientific knowledge is nothing but a product of social forces. It has encouraged similar exaggerations in theology. Consider the following remarks, which are put forward as though they represent a theological consensus:

... we are aware in ways our foremothers and forefathers were not that theology is a constructive enterprise and that Christianity is but one religion among many.

As almost every contributor to this volume has stressed ... the human "world," whether religious, political, sociological, or personal, is a constructed world and hence a relative one. Since the Enlightenment and especially since Immanuel Kant, it has not been possible to turn to a deposit of faith in scripture or tradition and find there an absolute or certain basis for religious truth. We have come to realize that there is no naked eye, no innocent eye, that all our ways of being in the world are *our* ways, and that the ways in which we construct our world are determined by our time and place.[4]

The claim in this passage is so common in theology today that it is important to uncover two mistakes in the reasoning. First, although Kant's name is invoked here and frequently among other theologians with this outlook, Kant's own philosophy is not the basis of the claim. According to Kant, from our constructed world we have no clue whatsoever about reality. But our author, in spite of having invoked Kant, nonetheless asserts that the essence of Christianity is

not any book or doctrine or interpretation, but the transformative *event* of new life, a new way of being in the world that is grounded in the life and death [and resurrection?] of Jesus of Nazareth . . . *as event* it stands behind, beneath, and before all our constructions of it.[5]

For Kant an "event" is a product of our rational faculty. Within Kant's epistemology the life and death of Jesus of Nazareth "as event" is no less a construction than anything else that happens.

In addition, Kant's epistemology does not imply relativism. For Kant there are no rival mathematical or scientific constructions. Euclid's geometry, other branches of mathematics, and the principles of Newtonian science are true for all human beings. We cannot, therefore, simply say, "the human 'world,' . . . is a constructed world and hence a relative one."

Second, according to the author, if there is no "absolute or certain basis for religious truth," the situation is one of relativism or even "radical relativism" (see her next paragraph).

But what is meant by an "absolute or certain basis"? What would it be to have that in any domain, not just a religious one? For Descartes, Spinoza, Kant, and some others in modern philosophy, it means that the ground for a claim must be such as to rule out any possibility of doubt about its truth because the evidence or intuition shows it to be true by necessity. Given the evidence or intuition, it is impossible for the claim to be false. One of the achievements of philosophy in this century has been to show that there are no claims which are true by necessity in any area of inquiry, including science.[6] This does not mean that none of our claims lack sufficient rational grounds to be warranted. Relativism cannot be inferred from the fact that our claims to knowledge do not have a foundation of truths that are true by necessity.

The author's argument must then be the following one: (1) Since there is "no naked eye," our worlds are constructed ones. (2) Our constructed worlds "are determined by our time and place." (3) There is no absolute or certain basis on which to determine which of the different worlds is true. (4) The situation is one of radical relativism.

Again the logic is incorrect. We may distinguish between having sufficient grounds to *warrant* the affirmation of a claim and having sufficient grounds to *compel* affirmation of a claim. I may have sufficient grounds to assert a truth-claim but not have grounds which show another person that what I assert is true because the grounds do not compel assent. This is true whether the other person shares or does not share my "constructed world."

Since there are sufficient warrants to affirm claims, even though the warrants do not always compel everyone to affirm the claims, we are not in a situation of "radical relativism." That is, we are not in a hall of mirrors without any sound basis for judging between reflections and the objects reflected. That people have different beliefs and convictions in the same and in different cultures is an important social, moral, and religious consideration, but it does not mean that we are in a Kant-like enclosed world of appearances, nor that we must have an "absolute or certain basis," either in the sense of claims that are true by necessity or in the sense of warrants that compel assent, in order to be able to make rational, warranted assertions.

Finally, there is an interesting shift in the quoted passage from "the ways in which we construct our world are determined by our time and place" to saying at the end of the paragraph, "we are selves-in-relationship from the very beginning to the end of our days and hence deeply influenced in ways beyond our knowing or control."[7] There is a vast difference between being "determined" and "being influenced." The former reduces our outlook to nothing but a social construct; the latter is far too weak to transport us into a situation of "radical relativity."

There is a marked tendency for those who begin by thinking that our understanding of the world is directly read off the world to lurch to the opposite extreme when they realize that our sense organs, brains, and culture all affect our perception and understanding. Our contact with external reality is mediated but that is not to say that we are totally enclosed within our subjectivity, nor that all our claims are reducible to socio-cultural accounts, nor that we need to find "an essence" that is not a mediated reality, as if only in this way can we escape from being enclosed within our own thoughts.

There is room for several intermediate positions between naive realism ("an unmediated reality") and relativity ("enclosure within our constructed worlds"). All that we are entitled to infer from the general fact that all knowledge is socially mediated is that some intermediate position between the extremes of naive realism and relativity is correct. We are not cut off from reality, as we indicated above in connection with the strong program in sociology of science.

We may make the same point more simply. Consider the way a blind person uses a cane to find his or her way around. The cane does not enable the blind person to say all that is true of what is touched with it. One cannot use it to measure the temperature or weight of things. What one knows of reality by use of a cane is limited to what a cane can mediate. Likewise, our various sciences use human sense organs, tools and instruments, words, and socially formed minds to probe the universe, just as a blind person uses a cane. The claims which can be made on this basis are incomplete, tentative, and corrigible, but they nonetheless are reliable ways of understanding the world, just as a blind person's cane is a reliable way of finding his or her way about. Precisely where we are on the continuum between naive realism and utter relativism in the case of each particular kind of inquiry is a matter of detailed study of that inquiry. But the analogy with a blind person's cane shows that we should not jump to the extreme of relativism when we learn that "there is no naked eye."[8]

From what has been said, it is clear that we should not identify reason and proper procedures with any one kind of "probe." Claims about reality should not be dismissed as beyond the pale of reason simply because their grounds are different from the kind of grounds used to support claims in the sciences. Faith differs from the procedures in the various sciences or other disciplines, including philosophy, but this does not imply that faith involves no reasoning. We will now consider the role reason does play in Christian faith and in this way show why faith is reasonable.

II

Basil Mitchell has suggested that

there is a continuum of rational disciplines from physics and chemistry through the biological and social sciences to the humanities and metaphysics. At the scientific end of the spectrum there are certain fairly precise patterns of argument possible (largely because of restrictions upon their scope) which it is tempting to equate with rationality as such. But at each stage in the continuum, not excluding the first, there is discernible a broader type of rationality in which rival explanations are canvased and defensible choices made between them. The degree of analogy between each stage and the next, and the evident continuity between them, make it implausible to suggest that at some point in the sequence we encounter a decisive break such that, up to that point we have been making reasonable judgments; beyond it only existential decisions—or something of the sort.[9]

The work of the late Michael Polanyi illustrates one attempt to specify a broader type of rationality within which all inquiry takes place. Polanyi argued that it is not only in religion that faith and reason have been set in opposition but that this has happened in every domain of inquiry. All belief has been reduced to the status of "an imperfection."

We must recognize belief or intuitive apprehension once more as the source of knowledge from which our acts of discovery take their rise, for it is in belief that we are in direct touch with reality, in belief that our minds are open to the invisible realm of intelligibility independent of ourselves, and through belief that we entrust our mind to the orderly and reliable nature of the universe.

Behind and permeating all our scientific activity, reaching from end to end of our analyses and investigations, there is an elemental, unshakeable faith in the rational nature of things, but faith also in the possibility of grasping the real world with our concepts, and faith in the truth over which we have no control but in service of which our human rationality stands or falls. Faith and rationality are intrinsically interlocked with one another. No human intelligence, Polanyi claimed, however critical or original, can operate outside such a context of faith, for it is within that context that there arises within us, under compulsion from the reality of the world we experience, an operative set of convictions or a framework of beliefs which prompts and guides our inquiries and controls our interpretation of data.[10]

As we pointed out in Chapter One, these convictions formed part of the vital context which allowed modern science to arise in the seventeenth century. Furthermore, there are several parallels between faith in Christianity and Polanyi's account of a faith which gives a context of rationality for all inquiry. First, in both there is the belief that an interaction is taking place between human beings and that which is a reality independent of human beings. In the case of Christian faith, the reality is God. In the case of physical science, the reality is nature. Second, in both faith is not in opposition to reason, as if we turn to faith because of an imperfection in our knowledge. Rather, the entire domain of rational inquiry relies on faith that interaction takes place with an independent reality, one that is orderly and that guides us reliably toward knowledge. Third, Polanyi was aware of the fact that both theology and physical science have distinctive procedures because the realities with which they interact are very different. Theology is concerned with the source of all reality and the revelation of its intentions for us; physical science is concerned with the workings of the universe. Fourth, to interact with God so as to come to the conviction that there is a God and a God such as Christianity claims there is, requires a particular personal preparation, as we have seen. Likewise, to do a particular science requires a specific personal preparation. To grasp the results that have been achieved by a science and to contribute to its development require a personal development in a discipline that is appropriate to the realities that science investigates.

The degree of agreement within the physical sciences is thought to mark them off absolutely from theology, and in various degrees from other disciplines. As Mitchell notes, this is largely because their scopes are severely restricted. Not only are all questions of value excluded, but only quantitative relations are considered. Even so, serious disagreement has arisen over the interpretation of quantum mechanics.

The bases of the most widely accepted interpretation of the quantal formalism were laid in discussions between Werner Heisenberg (1901–76) and Niels Bohr (1885–1962) in Copenhagen in the winter of 1926–27. This interpretation, often called "the Copenhagen interpretation," continues to meet strong opposition from many physicists and philosophers. Bohr's own interpretation went in the direction of a fundamental principle, which he claimed applied to every domain of inquiry, namely, the principle of complementarity. Heisenberg claimed that the quantal formalism could not be regarded as a description of nature in the same sense as classical physics. What it described was not nature as such but nature as exposed to our method of questioning. It was not a symbolic representation of nature but the interplay between nature and human beings. Erwin Schroedinger (1887–1961), the creator of wave mechanics, along with Einstein claimed that the Copenhagen interpretation violated basic assumptions of science: that nature is comprehensible, that our experiences of it may be ordered, and that the knowing subject may be left out of the picture. Still others have thought that quantum physics contains no philosophical assumptions and has no philosophical implications. As far as they are concerned, only experimental data exist; nothing else spoken of in theories need be thought of as existing.[11] One may continue to insist that there is no disagreement here by saying that everyone agrees on the experimental data and that the interpretation beyond that is not science but philosophy. But in that case it is evident that a number of scientists are doing philosophy and doing it because of questions that have arisen from their scientific work.

One of the reasons that theology is not widely recognized as being on a continuum of rational inquiry, participating with all other inquiries in a broader type of rationality, is our high degree of specialization. Few people are deeply informed about the procedures of other disciplines, especially when they are distantly separated along the continuum of inquiry, as are the natural sciences and theology. But there are a few pioneers who have found significant similarities in reasoning between physics and theology, even though each asks very different questions and uses different procedures with respect to the common universe they both investigate. For example, W. Jim Neidhardt, a member of the physics department of the New Jersey Institute of Technology, literally went back to school to gain a substantial competence in theology. With a sophistication rarely to be found in publications on the relation of science and theology, he has uncovered similarities in reasoning between particle physics and divine predications (the theory underlying applying various attributes to God's nature) that are rich and complex in detail. He believes that the similarities he has specified point "toward an underlying unity in the thought patterns of theologians and natural scientists." [12]

Even more important for us is John Bowker's explanation of the division between religion and all other forms of inquiry. According to Bowker, over the last four hundred years there has been a gradual differentiation and divergence in interests between religion and university disciplines, rather than a replacement of faith by rational inquiry. Religions (and not just the Christian religion) became differentiated from other inquiries by their continuing focus on the more intransigent limitations of human life, such as evil, suffering, and death. Religions developed an understanding of reality that primarily, though not exclusively, concerned these intransigent limitations, and acted as guides in the construction of life ways to deal with them. Scientific traditions have increasingly focused on limitations that have turned out to be less intransigent, such as the inability to fly and the limited range of sounds and colors the unaided senses can detect. Their more easily discerned successes have elevated the sciences above religion in the community concerned with inquiry and also encouraged the tendency to think of scientific activity as the only rational and reliable procedure. [13]

Religious faith will appear to consist of blind, unfounded opinions when it is evaluated solely by procedures and standards employed in disciplines which exclude the very matters that are the primary concern of a religion. For example, the last chapter stressed that faith is to consent to the good that God would do us. If all rational inquiry is value-free, as is so often claimed today, how are we to make an inquiry into the goodness of the alleged good that God would do us? Neither consent nor rejection can be rational when "rational inquiry" is identified with procedures and standards of inquiry which exclude values and the rationality of the endorsement of any values.

As we explained earlier in Chapter Six, the "heart" is a metaphor for our response to good and our quest for what would give us our well-being. As we argued in Chapter Five, no agent insofar as he or she is rational can ignore the fact that many human beings are looking for what would give them well-being, a well-being that is unlikely to be realized if this universe is all that there is. The exclusion of matters of the heart from many university disciplines is legitimate because of the nature of the questions they investigate. But this exclusion from many university disciplines does not put the search for what satisfies the heart beyond the scope of rational inquiry. Nor does it render the response to the good God would do us a nonrational response. The role of reason in Christian faith may be illustrated with Pascal's famous distinction of three orders: body, mind, and heart.

According to Pascal, we cannot discover or demonstrate some of the major claims found in the book of Scripture, namely that we are created in God's image, fallen, but redeemable through Christ. To require people to affirm this before they recognize by reasoning some of the paradoxes of human nature and the human condition is to subject the mind to tyranny. It is to compel it to assent.

The way of God, who disposes all things with gentleness, is to instil religion into our minds with reasoned arguments and into our hearts with grace, but attempting to instil it into hearts and minds with force and threats is to instil not religion but terror (*Pensées* 172).[14]

According to Pascal, Christianity enables us to understand our nature. In a number of paradoxes Pascal shows that we are a riddle to ourselves and do not understand what we are. On the one hand, we have reason and can achieve remarkable things; on the other hand, in making judgments, our reason is thrown off by the most irrelevant factors (see, for example, *Pensées* 44). More significantly jarring is the paradox that we who have such greatness can be utterly destroyed by the slightest imbalance in our bodies or crushed as easily as an egg.

Man is only a reed, the weakest in nature, but he is a thinking reed. There is no need for the whole universe to take up arms to crush him: a vapour, a drop of water is enough to kill him. But even if the universe were to crush him, man would still be nobler than his slayer, because he knows that he is dying and the advantage the universe has over him. The universe knows none of this (*Pensées* 200).

We are both great and insignificant, and our greatness and insignificance do not fit together. They are truths which no philosophical or psychological theory has been able to render compatible. Either of the extremes may be stressed but always to the neglect of the other. With Descartes, reason is our defining characteristic, so that our essential nature is not subject to physical destruction; with Freud our affective, irrational, animal side is uppermost. The first theory stresses our greatness; the second our insignificance, yet neither theory can be sustained. When we try to affirm our greatness, our lower selves and the vastness of the universe pull us from our lofty heights. When our insignificance is stressed, our distinctiveness from the rest of nature resists this reduction ("he knows . . . the advantage the universe has over him. The universe knows none of this"). However small and irrational we may be, we are also able to become aware of our smallness and irrationality, so that our greatness cannot be utterly undermined by the irrationality of our passions or the vastness of the universe or the ability of a tiny part of it to kill us. But we cannot conclude that we are immensely significant because of our irrationality, smallness, and vulnerability. Our nature has both of these extreme features, and they push us in opposite directions, so that as soon as we go in one direction, we are driven back toward the other. We cannot find a compromise by saying that we are neither great nor insignificant but something in between simply because we indeed are both great and insignificant and these cannot be blended any more than can oil and water. No philosophical or psychological theory has been able to tell us what we are: great or insignificant.[15]

But Christianity by its recognition of two realms, the natural and the divine, can make sense of these extremes. According to Christianity, we are natural beings with a supernatural destiny. However much we exceed other creatures, we cannot sustain our sense of greatness and significance on the basis of our natural endowments because of our limitations and mortality. A greatness based on our supernatural destiny, however, is not affected by them. When our greatness is based on God's gift of eternal life, whose realization begins here and now but which has its full fruition in the kingdom of God, it is not affected by nature's vastness or our natural limitations. God's gift or intention as the basis of our greatness introduces another level into our understanding of human beings. It enables us to see that although our greatness based on our reason and our achievements is easily deflated by the fact that we are natural beings, our greatness based on our having a supernatural destiny is secure.

As long as we stay on one level, the natural, we cannot find a resting place because we ceaselessly go up and down in our self-evaluation. We are haunted by a sense of significance, yet we are mocked by obvious facts. We cannot know what we are or understand ourselves. But as soon as a supernatural level is introduced, we can cease the vain attempt to determine what we are by staying on one level and being forced to go back and forth between two extremes. Our true nature includes a supernatural destiny, a greatness beyond the ceaseless seesaw because its basis is another level of reality (see *Pensées* 131).

Christianity also explains why human beings have the incompatible

features of greatness and insignificance. Our limitations and vulnerability, which constitute the basis of our insignificance, and our reason,
which constitutes the basis of our natural greatness, are accounted for
when viewed from a supernatural perspective. As mere creatures we are
limited and vulnerable as are all creatures in their different ways. But as
creatures made in God's image, we are able to reason and to relate to
others on a personal basis. Our natural greatness is seen in relation to
God's nature, and that natural greatness has been conferred as a reflection of our supernatural destiny: to be related to God and to obey God
freely.

We tend, however, to use our natural greatness for self-elevation, ig-
noring the fact that we are great only because we are made in God's
image. Our natural greatness leads us to pride, that is, to an attempt to
base our status on our own powers without any reference to God. Our
natural powers blind us to our true greatness. God's good gift of natural
powers becomes a barrier between us and God. We therefore need to
realize and constantly to be reminded that our natural greatness is the
result of our supernatural origin and destiny. Our natural greatness,
because it can fill us with pride, must be seen in relation to our limitations and vulnerability. We must keep in mind our insignificance in a
vast universe, the fallibility of our judgment, and our susceptibility to
microbes and viruses. Yet our insignificance cannot be allowed to dominate our views of ourselves lest we sink into despair. The disparate features of our nature are to be used to counter each other so that we
become neither blinded by pride nor sunk in despair.

Pascal does not claim that the Christian resolution of the paradoxes
of our nature proves that there are two realities, natural and divine, but
that to consider two kinds of reality makes sense of what otherwise
baffles us. Christian truth, which we receive by faith, does give us illumination. It does inform the mind and provide understanding that is
not otherwise available to us. Ultimately, the incompatibility of our
greatness and our insignificance so baffles us as to make us receptive or
open to a supernatural understanding of ourselves. It is by this kind of
reasoning that we are pressured by our reason to become open to what
is above reason's ability to discover or demonstrate as true.

Pascal points not only to the paradoxes of our nature but also to the
paradoxes of our condition. For example, we are inconstant. Pascal
writes, "A trifle consoles us because a trifle upsets us" (43). Were we more
stable and more in control of ourselves, a trifle could not console us.
That it does shows us how easily we are upset. We are also plagued by
boredom and anxiety from which we constantly seek diversions. "If our

condition were truly happy we should not need to divert ourselves from thinking about it" (70).

Even though, as we have indicated earlier, we cannot comprehend how sin originally arose or how it arises in each person today, the Christian doctrine of sin gives us an understanding of our condition of inconstancy, boredom, anxiety, and unhappiness. We are this way because, not being directed toward God, we think we can determine for ourselves the path to our well-being. Without this explanation, our wretchedness remains incomprehensible to us; for we are unhappy in a particular and peculiar way.

Who would think himself unhappy if he had only one mouth and who would not if he had only one eye? It has probably never occurred to anyone to be distressed at not having three eyes, but those who have none are inconsolable (117).

All these examples of wretchedness prove his greatness. It is the wretchedness of a great lord, the wretchedness of a dispossessed king (116).

Our unhappiness is such that it points beyond itself to a greatness, and the greatness it points to is a supernatural one. We suffer from an unhappiness that is similar to that suffered by those who once were great but now are fallen, of those who have lost what they once had and now are inconsolable. For ordinary people to feel this kind of wretchedness makes no sense from a natural perspective. But from a higher perspective it does: the perspective that says that our happiness is to be found in obedience to God, who seeks to do us good. Through our failure to obey, we are wretched, subject to inconstancy, boredom, and anxiety, in need of diversions to keep us from thinking about and feeling our wretchedness.

The claims that we are created in God's image, fallen, but redeemable through Christ, are not demonstrable by reason. Christianity claims that they are revealed by God's inspiration to a very few chosen people, who have passed them on through the communities of Israel and the church. But to expect a response of faith to these claims before our minds recognize the paradoxes of our nature and condition is to expect a blind submission. The proper response to Christian claims is indeed faith but only after we have recognized with our minds the incomprehensibility of our nature and our own wretchedness. Then we can see by reason the coherent picture of ourselves which Christian truth gives us as it enables us to understand those paradoxes which perplexed us and left us in our wretchedness without hope of remedy. Even though faith is not produced by reason, our faith is reasonable because Christian claims illumine the mind on matters that otherwise baffle us. Without such illumination, faith is improper because it is blind, that is, based on such things as craven fear or a mistaken idea that Christianity promises earthly rewards.

Earlier we examined at length the fact that the members of the universe do not explain why we have this universe or any universe at all. Here too the human mind encountered a limit beyond which it has not been able to go. Often we ignore this limit. Many people take it for granted that science can explain everything because it has been so successful and because the deity of natural religion has been undermined. They, like so many practicing scientists, forget that science takes the existence of the universe for granted. Because scientific procedures are geared to study the relations between the members of the universe, when the question arises as to why nature has the particular order it has, the question is discussed in terms of whether the universe was designed, not its contingency.

Philosophically the only way to deal with the contingency of the universe (why does nature have this order, rather than another? and why does the universe have any members at all?) is boldly to assert that the universe must have a source in a being that accounts for its own existence. But the principle of sufficient reason, which enables such a claim to be made, is not a principle which we are compelled to hold. It rests on the conviction that the universe must be intelligible and not just a brute fact.

The book of Scripture, though not initially nor primarily directed toward seeking to explain why we have this world or any world at all, nonetheless answers these questions. To have faith is to receive illumination concerning the universe. We do not have to settle for a universe that is a brute fact. We have an understanding of the universe in which it is not the highest or the best reality, and we have this understanding without claiming that a disputed philosophical principle must be true. By the exercise of our minds we see the legitimacy of the questions, why they are not answered by our science, and why they are not determinable philosophically. In addition, the answer we get from Scripture is not merely "a being which has the reason for its existence in itself." Rather, the source of all things of which the Bible speaks is One who also gives us a destiny.

Even though the affirmation that God, not the universe, is the highest and best reality requires faith, that affirmation is not wholly discontinuous with the order of the mind. Otherwise its affirmation would not have borne such fruit in that order. It has been a major ingredient in the very origins of classical science and has had immensely fruitful effects on the scientific study of the universe.

Faith instead of being a compelled submission to an authoritative revelation is rather a positive response to a source that gives immense understanding of matters which concern us greatly. If religious claims are excluded by a narrow view of what is reasonable, we cut ourselves off from a source of considerable understanding as well as guidance and direction for our lives.

III

The nature of faith and its relation to reason are frequently misunderstood because of a particular understanding of the phrase "leap of faith." The phrase is usually taken to mean that since all the available evidence falls short of establishing the truth of Christianity, we must leap the gap between evidence and truth. It is rather like Lou Costello's joke. He showed Bud Abbott a gun, which he said was wonderful. "What's so wonderful about it?" asked Abbott. "It shoots bullets for eight miles and throws rocks the rest of the way," was the reply. So too with religion. Because the evidence falls short, faith has to take us the rest of the way.

This is to treat faith and reason as belonging to the same order. The evidence cited for the belief gives Christianity some rational basis and makes the leap beyond evidence a less serious violation of the commitment to rational inquiry. But Christian faith is not a leap *within* the order of the intellect, a leap which violates the very essence of that order. The leap of faith is a leap *from* the order of the intellect to the order of the heart. We leap because we recognize the reality of the domain of the heart, not because there is a shortage of evidence.

We recognize the reality of the order of the heart when we realize that we cannot achieve the well-being we seek from possessing those goods which can be gained by power and wealth (the order of the body) and when we realize that all questions of value and self-evaluation are legitimately excluded from consideration within the order of the intellect. Faith is called a "leap" because there is a chasm between the orders of the body and the intellect and the order of the heart, which can be spanned only by a change in outlook and concerns.

This change cannot be compelled by frustrations and misery at the level of the body, nor by arguments at the level of the intellect, although both supply excellent reasons to make a change. Our desire for our well-being can provide us with a great deal of motivation to change. But still it is we ourselves who must open our hearts and give our consent to the good that God would do us, the good that is portrayed in the Bible and taught by the churches.

The difficulty in making the transition to the order of the heart is similar to the parallel difficulty in making the transition from the order of the body to the order of the intellect. Those who belong to the order of the body are blind to the greatness of the intellect because they are fully occupied by practical needs and appetites. Teachers know how difficult it is to get students, legislators, foundations, and other benefactors to value intellectual achievement for its own sake, rather than solely in terms of its practical uses.

Likewise it is difficult for those who recognize the greatness of the order of the intellect to realize that the concerns of the heart are not like those emotions that interfere with the proper working of the mind. The desire for our well-being, when purified of the desire for earthly prosperity and worldly success, points toward an order that is above the order of the intellect, not below it. Because faith is neither below nor on the same level as the order of the intellect, it does not interfere with honest inquiry.

We respond to Christian claims with faith because they give us an understanding of our universe and of ourselves and provide us with a path to our well-being. Faith does not make its first appearance because there is a shortage of evidence. It begins with our consent to the good God would do us, is purified with the continuing acceptance of God's judgment, and grows into maturity with the acceptance of unavoidable suffering and participation in the life of the Christian community. To achieve this understanding, our minds must be active, but we must also be open to the concerns of the heart. The exclusion of values from the natural world by modern physics when it dispensed with an Aristotelian teleology has greatly reinforced the resistance of those engaged in intellectual inquiry to the stirrings of the heart.

If faith belonged to the order of the intellect, it would be inversely correlated with the evidence for Christian claims. But faith understood as belonging to the order of the heart is not lessened because of an increase of favorable evidence for religious claims. Our consent to the good God seeks to give us is indispensable however much evidence or warrant for religious claims increases.

In academic circles today, the "leap of faith" is most closely associated with Søren Kierkegaard (1813–55). Kierkegaard rejected the practice of those theologians and philosophers who tried to use Hegel's philosophy of history as a foundation for Christianity. In his *Philosophical Fragments, Concluding Unscientific Postscripts,* and *Training in Christianity,* Kierkegaard refers to this as "the way of speculation" and more generally "the way of objectivity." This corresponds to Pascal's order of the intellect.

Kierkegaard argues that if Christianity is true, there is so much at stake for us personally that nothing less than certainty is able to satisfy us. Because Christianity claims that God became human, we can never establish its truth by historical study, partly because historical arguments never give us certainty, and partly because even the contemporaries of Jesus were unable to perceive his divinity. Nor can the incarnation be inferred from scientific or philosophic principles because God freely chose to become human. Historical study and philosophic speculation can never close the gap between the claim that Jesus is God incarnate and the evidence for the claim. The size of the gap between the claim and the evidence is irrelevant because the claim has revealed such an enormous good that our concern for our well-being can no longer be satisfied with anything less than certainty.

Kierkegaard argues that another route, that of subjectivity, can give us certainty. By subjectivity Kierkegaard means the human subject, in contrast to objects. The way of subjectivity refers to the state or condition of people, in particular the validity of their lives. It is through an examination of the validity of our lives that we are able to gain certainty.

In a series of "aesthetic" works Kierkegaard gives an analysis of the aesthetic form of existence which is so brilliant and contemporary that few people are able to read his accounts of it without recognizing a significant part of themselves. Kierkegaard seeks to exhibit the instability of an aesthetic form of life and show why it cannot be sustained. Although it is attractive because it is a way of life that is based on self-gratification, in time it becomes boring. It requires progressively desperate measures to keep boredom at bay. If persisted in, the aesthetic life leads to apathy and despair.

Kierkegaard claims that those who belong to the way of objectivity conceal the fact that we are existing individuals who cannot find our well-being aesthetically. If we examine our lives thoughtfully, we shall find ample reason to desire change. That change can only be made by leaping from the aesthetic life and from speculation to embrace by faith the promises of God.[16]

Kierkegaard argues that we resent not being able to comprehend God by our intellect and establish God's existence, covenant with Israel, and incarnation by evidence or philosophical inferences. Faith seems an absurdly weak basis for such claims and for making the changes in our lives that following Christ requires. We are frequently tempted to base Christianity on historical reconstructions of biblical history, philosophies of history, general philosophic principles, and the like. But these always reduce the Christian religion, our understanding of God, and God's intentions to the limits of what is humanly comprehensible.

Once we see that the intellect is not able to satisfy the concerns of the heart, and take into account the biblical teaching that God is above the power of the mind to comprehend, we recognize the appropriateness of faith. We may embrace God with all our heart, mind, soul, and strength because God is accessible to us through the good God promises to give us. At least God is accessible to those who overcome their resentment of being utterly dependent on deity for their well-being.

We have examined Kierkegaard's account of the leap of faith because the phrase is widely associated with him, but it is not necessary to accept its details in order to recognize that the leap of faith is a move to another order of reasoning.

Many religious people, including theologians, fail to realize that Christian truths are "above reason." This is evident in the recurrent dispute between those who think that the gap between evidence and truth is so small that faith is more like a step than a leap, and those who think the gap is so large as to require a wholesale reconstruction of theological claims. The former are usually thought to be conservatives and the latter liberals. Actually both make the same fundamental mistake about the nature of faith and the role of reason. They differ only over the size of the leap, not the direction and nature of the leap of faith.

Chapter Eight

Reason and Revelation

In the previous chapter we examined various philosophical views of the nature of reason and argued that to have faith is not to violate reason, even though faith is above reason, but that reasoning is involved in faith itself. In this chapter we will examine the way theology characterizes reason with the intention of showing that faith is not opposed to reason but that faith is reasonable in the sense of being the appropriate way to respond to revelation because God has *freely* chosen to make divine intentions known.

I

There is considerable disagreement in theology about the nature of revelation.[1] But for the purpose of showing that faith as a response to revelation is not opposed to reason, we need to consider only a few generally accepted features. In revelation God makes manifest divine purposes or intentions, and in that manifestation God has the initiative. For example, God calls Abraham and Sarah to leave Ur and tells Abraham that he will be the founder of a new race, to whom God will be bound by a covenant. God will bless this people and through them all people will be blessed (Gen. 12:1–4). The attempt of Abraham, Sarah, and their descendants to live in accord with this covenant leads to a richer and deeper understanding of God's intentions and ways of fulfilling them.

Revelation is not a one-sided activity, with God revealing and human beings merely responding to what is revealed. Rather revelation is the result of an *interaction* between God as God seeks to realize divine intentions and the people of Israel as they seek to discern those intentions in the concreteness of their history as a people. Their understanding of God shows their limitations as well as their greatness.

For the Israelites, to have faith is to believe that God seeks to bless them and, through them, all people. Their faith does not begin with such questions as, Why is there a world? Why is it so ordered? What are the relations between its members? What is the nature of human well-being? Their beliefs about the physical universe and human beings grow out of their concern with the covenant God made with Abraham and its meaning. Faith is contrasted to improper responses to the covenant, such as faithlessness, ingratitude, foolishness, and hardness of heart. These are all forms of unbelief. As time went by, the Israelites developed traditions. Faith involves learning from tradition, that is from the experience and testimony of others, largely enshrined in sacred writings and transmitted in worship. Tradition tends to be conservative, but it is not blindly accepted. It is used to interpret and better understand the significance of the lives of those who do and those who do not live under the covenant, and it is occasionally recast in light of experience and new knowledge.

For the early Church Fathers the revelation of God's intentions in the Old and New Testaments is *above* reason. From an examination of nature and history, it is not possible to discover God's intention to make a covenant with Israel, nor that there would be a Messiah, nor that the Messiah would be the Word of God incarnate. These matters depend on the free choice of God. They are not etched in the created order and thus discoverable through an examination of nature.

There may be intimations of God's intentions in the history of various people. God's involvement with the Jewish and Christian people does not preclude God's involvement with others. But theologians through the ages have usually thought that to detect those intimations a knowledge of God's intentions manifested through Israel and Christ is required. This was not necessarily said in an imperialistic way. For example, in the New Testament Peter, who is utterly devoted to Jesus as crucified and risen Lord, achieves a new and better understanding of God's covenant with Israel and the new covenant in Christ through contact with a Roman centurion. Both Peter's and the centurion's understandings of God and divine intentions are expanded through the encounter (Acts 10:1–35).[2]

Such episodes in the New Testament should guide Christians in their relations with people of different faiths. As we shall see in the last two chapters, new understanding and appreciation of other faiths can result from irenic and honest interreligious and intercultural dialogue. Christians believe that this is possible because the Christ is the incarnate Word of God who is present universally. However that may be, since earliest Christian history it has been held that the interactions between God and the Jewish people as presented in the Old and New Testaments supply an understanding of God and divine intentions in the concreteness of that people's history that cannot be found by an examination of the physical universe nor detected with nearly as much clarity and fullness by an examination of the history of other peoples. This is why it is said that God's intentions, as they are revealed in the history of Israel and in the person of Jesus, are "above reason."

In Greek philosophy reason is generally regarded as a faculty that is like a tribunal that is able to make judgments unaffected by the senses and the experiences of historical and social existence. It is even regarded as able to generate independently of the senses or to grasp through the senses the basic and fundamental structure of reality. This conception of reason lies at the basis of the work of Descartes, Kant, and Hegel and those influenced by them. When John Locke became convinced that it was impossible to find certain foundations for knowledge in reason, as Descartes and Spinoza had attempted, he argued that we could find a foundation for knowledge in sense experience. Nonetheless, he continued to hold a view of reason that had many of the features of Cartesianism. Those who followed Locke's lead have continued into this century. Bertrand Russell (1872–1970) in his "logical atomism" phase and the logical positivists were major representatives of it.

The early Church Fathers have this sense of reason in mind when they say that revelation is above reason. A divine covenant and divine interaction revealing God's intentions in the concreteness of a people's history are not the sort of things reason so conceived can discover or generate from its own nature. Reason deals with what is eternal and unchanging. That the eternal Logos, a concept in Greek philosophy, should become a human being, as the prologue of John's Gospel asserts, is absurd to anyone acquainted with ancient Greek philosophy. This led Paul to say that the gospel is foolishness to the Greeks.

In recent years this conception of reason has been violently repudiated by deconstructionism, especially in the works of Jacques Derrida, and in America as a reaction against both idealism and the attempt to replace it with an empirical, in contrast to a rational, foundationalism.[3]

The theological view that faith is above reason does not rely on the ancient Greek philosophic understanding of reason. It rests on the freedom of God, whose intentions are recognized only as God reveals them to those to whom God seeks to make them known. In fact, foundationalism in both the ancient Greek form and in modern philosophy has been a basis for attacking the reasonableness of Christianity. It not only led Paul to say that the gospel was foolishness to the Greeks but was the basis of the most important philosophical attack on the Christian faith in ancient times that led Origen (c. 185–c. 254) to reply with a defense in his work *Against Celsus*. If reason or sense experience can establish the foundations of all knowledge, then Christian revelation is examined to see whether it conforms to the principles of all knowledge. Since it is a revelation, dependent on the free action of God, it will, of course, not fully conform to those principles. Faith as the basis of revelation will accordingly be characterized as outside the boundary of acceptable grounds for truth-claims.

Rather than be disturbed by the recent displacement of foundationalism, as was apparently the author of the passage from an introductory textbook on theology which we examined earlier, Christian theologians ought to be glad to be rid of a thorn in its side since ancient times. They need not endorse irrationalism nor relativism but may rejoice that the contingency of the universe and the socially mediated character of our knowledge undermine any foundationalist project and the narrow views of reason and rational grounds that have historically resulted from foundationalism.[4]

The encounter with Greek philosophy led the early and medieval Church Fathers to speak of God as above reason not only because God's intentions are uniquely revealed in Israel's history and in Jesus but also because God's nature is "hidden." As we mentioned earlier, no causal relation within the universe is the creative relation between God and creatures because God, as the source of all, is not a member of the universe. The causality of God's creative action is hidden in impenetrable mystery. To state these claims and to seek an adequate theological formulation requires us to use our minds. But we are reasoning about a reality who is in a different category from the gods of ancient Greek and Roman religion, the various conceptions of ultimate reality in ancient philosophy, and the universe itself because God, as the self-sufficient source of all, is not a member of the universe. Although God's nature is beyond or above our power to comprehend, God makes God's intentions known. Even though we cannot comprehend God's nature, we can reason about God because of these intentions and understand why God's nature is incomprehensible to us.

When revelation is contrasted to reason, it should be borne in mind that we are dealing with what is available to us by God's initiative in making a covenant with Abraham and in becoming incarnate in Jesus and by the interaction between these divine initiatives and the ancient Jews. Because knowledge of these divine intentions is unavailable in whole or in part from an examination of the natural world and the course of other people's history, we are to respond to them with faith.

Faith is "above reason" because it involves consent. Consent involves a decision, or an act of will, to seek our well-being in the good God seeks to give us and to realize it according to God's ways. But to consent to the good God gives us is not an arbitrary decision, devoid of reason, even though faith, because it involves yielding our allegiance, is beyond the mere exercise of reason. Unfortunately, to base Christian faith on an act of the will is frequently understood in the academic community and in theology itself to mean that there are no rational grounds for having faith, or at least not sufficient rational grounds to warrant having faith. Faith becomes opposed to reason.

What has encouraged intellectuals to think of the will as acting arbitrarily or as expressing mere personal preferences? Alasdair MacIntyre in his widely discussed book, *After Virtue,* credits Kierkegaard with being a prophet of the contemporary world because he unmasked the absence of any rational grounds for ethics. Kierkegaard stressed decision, rather than reason, as the foundation of ethics and religion. They are a matter of personal decision.

Although this is not an accurate account of Kierkegaard's views, MacIntyre accurately describes the way the will is regarded today. Iris Murdoch in her essay "Metaphysics and Ethics"[5] argues that in order to protect our freedom to choose between alternatives, both Sartrean existialism and English-speaking ethical philosophy have construed the will as conferring value, rather than recognizing it. They have excluded the possibility of the sovereignty of good because the reality of good would determine the will and, in their view, destroy freedom. They have so neglected both moral development and deterioration that people are viewed as no more than a will that is "needle-thin." When our search for our well-being and our personal history are excluded from consideration, human decisions have no grounds and indeed can only be understood to be arbitrary. The will is isolated from any reasoning or experience as a basis on which people act and make decisions. A faulty understanding of freedom is also involved. Freedom is understood exclusively as having a large range of alternatives from which to choose. In order to protect the freedom of the will to choose as it wishes, good is defined as only what we choose to designate as good. This is to put the cart (freedom) before the horse (good). Freedom should be understood as liberation from a bondage to one's past history and egocentric outlook and the capacity to yield to a good that is a reality.

Faith, or consent to the good God seeks us to have, involves the will, but not a will uninformed by reasoning nor a will devoid of the concerns of the heart. A narrow sense of reason, combined with a faculty psychology, treats the concerns of the heart as emotions that entice us to believe what we want to believe. If this discussion has helped to free us of a narrow view of reason and a faculty psychology which isolates reason, feeling, and will, we should be able to recognize in the following recapitulation of the nature of faith that faith itself involves reasoning and does not stand in opposition to reason.

Human beings are goal-seeking. Because our goals are numerous and in some instances conflicting, we must attempt to order them into some rational plan. To estimate rationally how we should arrange our priorities, we must consider which goals we may realistically pursue with some chance of success. This estimate is greatly affected by whether or not the universe is ultimate. This fundamental issue cannot be settled scientifically or philosophically. Whether we should or should not restrain our aspirations cannot be scientifically or philosophically determined.

We may progress beyond what we can learn from science and philosophy by considering the claims of Christianity. We may examine what is said by Christianity to see what it offers us. The examination is to be made with our minds, but our minds are to be motivated by the desire to find our well-being. That is to say, we are to reason with an open heart. Whether we find God as presented by Christianity attractive or not depends largely on what we care about. If we belong to the order of the body, we will find God attractive for the wrong reasons. But if our hearts have been purified to the extent that our well-being cannot be gained by what force and wealth can secure, we ought to find God as spoken of in Christianity attractive.

In our continuing concern for our well-being, our minds are engaged as we consider whether following God's ways indeed leads to our well-being. We wrestle with the requirement that we love justice, learn the significance of suffering, and seek to realize a community life. Our minds are used throughout this process. For those who are seeking their well-being, who find God as spoken of in Christianity attractive, and who give their consent to the good God seeks us to have, faith is not opposed to reason but is itself permeated with reasoning.

But faith is above reason, as we have pointed out, because the material concerning God's intentions as confessed by Israel and the Christian church is not available from a study of nature scientifically or philosophically. Nor is that material convincing to the mind of a person with a closed heart who examines it historically.

Perhaps a brief examination of Plato will help us to recognize that faith itself involves reasoning. Since Plato lacks a knowledge of Christian revelation, theologians would say that the basis of his claims must be reason. Yet we find that Plato wrestles with all four of the aspects of faith that we have described.

1. Plato is deeply concerned with human well-being and where it may be found. He writes extensively about the need to free ourselves from the seduction of our appetites. As mentioned earlier, he says that we are like leaky vessels. We keep seeking to fill ourselves by the gratification of our appetites, but we never become full. Strong drives to acquire wealth and power frequently stem from the desire to gratify our sensuous ap-

petites. If our sensuous appetites become dominant, we become slaves to our appetites. Our lives become disorderly and miserable. We become like a city torn apart by civil war.

2. Plato's name is virtually synonymous with a concern to understand the nature of justice. He argues that we cannot find our well-being unless we are just, nor have an optimally desirable society unless the community is justly ordered. In the *Republic* he describes the training in virtue that is needed for the governing class. But people who are entrusted with the supreme power of state must have a special kind of knowledge, not mere training in virtue. This knowledge can be gained only by *metanoia*, a turning from the sensible world toward the supersensible realities on which it depends for its order and goodness. For Plato the pinnacle of knowledge is the form of the Good, which is above justice. All other forms participate in it, and it is the source of all other goods and the principle which renders them harmonious.

Philosophy is described by Plato as the practice of dying, that is, turning from sensuous appetites, worldly power, and wealth toward the supersensible for our well-being. The conviction that our well-being is to be found in justice and the search for such knowledge is motivated by love. Plato points out that philosophy means a love of wisdom. According to the *Phaedrus* and the *Symposium,* love is sent "from above" in order to lead us from sensuous concerns to that which is the source of the limited beauty and goodness of sensible things.

Plato does not explicitly consider forgiveness, but he clearly believes in justice. No one is able to escape the consequences of their evil. It is primarily because we ought not to be able to escape the consequences of our evil deeds simply by dying that Plato believes in a life beyond our earthly death. Conversely, he believes that a just person ought to be rewarded. Because of his confidence in the reality of justice, in the *Phaedo* Socrates goes serenely to his death even though he realizes that the arguments he has just given for the immortality of the soul are not particularly good ones.

3. Plato is also concerned with suffering. In the *Republic* Plato argues that an unjust person could not be happy in this life. The tyrant, who can gratify the passions unchecked, finally becomes a slave of the passions. A just person, even though he or she has self-control, suffers in an unjust society. How can being just be good for us? Plato argues in the last book of the *Republic* that, even though injustices cause us to suffer, they cannot make us evil without our own consent. We may, therefore, endure suffering without fear that it can cause us the injury that committing evil does.

4. We have already mentioned Plato's interest in the realization of a

just community. It is the focus of his two longest works, the *Republic* and the *Laws*. Both works are monuments to the difficulty even to conceive in outline a just community, must less to achieve one.

There is also a powerful sense of service to the community. In the *Republic*, for example, Plato has an allegory in which the sensible world is described as a cave. The person who has turned from the illusion that the sensible world is the ultimate reality emerges from the cave and sees the sun, a symbol of the form of the Good. Although it is joyous to be above ground in the presence of the Good, the person returns to the darkness of the cave in order to help order human affairs as justly as possible.

In their consideration of human well-being, the nature of justice, the role of suffering, and the just community, both Plato and Christianity use reason as well as myth (in Plato) and faith (in Christianity). Faith is not blind nor a response devoid of the use of reason.

The development of a mature faith does not exhaust the role of reason, however. A Christian may learn a great deal about the good that is to be found in obedience to God, love justice, achieve considerable maturity through suffering, and love his or her neighbor to an impressive degree, without being well-informed in philosophical theology or other divisions of academic theology, biblical studies, and the like. In every Christian's faith there is considerable understanding, but as we shall see in the next three chapters, faith seeks more understanding than is needed to achieve a mature faith.

II

We have shown that Christian claims about the universe as a whole and our own nature and condition enable us to understand the contingency of the universe and ourselves. These are intransigent limitations, to use Bowker's expression. The contingency of the universe is recognized today in philosophy. Within the sciences it is rightly regarded as beyond scientific methods of inquiry. There are only three possible ways to deal with the intransigent limitations of our nature and condition which, according to various religions, indicate a transcendent dimension in human life: to *deny* a transcendent dimension, to ignore a transcendent dimension in human life as much as possible, or to recognize the limitations of the social sciences and philosophy in pronouncing definitively one way or the other on the existence of a reality beyond the universe impinging on human life.

But as important as developments in physics and biology have been, a development within the church itself has caused believers more concern.

The use of historical-critical methods by biblical scholars has tended to undermine the confidence of believers in the credibility of the Bible as a divine revelation. This has been more true for Protestants than for Roman Catholics because of the particular role the Bible plays in Protestant Christianity.

Classical science and philosophy have affected biblical criticism, however, because a scientific view of the universe allegedly excludes the possibility of divine action in the workings of nature and the course of history. The problems of interpreting a book that is saturated with accounts of divine agency in nature, history, and individual lives have increasingly exercised biblical scholars in modern times.

To treat the nature and significance of critical biblical methods would lead us well beyond the scope of our inquiry into the reasonableness of Christianity. We shall treat the general issue of divine action in nature, history, and individual lives in the next chapter. Here we shall consider only how historical inquiry impinges on the truth or falsity of the Bible.

It is generally agreed that historical investigation has led to a recognition of legends and myths in the Bible, and that this does not mean that they cannot serve to reveal God's intentions, as we saw with the story of Adam and Eve. Historical evidence may lead to a reinterpretation of the Bible and significant modification of Christian doctrines. In principle, historical investigation could lead to a rejection of even the central belief of Christianity, namely, that Jesus is the incarnation of the Word of God. This would happen, for example, were it determined that Jesus was a charlatan, collecting large sums of money which he secreted in Damascus with the intention of having a spree with his disciples. As we noted in the Introduction, Austin Farrer said that "we must have no bogus history."

The critical issue is to decide what we may affirm. May we reasonably affirm only what historical evidence warrants, or may we reasonably affirm what the Bible teaches on the ground that the Bible is a revelation even when its affirmation is not warranted by historical evidence?

This question arises because there is often not enough relevant data available for a historian to make a judgment on what the Bible says. Sometimes it arises because, given the limitations of historical study itself, historians are unable to achieve a consensus. Even more significantly, it arises because the Bible claims that a transcendent reality is revealing its intentions. Let us see the significance of this claim on the critical issue by focusing on the Gospels.

The significance for historical inquiry of the claim that the Bible is concerned with a transcendent reality is nicely suggested in a remark by Wittgenstein.

We had a discussion about the difficulty of reconciling the discourses and history in the fourth Gospel with the other three. Then [Wittgenstein] suddenly said, "But if you can accept the miracle that God became a man all these difficulties are as nothing, for then I couldn't possibly say what form the record of such an event would take."[6]

We normally judge the accuracy of a report in terms of its agreement with other reports. Quite naturally we take the differences between the synoptic Gospels—Matthew, Mark, and Luke—and the Gospel of John seriously, as well as the discrepancies among the synoptic Gospels themselves. But one of the difficulties we have with knowing what to make of these discrepancies is that the Gospels are an unusual form of writing. Drury apparently annoyed Wittgenstein because he spoke as if there were an appropriate standard available by which to evaluate the soundness of the claims made by the Gospels. For Wittgenstein, their claim that Jesus was God incarnate showed that this was a serious mistake. There is no other writing which has tried to express this, and we have no recognized basis to specify what form an account of such a person should take.[7] Wittgenstein himself confesses that he has no idea what form such an account should take.

Let us examine the task which the Gospel writers undertook in order to appreciate the immensity of the task and the greatness of their achievement. An analogy based on geometry may help. Imagine a flat surface, such as a sheet of paper, which in geometry is a plane. Let us assume that everything which we can experience is on that plane—the human plane, so to speak. If there is a divine reality, it is another plane. We would have no experience of it unless it intersected our own plane. According to plane geometry, the place of intersection of two planes is a straight line. The line is a member of both planes; yet it is a single line. It is part of both a human and a divine plane. Most of the divine plane of which it is a part is outside the human plane. We cannot experience the whole of the divine plane, but we can experience Jesus as the Word of God incarnate on the line where the divine plane and the human plane meet.

Let us now see the relevance of this for the issue of the historical warrants for Christian affirmations. Consider the narrative of Jesus' crucifixion, which is the longest single section in all four Gospels. Even though virtually our only written source is the four Gospels, historians do not dispute that Jesus was crucified. Crucifixion was a common way to execute criminals in the Roman Empire, and what the Gospel stories say about Jesus make it quite likely that he would fall foul of the authorities. We have no record that anyone has ever disputed the claim.

The significance of his death, however, is not accessible to historical inquiry because the significance of that death largely depends on *who* it was that died. Whether it was the Word of God, a reality on a plane that is not our own, which degraded itself by becoming a member of our plane, and in that condition allowed itself to suffer at the hands of its own creatures, in order to redeem them from sin and death, cannot be determined by historical investigation. That it was the Word of God incarnate that died cannot be historically warranted because historical study cannot establish that Jesus is the intersection of two realms, the divine and human.

It might be possible to refute the claim indirectly by showing, for example, that Jesus was not crucified, or that Jesus' own self-understanding was such that it undermines his disciples' understanding of the significance of his death. This was tried in the nineteenth century by drawing a distinction between the religion *of* Jesus and the religion *about* Jesus. But the distinction has not been sufficient to undermine or seriously threaten the disciples' views of the significance of Jesus' death.

Let us now see how the incarnation is conveyed or portrayed in the Gospels. Consider Mark's story of the healing of a paralytic (Mark 2:1–12). When the paralytic's friends lowered him into the room through a hole the roof, which they had made because the large crowd around Jesus prevented them from approaching him directly, Jesus said to the man, "My son, your sins are forgiven." This aroused some of the scribes. "Why does this man speak thus? It is blasphemy! Who can forgive sins but God alone?" Jesus, perceiving this, said, "Which is easier, to say to the paralytic, 'Your sins are forgiven,' or to say, 'Rise, take up your pallet and walk'? But that you may know that the Son of man has authority on earth to forgive sins"—he said to the paralytic—"I say to you, rise, take up your pallet and go home."

Does the healing of this man establish that Jesus has the authority to forgive sins? In spite of this display of power, it is possible to continue to hold to the view that only God forgives sins. According to the Gospel writers, the ability to heal and perform other wonders is not unique to Jesus. For the Jews, extraordinary power does not prove that a person is from God, much less that he or she is God. Satan also gives people the power to perform extraordinary deeds. Accordingly, Jesus was frequently accused of being from Satan because he did things which ran counter to the Jewish Law, as interpreted by the authorities, such as healing on the Sabbath and claiming to forgive sins.

The healing of a paralytic is the sort of thing that can be observed. So too is claiming to forgive sins. But that Jesus actually can forgive sins is not. Historical investigation might determine that the promised figure "Son of man" as portrayed in the Old Testament would have authority to forgive sins, but it cannot determine that there is such a being as a divine "Son of man" or that Jesus is that person.

History, like science, is limited to the study of the relations between members of the universe. Earlier we saw that science takes the existence of the universe for granted and studies the relations between its members. The relations between its members are what we mean by physical relations. The creative action of God is not a physical relation because it is not a relation like those between members of the universe. By its very nature science does not and cannot study divine creative action because science studies physical interactions and God does not physically interact with the universe.

History is concerned to understand events in terms of relations between human beings and the effects of other members of the universe on them. Historical explanations include a consideration of people's motives and actions. But in addition, historical explanations emphasize larger geographic, economic, and social conditions, of which people at the time of their acting are often not aware, and which greatly condition, but not necessarily determine, the human actions taken. At this level historians seek to find those forces which might give some pattern to history, without necessarily believing they have found laws by which history is determined.

It is possible to operate at still another level on which the significance of events is explained in terms of divine providence. For example, one can regard the waning years of the Roman Empire as the judgment of God on a culture, or as the best civilization that the wills of humans and various other factors allowed divine providence to achieve at a particular juncture of history; or even as the way to a better, more just society because human resistance had closed a shorter, easier route to it; or indeed as all the above. Such a consideration of the significance of events does not ignore or set aside historical explanations based on human choices, and on lawlike conditions such as geographic, economic, and social conditions.

In modern times, however, the historian works under several self-imposed limitations. Historians have accepted the assumption of the Enlightenment that to follow reason ideally results in universal agreement. In order to achieve a greater consensus, historians have limited themselves to certain kinds of tangible data. This allows an easier and wider communication among historians, and a wider range unanimity, but at the price of excluding questions concerning the religious significance of events and human life because these are not subject to a technique that gives desirable but limited results.

As Herbert Butterfield, the eminent Cambridge historian, put it,

Greater degrees of certainty, more practicable forms of communicability and a wider range of unanimity can be achieved when the enquirer performs this act of self-limitation—when he asks what is the pressure of steam that a given task will require in a given engine, or enquires what was the effect of the influx of American silver on the French wars of religion in the sixteenth century. But these are not the really momentous questions upon which all human beings have to make their decision; and the technical student in any branch of science or learning is arguing in a circle if he thinks that his researches have in fact eliminated from life the things which for technical reasons he had eliminated in advance from his consideration.

The truth is that technical history is a limited and mundane realm of description and explanation, in which local and concrete things are achieved by a disciplined use of tangible evidence. . . . When the events have been laid out by the technical historian, they may be taken over by the Catholic or Protestant or atheist—they are equally available for Whig or Tory. Each of these can add his judgements and make his evaluations.[8]

Because historians operate within these self-imposed limitations, Jesus' claim to forgive sins can never be warranted by any historical account.

We may point out explicitly how a Gospel writer portrays a divine dimension in an action on the human plane. The claim to forgive sins, though scandalous to some of the scribes, could be passed over rather easily and not taken seriously as something one might believe. Healing a person put those who witnessed it in the situation of having to make a judgment about Jesus. Was he from God or from Satan? But when the claim to forgive a person's sins is followed by the healing of the person, the claim to forgive sins cannot be ignored. The only options left for those who witness it are either that Jesus is from Satan or that Jesus shares in the power that hitherto has been considered exclusively God's. The claim to forgive sins coupled with the healing of a paralytic does not allow those who do not believe that he is from Satan the relatively comfortable option that he is from God. Jesus, as he himself pointed out, cannot be classified with John the Baptist, Elijah, or one of the prophets. They story of the healing of the paralytic shows one way that a Gospel writer portrays the actions of a human being performed on the human plane as actions of God incarnate. This is the form the record of divine incarnation takes.

Wittgenstein remarks in one of his notebooks that since the four Gospels attempt to portray one who is the intersection of two planes, the divine and the human, a historical account would be inappropriate and misleading.

God has *four* people recount the life of his incarnate Son, in each case differently and with inconsistencies—but might we not say: It is important that this narrative should not be more than quite averagely historically plausible *just so that* this should not be taken as the essential, decisive thing? . . . What you are supposed to see cannot be communicated even by the best and most accurate historian; and *therefore* a mediocre account suffices, is even to be preferred. For that too can tell you what you are supposed to be told. (Roughly in the way a mediocre stage set can be better than a sophisticated one, painted trees better than real ones,—because these might distract attention from what matters.)[9]

From the standpoint of writing a history about Jesus, the writers of the four Gospels do not score high marks. But even if they had written an excellent historical account of Jesus, such an account would fail to serve their main intention. The portrayal of the incarnation is beyond the scope of a technical historical account, just as the creative action of God is beyond the scope of physics and other sciences.

If we are seeking our well-being, as any sensible person ought to, an examination of the Bible and the interaction with the Christian community will lead us sooner or later to the question Jesus' disciples faced: Who do you say that I am? If we respond in Peter's fashion, "You are the Christ, the Son of the living God" (Matt. 6:16), it will not be because anything on the human plane makes that confession historically mandatory nor a commitment to Jesus as the divine one historically warranted. Faith is not a substitute for the absence of a historical warrant but a discernment of God's intentions by one who is interacting with God.

History is, nonetheless, indispensable to Christianity. God's choice to reveal divine intentions through interaction with particular people, first Israel and then the Christian church, in the concreteness of their corporate lives, has been offensive to people from ancient times. The offense is reflected in a remark by Ambrose, the great bishop of Milan, whose sermons Augustine heard while still a pagan, "God has chosen to save us through a people, not through dialectic."

By dialectic Ambrose means the Neoplatonism that was very strong in his day among intellectuals in the Roman Empire. For the Platonists, as they were called, divine truth was not concretely embedded in history nor in a person. It was utterly beyond the parameters of their thought. Augustine, who was led through a study of the Platonists to recognize a transcendent reality, remarked after he had become a Christian that the Platonist had everything but an incarnation of the Word. As Augustine matured in the Christian faith, he displayed in his *Confessions* and even more fully in *The City of God,* his discovery of the reality of historical existence, with divine intentions being revealed and realized in the life of individuals, peoples, nations, and entire civilizations. He impressed this on Western Christianity and Western culture.

During the Enlightenment (c. 1600–1800), when the foundations of the modern mentality were laid, there was a rejection of the historical nature of religion and of Christianity in particular. As we saw, natural religion was based solely on the book of nature because it was thought that the vital truths concerning God must be accessible to people in all times and places and directly accessible to every rational human being. A historical revelation of divine truths to a particular people, embedded in the concreteness of their history, was to many intellectuals an utterly unreasonable way for God to make Godself known. The alleged clarity of the book of nature was to be immeasurably preferred to the obscurity of the book of Scripture. This attitude is nicely captured in one of Rousseau's sallies. If God had something vital for Jean-Jacques Rousseau to know, God would not address Jean-Jacques Rousseau through Moses.

But Christianity is a historical religion because God's intentions are not locked into a never-changing natural world order. They are not read off a common structure embodied in every society. They cannot be discerned from lawlike patterns which may be found in the flow of the history of every nation or civilization. God freely creates and freely calls people to realize divine intentions. It is by working with people that God enables people to find their well-being.

Because God has made divine intentions known to us in and through a particular people and above all a particular person, historical investigation, though limited, provides vital knowledge. For example, without it we would not know what a Pharisee or a scribe was, nor understand nearly so clearly what was at stake in the various confrontations Jesus had with them. We would not know what the titles that were applied to Jesus signify, such as Messiah. Without that, we would not realize that Jesus modified their meaning nor the importance of those modifications. We would not realize that the focus of attention of the first six books of the Bible is the covenant with Abraham, not speculation concerning why we have a universe, even though the Bible, as we now have it, begins with two creation stories. The differences between the synoptic Gospels and John's Gospel, as well as between the synoptics themselves, are significant because they enable us to recognize different emphases given to the significance of Jesus.

A better understanding of biblical teaching is possible when we know something about the author, the intended readership, and the circumstance of composition of each book. The older, fourfold method of biblical interpretation—namely, the literal, allegorical, moral, and anagogic (mystical), as used in the Middle Ages—no longer retained the historical dimension fostered by the early biblical school at Antioch in the East. Its recovery by Christian humanists of the Renaissance enabled people to read Paul's letters, for example, as addressed to particular congregations in particular historical circumstances. This historical awareness has helped to keep the mainline Protestant Reformation and the Roman Catholic Church after the Reformation from falling prey to rampant apocalypticism (the immanent destruction of the world) which during the Middle Ages periodically swept the church, as it does today in those Protestant denominations that still have not learned to appreciate the value of a historical approach to the Bible.

Because the intentions of God are revealed through interactions with human beings, history is more significant for Christianity than are philosophy and science. I have discussed recent developments in philosophy and science at much greater length in this study because they have discredited the modern belief in a self-contained universe. An open universe enables us once again to conceive of God's action in history, as we shall show in the next chapter.

Chapter Nine

Divine Agency in a Scientific World

We have already described the way classical science changed the relation of the two books of God. The Deists elevated the book of nature over the book of Scripture. According to them, we may deduce from the existence and order of nature that there is a Creator who has given nature its laws. But the relation of God to the events of the physical universe had to be reconsidered because the new mechanistic science described the physical universe as self-sufficient in its operations. Once the universe was designed and created by God, it operated on its own through the causal impact of matter upon matter. The universe was pictured as a great machine in which things moved by impact. Extension, figure, and motion were thought to be the essential properties of matter. Given the position, mass, and motion of any body, and the force or forces acting on it, its resultant path, velocity, and position at every instant of time could be calculated with exactness.

As we have seen, according to Newton the universe in its operations was not quite self-sufficient. For example, there were slight irregularities in the orbits of the planets which would in time cause the solar system to collapse. Unless those irregularities were corrected by divine intervention, the solar system could not continue indefinitely. Newton claimed that God's correction of the irregularities in planetary orbits from time to time is not a violation of nature's laws because God's actions help to sustain the regularity of the solar system. The was but one of several things which God must do in order to keep the machine in running order.

As we saw in Chapter Two, this understanding of divine action in nature became untenable as various alleged gaps in nature's operations were filled by scientific discoveries. For example, the alleged irregularities in planetary orbits, which so troubled Newton, were found to be periodic, that is, they righted themselves in the long run.

We have shown, however, that scientific accounts of the relations between members of the universe do not replace God's activity. Our sciences take the existence of the universe for granted and study the relations between its members. Divine creative activity and a complete scientific account of the relations between the members of the universe do not exclude each other because different kinds of causality are involved in each case: the constant creative activity of God that gives each creature its existence and nature, and the causal relations between creatures studied by the sciences.

But how does God achieve God's purposes or intentions? If God's intentions were confined to bringing about physical events, it would be possible to say that God achieves God's intentions through the natural operations of the physical natures God gives to creatures. But God is concerned with what happens in history and to individual lives as well. How does God act *within* the universe to bring about singular and personal events in contrast to those regularly occurring events of the natural world, which God produces through divine creative agency?

This question has caused considerable anxiety among theologians because of a particular picture of the physical universe. Although our scientific ideas about the nature of matter soon outstripped those crude mechanistic ones formed in the seventeenth century, the picture of a universe ruled by causal laws that determine precisely all physical events continued to dominate the sciences until the advent of quantum mechanics in this century. It still dominates our intellectual culture at large, and it is a very powerful force in theology.

The idea that the physical universe is ruled by causal laws results in a dilemma for theologians. On the one hand, the laws of nature decree that all physical events are determined by other physical events. On the other hand, the Bible reports that God brought about extraordinary physical events (that is, events which do not appear to conform to the laws of nature) in order to intervene in history (e.g., parting the Red Sea to rescue the Jews fleeing from the Egyptians).

Deists were delighted with the exclusion of particular divine actions in the name of science because it supported their claim that the book of nature is more reliable than the book of Scripture. It was only a matter of time before Christian theologians, who accepted the view that God does not intervene in the physical universe, concluded that God does not intervene in history. David F. Strauss was the first to claim that the New Testament accounts of Jesus as a supernatural being who performs miracles and is raised from the dead are mythological. In the introduction to his *Life of Jesus* (1835) he roundly declared,

We may summarily reject all miracles, prophecies, narratives of angels and demons, and the like, as simply impossible and irreconcilable with the known and universal laws which govern the course of events.[1]

Strauss' radical claim was not accepted by most biblical scholars, but it lay behind much of the nineteenth-century attempt to find the historical core that underlies the Gospel accounts of the life of Jesus. But, as Rudolf Bultmann pointed out, the causal order is disrupted not only by miracles but by any divine action within nature and history. Bultmann, who accepted "the causal nexus" as inviolable, therefore concluded that all biblical claims of divine action in nature and in history are mythological.[2] He restricted God's agency to acts of grace that enable people to make a transition from inauthentic to authentic existence. But if nature and history are closed to divine agency, then to be consistent, Bultmann ought to have said that the lives of individuals are closed to divine agency as well.

Bultmann and those who have sought to square the Bible with modern science so that "modern man" can believe the gospel with intellectual integrity are misinformed about the implications of modern science. We shall first describe that misunderstanding and then show how divine activity may be conceived with a postmodern understanding of science.

I

C. C. Gillispie in his history of science describes the introduction and advance of science as "the edge of objectivity." Physics and chemistry are "objective," that is, they are about the relations between objects. The laws and theories that state and explain the relations between objects, completely omit any references to human subjects. It was not only God but also human beings who were superfluous. Because they are personal agents, acting purposively and freely, they are alien to the mechanistic and deterministic universe which seventeenth-century science was thought to have unveiled. It was not only divine but also human agency that seemed to be impossible in a universe ruled by causal laws that hold by necessity.[3]

Descartes proposed a radical solution: human beings are not essentially material but essentially minds or nonmaterial substances. Even though each of us inhabits a body, our thoughts and behavior are not determined by the material world which impinges on our body. According to Descartes, we bring about events in the physical world through our bodies. But he was never able to show, given his understanding of the properties of bodies and minds, that this was possible. Kant's division between phenomena and noumena, in which we as phenomenal beings are determined but as noumenal beings are free is another attempt to retain belief in human freedom in a scientifically conceived universe.

Human freedom, however, can be maintained without resorting to the desperate measures of Descartes and Kant. The causal laws formulated in the natural sciences do not render human freedom and human agency impossible, nor do they exclude the possibility of divine agency within the universe.

In the first place, scientific laws, such as Galileo's law of falling bodies, are formulated for closed systems. Unless interfered with by such things as air resistance, a body will fall in accordance with the formula $s = \frac{1}{2} at^2$ (s = distance, t = time, a = acceleration at sea level). That is, a body will fall a particular distance at a particular acceleration during a particular time interval at sea level, only if everything else that can affect its fall is excluded. But, in fact, a billiard ball rolling down an inclined plane will not descend with the acceleration Galileo's law specifies because of the effects of air resistance and friction. We can, of course, calculate these effects by applying other laws of classical physics. The effects of a person touching the ball can also be calculated. But neither Galileo's law nor the remaining known laws of nature cause a person to decide to touch the billiard ball, any more than they cause a person to purchase billiard balls from a store and to build an inclined plane on which to roll them.

Galileo did not include human agency in the formulation of his law because the law specifies the relation between a specific set of factors—time, distance, and acceleration—and those factors only. He did not exclude human agency from the formulation because he thought that human beings are unable to affect the acceleration of falling bodies. Rather Galileo's law of falling bodies, like other scientific laws, is stated for systems closed to any influences other than those specified as relevant to the relations codified in the laws. Other scientific laws take more factors into account than does Galileo's law of falling bodies, but they also do not include the human factor in their formulations for closed deterministic systems. But neither Galileo's law of falling bodies nor any other scientific law excludes the possibility of human agency in bringing about physical events.

In Galileo's law of falling bodies the relations between time, distance, and acceleration for any falling body at sea level are precise. It permits the precise determination of any one of the parameters when the other two are known. This is true of all causal laws; they state precise determination. But causal laws that state the precise relations between various parameters do not entail determinism, that is, a universe in which every event is brought about by the nonhuman conditions specified by causal laws. Our natural sciences are incomplete, but even if they were complete—so that every relation between every nonhuman factor of the universe were known—this would still not mean that every event in the universe is brought about by nonhuman factors. Scientific laws are formulated without taking human agency into account because the relations specified between parameters are ones that hold unless human agency is exercised on them. Scientific laws do not imply that every event in the universe is bought about solely by the factors specified in those laws and by those factors only. The precision of causal laws poses no threat to human agency or human freedom. A misunderstanding of the nature of scientific causal laws, together with the misleading picture of the entire universe as a machine, created the bogy of determinism.

With the progress of science, various closed systems have been broadened as more and more factors have been taken into account. But this does not give us a reason to say that human freedom is not possible in a scientifically conceived universe. It is utterly unwarranted to assume that because we have been able to include more and more factors in scientific laws that we shall be able one day to include the human factor in our scientific laws. Likewise, it is utterly unwarranted to assume that because the natural sciences have found precise causal laws, we must, to be truly scientific, postulate that human agency must be reducible to similar causal laws. We have no scientific reason for either of these assumptions.

As Pierre Duhem, the great physicist, put it,

Imagine a collector who wishes to arrange sea shells. He takes seven drawers that he marks with the seven colors of the spectrum, and you see him putting the red shells in the red drawer, the yellow shells in the yellow drawer, etc. But if a white shell appears, he will not know what to do with it, for he has no white drawer. You would, of course, feel very sorry for his reason if you heard him conclude in his embarrassment that no white shells exist in the world.

The physicist who thinks he can deduce from his theoretical principles the impossibility of free will deserves the same feeling. In manufacturing a classification for all phenomena produced in this world, he forgets the drawer for free actions.[4]

The second reason causal laws in the physical sciences do not imply that human and divine agency cannot bring about events in nature is that causal laws and intentional actions are different kinds of accounts. This can be explained by an example given by G. E. M. Anscombe and developed by Robert King.[5] A man is pumping poisoned water into the water system of a house in which some people are plotting a war. Suppose we ask the man what he is doing. He answers, "Pumping water." If we ask, "Why?" he may answer, "To poison the people who live there." If we again ask him why, he may reply, "Because they are plotting a war, and by poisoning them I am helping to prevent a war." If pressed further, he might say that what he is doing is working for peace. He might even go so far as to say that what he is doing is working for the kingdom of God.

The series of questions lead the man to reidentify what he is doing within a broader context: pumping water, poisoning people, preventing war, working for peace, working for the kingdom of God. Each is both an end and the means to another end. He is pumping water in order to poison some people in order to prevent war in order to further the cause of world peace in order to further the kingdom of God. We may sketch them as series of concentric circles, with each end in the series being included in the next. All of the answers to our questions identify his intentions, which tell us what he is doing when he is moving a pump handle up and down and explain why he is doing it.

The pump handle going up and down is an action—it is something a person does—and so the explanation of the movement of the pump handle is a personal one. We can determine the amount of energy the man uses in order to pump the handle up and down by using general impersonal laws. But we have no impersonal explanation for the agent causing the pump handle to go up and down. An impersonal explanation of a pump handle going up and down is possible if the handle is connected to a rod, which is moved by an engine. But then the movement of a pump handle would not be an action. We would not be able to say that a man is seeking to poison some people in order to prevent war, etc. It would only be an action if the man connected the machine to the pump handle with those intentions.

How a pump handle moving up and down causes poisoned water to get into the water system of the house is explained by an impersonal account about air pressure, gravity, and the like. But what is being done is identified and explained by the agent's intentions. Impersonal explanations do not rule out human agency. We need personal explanations to explain the cause of some events. In our example, a man's actions cause a pump handle to go up and down, and his intentions give us the reasons it is made to go up and down.

For most of the history of the universe, however, human intentions do not explain events. According to our scientific cosmology, our present cosmic order began approximately twenty billion years ago. Only within the last few million years did human life appear. Most human activity is confined to bringing about events on or near the earth's surface. The success of science in discovering many relations between impersonal factors made plausible the claim that personal explanations are not fundamental. That is, human actions would eventually be wholly explicable in terms of impersonal explanations. But when it is understood that personal explanations are necessary in some instances to identify *what* is happening, the claim that with the progress of science personal explanations will eventually be completely replaced by impersonal ones loses its plausibility.

William G. Pollard, a nuclear physicist, has argued that the uncertainty principle in quantum mechanics shows that human freedom is possible. According to the uncertainty principle, it is not possible to determine simultaneously with precision the position and velocity of particles at a subatomic level. This lack of precision at a subatomic level has led many people to infer that events at a subatomic level are not determined. From this, Pollard infers that there is room for human freedom and divine agency in a scientifically conceived universe.[6]

But as we have seen already, it is a mistake to think that the precise relation between the factors included in classical scientific laws means that every event in the universe is determined, that is, brought about by the nonhuman factors specified in classical physics. The precision of the relation of factors in scientific laws does not imply that human beings are unable to affect the outcome of physical events. Although the impossibility of determining simultaneously the position and velocity of particles at a subatomic level has enormous implications for physics and beyond physics—many of which are controversial—it is irrelevant to the issue of human agency or freedom.

What has been said about the relation of scientific causal laws and human agency is applicable to the relation between scientific causal laws and divine agency. For the causal laws of classical science to exclude the possibility of divine agency, so that God does not and cannot affect the outcome of any events, classical science would have to exclude human agency as well. But the existence of precise relations between the factors of scientific laws does not entail that human agency does not affect the outcome of physical events. It does not therefore mean that divine agency cannot affect the outcome of physical events. The precise relation between the factors formulated in scientific laws does not close the universe either to human or divine agency.

II

For examples of human agency affecting the outcome of events we do not need to turn to subatomic physics or to billiard balls rolling down an inclined plane. In our everyday life we are familiar with human agency bringing about events, from turning on a stove to cook a meal to turning the pages of a book.[7] Examples of divine agency, however, are not as obvious as those of human agency because God's creative activity is not external to the universe, as is our relation to such things as stoves and books. It is not as if there are two separate realities, God and creatures, externally connected by a cause and effect relation. God's creative activity is the continuous action whereby creatures exist. Every creature is what it is, with its powers of operating, because of the creative activity of God presently in action. On the one hand, God is as near to us as the molecules and cells of our bloodstream because God is their present creative source. When we resist God's will, our very power to resist comes from God's grace by which we are existing, acting beings. On the other hand, even though God's creative activity sustains all the members of the universe, creatures are not part of God's own being. The members of the universe are realities, not fake products of a magic show, because they affect each other and thereby affect the outcome of events by this activity. God respects their agency; that is, God does not override their natures as God weaves their various powers and activities together to achieve God's purposes.

We may picture God's creative activity as operating in a vertical direction, active in every instant of time to sustain the existence of each member of the universe and the relations between members in past, present, and future states of the universe, and the causal activity of creatures on each other as operating in a horizontal direction. In the following figure, x represents creatures, >> represents causal activity by a creature on another creature, and ^ represents God's creative activity.

$$X \gg X \gg X \gg X \gg X$$
$$\wedge \;\; \wedge\wedge \;\; \wedge \;\; \wedge\wedge \;\; \wedge \;\; \wedge\wedge \;\; \wedge \;\; \wedge\wedge \;\; \wedge$$

As we saw in Chapter Two, in our scientific study of nature, we do not and should not expect to find any gaps filled by God in the ordinary operations of nature between the members of the universe. God realizes divine intentions through the activities of the members of the universe God creates. The activities of every created being are simultaneously their own activities and divine creative activities. We have what Austin Farrer calls "double agency." God enables the members of the universe to be what they are, and the members of the universe, acting according to their natures, cause the universe to develop in the ways cosmology, evolutionary biology, and history describe.

For example, let us say that God creates A and B. God makes them so that they can generate other beings. Let us say A and B generate C. It would be correct to say that A and B cause C, and also correct to say that C is caused by God through A and B, because for A and B and C to exist and to be causally related, God's creative agency must be operating.

C is caused both by the agency of A and B, and also by God because God's creative power is active throughout the process as the creative source of every member. All we perceive is the regularity of beings such as C following from beings such as A and B, but God's creative activity is present, though unperceived, in each creature's activities.

In the example of human agency, we said that a man moved a pump handle in order to pump poisoned water into a house in order to poison some people plotting war in order to promote peace in order to serve the kingdom of God. The man achieves his intentions by moving a pump handle. This creates a vacuum, and the air pressure moves water along pipes into the water system of a house. The pump, air, water, and pipes perform according to natural laws. The man uses their activities to achieve his goals. God too uses the natural operations of creatures to achieve God's intentions or purposes. God uses the activities of A and B to achieve God's intention that C exist.

God's agency is not as obvious as human agency, in which the outcome of events is brought about by moving a pump handle up and down or turning on a stove to cook a meal. We cannot detect the continuous causality of God *on its productive side* because it is not a relation between two realities, God and creatures. The creative activity is God positing others, not a relation between God and others *already* in existence. We can, however, detect divine activity through its *consequences* or effects.

First, the contingency of the universe is a consequence of God's creative activity. That is, we see that the members of the universe do not explain why we have these members, rather than others, nor why we have these members, rather than no members at all. This contingency is a manifestation or indication that the universe exists with the members it has because of God's creative activity.

It is a mistake to think that because God's agency in bringing about a specific event is undetectable from the event itself, God does not in fact act to bring about specific events in nature, in history, and in individual lives. As we saw earlier, if we seek to move from the order of the universe to a designer, it is always possible to argue that the order is a result of the inherent properties of the members of the universe, and there is no need to infer from the pattern that it is the result of an intelligence. But the picture of a universe made up of interconnected members, which fully account for the order we find, does not in the least dissipate the questions, Why this particular order, *rather than another?* and Why does a universe exist at all? When we take the universe as a whole, these questions about its order and existence arise. It is the contingency of the entire universe that allows, and to an extent confirms, the claim that the universe is created and ordered by God. As we have seen, any attempt to explain God's activity as filling gaps or supplementing laws of nature is a mistake.

Second, we are able to discern God's providential activity—God's intentions—from the patterns made by events in nature, history, and individual lives. In contrast to human agency in which we can sometimes easily tell from a specific event in relative isolation as, for example, the turning on of a stove, what a person intends to do, in order to detect divine agency, we need a larger number of events before a pattern emerges so that God's intentions become manifest. If we take a large enough sweep of nature, history, and individual lives, God's intentions become apparent in the results produced by many events. For example, in the case of biblical revelation, the significance of Jesus can be understood only with the larger context provided by the long history of Israel. With our present-day knowledge of cosmology and evolution, we can see that God has chosen to make human beings through the long process of many billions of years of cosmic development and millions of years of biological evolution. For us, this is a long time. But is it for God? It is said that what atoms are to physicists, galaxies are to astronomers. Size is relative to intentions. Time too is relative to the intentions to be realized. It seems that God has chosen to make human beings through a process which roots them in nature. This and other judgments about God's intentions are not infallible and may be revised in light of more knowledge about nature and history.

There are no gaps in nature, history, and individual lives because God achieves divine intentions by working with and through the members of the universe without faking the story. There is no faking because, in the relations between the members of the universe, what goes before affects what comes after. Likewise God does not force or violate the activities of the members of the universe in order to achieve divine intentions. As in a good novel, the events and characteristics of the characters are woven together in such a way that they cohere.

The fact that God's creative production of members of the universe and God's providential activity in bringing about specific consequences are not detectable from an examination of individual members of the universe or from single events taken in relative isolation has misled some theologians, such as Gordon Kaufman and Maurice Wiles.[8] They have questioned if not actually abandoned the biblical view that from time to time God acts in the world to bring about some specific events to achieve God's intentions or to make God's intentions known to particular people.

Wiles, for example, has argued that when people make claims about divine actions in the world, as we find in the Bible, what has actually happened is that they have simply latched onto some specific events as the result of divine action because in these events they have become aware of God's intentions. But God has not acted within the world to bring about those events. God's only activity is to keep creatures in existence, *with no variations in that divine activity.* There is no divine action *within* the world bringing about some events in contrast to others. When people speak as though certain events are brought about by God's activity in the world, they are merely responding subjectively to events which have no more claim than any others to be the result of God's agency. Once God has made the universe, God leaves it to run itself. God has made God's own existence and God's intentions for us accessible to us, and God leaves it wholly up to us to perceive and to actualize those intentions.

At bottom, Wiles shares with the seventeenth century Deists a crucial assumption. The Deists assumed that the creative action of God is *uniform.* That is, once God created the universe, God left it to run itself. They held this view of God's relation to the universe because they thought that seventeenth century science had revealed the fundamental properties of matter. For them, all matter was extension and figure, capable of motion and rest, and interacting by mechanical impact. Matter so understood is self-sufficient in its operations.

This view of matter has long been superseded, but the picture of God as outside the universe, unable to bring about specific events without disrupting its operations, continues to underlie and vitiate theological discussions of divine agency. It is operative in the work of Wiles. Unlike the Deists, Wiles does not think of God's creative activity as limited to the beginning of the universe, but God's creative activity is nonetheless uniform. God does not affect the outcome of events except indirectly through the original choice of the powers God conferred on the members of the universe.

If we accept this view of the nature of the members of the universe, the only way God could not affect the outcome of events is by intervening, disrupting the natural flow of events and introducing discontinuity in nature and history. The biblical accounts of God bringing about special events in nature, history, and individual lives become problematic in the minds of those theologians and biblical scholars who want to be intellectually honest. It leads to a definition of miracles as a disruption of the continuities of nature, and so lies behind David Hume's and Ernst Troeltsch's arguments against miracles. For them, historians seeking to reconstruct the past must judge the soundness of reports on the basis of what usually happens. Hume argues that we ought not to accept the soundness of any report of events that fall outside the regularly observed course of nature and human affairs. It is always more likely that the reports are wrong than that a miracle has occurred. Should an event occur which is beyond the bounds of our present understanding of the powers of members of the universe to bring about, it simply means that our sciences have not yet advanced far enough to explain how it occurred.

This Deistic view of the uniformity of God's activity has been broken by Austin Farrer's account of what it is that God creates. Farrer used the expression "activity systems" to describe the members of the universe. It is a highly general notion because it designates that characteristic which is shared by every member of the universe—animals, plants, organisms, cells, chemicals. The expression is based on the concept of human agency. Although human actions are personal, we can place all members of the universe on a continuum. If we remove the personal element from our activities but keep the feature we have in common with all members of the universe, we and they are active. Farrer, therefore, designates all the members of the universe as "activity systems."

Every activity system has an enduring pattern and interacts with other activity systems. Our bodies are made up of interacting activity systems, such as cells, that together make it possible for us to be personal agents. They also limit what we can do. The degree of self-determination possible for any activity system depends on the kind of system it is. A person is much more self-determining than a single-cell organism.

We need not follow in detail Farrer's account of activity systems. His main point is that every member of the universe is a distinct individual. Because everything is an individual, God can make an individual activity system or systems that differ in some respects from similar ones in order to affect the outcome of events. When God does this, God has not suddenly entered the universe because God is constantly active in giving each individual activity system its unique nature. God still achieves God's intentions with and through creatures' natural activities. This does not constitute an "intervention" or a "disruption" of any continuities because there is no requirement that God make every similar kind of activity system the same. God's constancy as the creative source should not be understood, as it is by Wiles and Kaufman, to mean uniformity of action. God's constancy is God's consistency of action. That is, in order to achieve God's intentions God consistently does not fake or force events. Because God does not create uniformly, God can bring about specific events in nature and history without violating or disrupting the created order.

But there are some self-limitations on what God may do. Even though every activity system is an individual, which may differ from other similar activity systems, the results God can achieve are limited by the kind

of universe God chose to make. God has chosen to make us free creatures. Because we are free, our responses to God's intentions are not
forced. Were they forced, our nature would be violated, which is the
same as to say that free creatures would no longer exist. Similarly with
subhuman agencies. Each must be allowed to be itself, that is, to act
according to its own reality. Otherwise it ceases to be. The very existence
or operations of physical energies means wear and tear and at times the
breakup of one activity system through interaction with other activity
systems. Living systems, in order to maintain themselves, eat other living
systems. Although the outcome of events are affected by God's agency,
there must be sufficient consistency in the divine agency for there to be
connections between creatures. That is, creatures must be affected by
what goes before and must affect what comes after them. Otherwise the
activity systems God makes are not real activity systems but fakes. This
would be a version of the God of the gaps. Instead of the situation in
which there is an absence of a member of the universe in a causal sequence, there would be the disengagement of a member of the universe
in a causal sequence.

We, as free agents, are rooted in nature. We evolved from it and are
affected by its workings. For example, we inherit our genes. They affect
what we can and cannot do and render us subject to illnesses, aging, and
death. God does not act so as to keep us from all illnesses and accidents,
any more than God acts to prevent all human activities that violate God's
intentions. God respects the reality of both subhuman and human systems of activity. Because of their reality God can achieve God's intentions
with and through their activities, and the way God achieves those intentions exposes us to injury and harm.

This understanding of divine agency does not exclude miracles such
as healings. As we shall see in a moment, they can occur without disrupting nature or history. But they will not occur frequently because the
good God seeks us to have is not limited to our physical well-being or
earthly prosperity. Consider, for example, Mark's account of the beginning of Jesus' ministry (1:14–45). People flock to Jesus in order to be
healed. During the night he leaves town and, only after a diligent
search, do the disciples find him. They complain, "Every one is search-
ing for you" (v. 37). But Jesus makes it clear that it is because people are
so intent on being healed that they will not listen to him. "Let us go on
to the next towns, that I may preach there also, for that is why I came
out" (v. 38). On their journey they meet a man suffering from leprosy
who begs Jesus to heal him. Jesus, moved by compassion, heals him but
sternly orders him to tell no one but a priest. But the man talks freely
about it so that Jesus cannot openly enter a town.

Jesus cares about people's physical health, but this is only one aspect of the kingdom of God. People can become so concerned with physical health that they use their religion to seek health and other material blessings without a significant interest in the kingdom of God. God's intention is that we seek God with all our hearts. If God were to give us earthly well-being whenever we asked for it, we would remain focused on limited goods and not the good of communion with God.[9]

We have extrapolated from the present as far back as some twenty billion years. This is possible because the natures God gives to nonhuman activity systems are basically uniform. God acts uniformly with nonhuman activity systems because God's intention of producing a universe with the necessary conditions for life to arise can be realized this way. Once human beings arise, the realization of God's intentions becomes more complex because human beings have a considerable degree of self-determination. This means that God does not have a blueprint for history or for individual lives. Rather, God interacts with human agents, seeking to realize God's intentions for them without violating their freedom. Our specific actions lead God to adapt the way God acts to realize the divine intentions for us.

This understanding of God's activity highlights our responsibility. Belief in God's providence does not mean that we simply leave everything to God. We may think in terms of a boat with two oars. One oar is pulled by us and one by the rest of God's creatures. If we do not act in harmony, then the boat will not go straight. If we are to live well and truly, we must act in harmony with God's intentions. We must seek to discern them through the fullest exercise of our minds in our study of nature, history, and human nature. We must also use our minds to the fullest in our study of the Bible and the life of the church. Only a heart that cares for God will make the effort, but without the effort to discern with our minds the intentions of God, we shall not be able to act responsibly.

But God's intentions are not easy to discern. The history of Israel is replete with partial and inadequate apprehensions of God's intentions by a people who are thoroughly convinced of the reality of God and of having a reliable, if only partial, grasp of the divine intentions. We also see how disastrously God's intentions were misread from nature's order by the exponents of natural religion, who understood them from an egocentric and anthropocentric viewpoint. But the main point we are making here is that unlike the case in which we can perceive the intention of human agents with ease from a relatively isolated event, such as turning on a stove, we need a large number of events to discern God's providential activities in specific events. Consider, for example, the incident reported in Genesis in which Joseph is sold into slavery by his brothers. It is only near the end of his life that Joseph realizes the way God used this event to save his family from starvation. Joseph tells his brothers, who are terrified that he will exact revenge on them for their terrible deed, not to be afraid because, even though they meant to harm him, God intended it for his and their good.

The discernment of God's providential actions is analogous to a situation faced by a naval engineer when doing the research for his dissertation. He sought to determine the height tides in the Gulf of Mexico would reach under various conditions, especially during hurricanes. Although the actions of the tides fall under the principles of Newtonian mechanics, until the advent of computers it was not possible to calculate the height of tides. But with computers it is possible to solve the simultaneous equations which give the effects of the myriad forces that act on waves. Yet at one point this naval officer was baffled. As the calculations were successively completed, several discontinuous lines were printed out onto his map of the Gulf of Mexico. He knew that the water could not jump, so to speak, from the end of a line to the beginning of another. He made the computer recalculate the data several times, but the results were the same. He was about to give up in despair, when he decided to feed in still more data. Suddenly a pattern emerged. The endings of the lines converged at a point. The reason for the convergence was that the tide was reacting to itself as a force. At first this led to discontinuous lines, but with the addition of more data, it became apparent what was happening.[10]

If a person can have difficulty detecting the pattern of tides when all the principles which govern the tides are known, and when the means of making calculations are available, it is hardly surprising that God's intentions for nature, history, and individual lives are for the most part unknown. With God, we do not have all the relevant principles, nor a means of calculation, so to speak. Yet some patterns have been discerned.

This account of God's activity holds to the view that God works with and through creatures to achieve divine purposes. It differs from the view held by Kaufman and Wiles. In their view, because people cannot normally heal blindness or leprosy by touch, or restore deranged people by speaking to them, the healings reported in the New Testament could not take place without violating nature and disrupting the continuity of history. But in my view it may be the case that holy people have the power to do these things. Their holiness is the result of their openness to God. Because we are all intended to become holy, to receive such power is not a violation of our natures. The exercise of that power by holy people is not a disruption of nature or history any more than is our affecting the acceleration of a falling object. Intercessory prayer may affect events because God attains God's ends with us and through us. Because of our prayers, God may act one way rather than another with and through creatures to achieve divine intentions. There is nothing uniform or automatic about the results of the actions of holy people nor the divine response to our prayers. Nor, according to my position, is it correct to infer that because you and I cannot turn water into wine, for Jesus to do so would disrupt nature. The Word of God incarnate may have that power, just as you or I have the power to turn on a stove. Likewise, the Word of God incarnate may have the power to command winds and waves.

In general we may say that God creates a consistent set of lawlike behaviors. As part of that set there are the known physical laws. These laws apply to a wide variety of situations. But in certain unusual situations such as creating a chosen people, revealing divine intentions in Jesus, and revealing the nature of the kingdom of God, higher laws come into play that give a different outcome than normal physical laws which concern different situations. The normal physical laws do not apply because we are in a domain that extends beyond their competence.

This is analogous to the way Newtonian laws operate within a certain domain (low speeds) but are only approximations to the higher laws of relativity that encompass all that comes under the purview of Newtonian laws and more besides.[11]

From the point of view from which I have been arguing, even the resurrection of Christ is not a disruption of nature. It may be as Peter said, ". . . it was not possible for him to be held by [death]" (Acts 2:24b). One who is obedient to God as Jesus is cannot be held by death. If we are in Christ, that is, made free of sin by him, then perhaps death will not be able to hold us either.

"Intervention" in the unacceptable sense means the filling of a gap of some sort in the operations of nature and history. In these examples there are no gaps. There are gaps only if it is assumed that what is true of the power of most people and things specifies the limits of what God can do through other people and other things. What happens is unusual, and so does not "regularly" happen. But there is no disruption of the continuity of nature and history.

My position does not commit a person to accepting all biblical events at face value. The Bible was not written as history. This creates great problems for biblical interpretation because our interests today are so historical. For example, the parting of the Red Sea may or may not have taken place. An informed judgment would require a general position concerning biblical interpretation. It may be that we can determine that the account of the Red Sea crossing was not written with the intent of reporting the parting of the Red Sea but is to be interpreted in the fashion of a legend, an allegory, or a literary form unique to sacred stories. We may, moreover, not be in a position to make a judgment on the matter; or we may find ourselves changing our minds from time to time as we formulate and reformulate our principles of biblical interpretation.

This chapter is an example of faith seeking understanding. Usually discussion of divine agency takes place as if the Christian faith were problematic, whereas this exploration is made after a case for belief in a God, whose Word became incarnate in order to redeem us, has already been made in previous chapters. Although my approach to the task of understanding the nature of divine agency is critical, the reflections are intended to clarify how we are to understand divine agency in light of the two books of God. In keeping with the approach of faith seeking understanding, the results of the exploration, like much of theology, are put forward tentatively, not dogmatically.

PART III

Christianity and Other Faiths

Chapter Ten

A Christian Theology of Other Faiths

During the Enlightenment there was immense confidence in the power of reason to establish decisively and with finality what is true in various areas of inquiry, including religion. This resulted in the creation of a natural religion. That is, it was thought that on the basis of reason alone, free of all need for faith in a revelation and any reliance on any church, the existence of a benevolent God and the nature of our moral obligations and rights could be established. Natural religion was said to contain the essence of religion. All particular religions, such as Judaism, Christianity, Islam, and Hinduism, were allegedly species of the genus natural religion. Only those aspects of the particular religions of humankind that agreed with natural religion were true; the rest of their contents were either superstition or superfluous and could be dispensed with by a rational person.

As we have seen, natural religion did not survive careful philosophical examination during the eighteenth century. Because the beliefs endorsed by natural religion were similar to some Christian beliefs, the collapse of the basis of natural religion was thought by many in the intellectual community to be the same as the collapse of the only reasonable grounds for Christianity as well. In Part I we saw why this is erroneous, even though the misperception continues to be quite widespread in universities. In Part II we gave a case for the truth of Christian beliefs.

But does this mean that all other religions must be false? That is not implied by the truth of Christianity. Are we then to say that all religions are equally sound? That is a very popular thing to say in university circles today, largely because we are suffering from a guilty conscience over Western colonialism. We do not want to appear to assert that the dominant religion of Western culture is superior to that of other cultures. But that is hardly a sound basis for saying that all religions are equally true. The failure of the Enlightenment's project to uncover the true religion on the basis of what reason can discover by an examination of the physical universe leaves us with no option but an examination of the major religions of our world in order to make any evaluation concerning their truth.

Since the Enlightenment's "universal viewpoint" (a viewpoint independent of all commitment) has proven to be illusory, an examination of various religions can only be made from a particular point of view. For example, we study various religions scientifically. That is, we seek to understand them from the point of view of history, sociology, psychology, philosophy, and other disciplines. But a scientific study of religion, however valuable it may be, of itself does not enable us to say that a particular religion is true. To be able to make a judgment concerning its truth or value involves the adoption of some convictions concerning the existence or nonexistence of a divine realm and concerning what is to be valued. The scientific study of religion, in order to be scientific, explicitly eschews such commitments.

We may also study various religions from the point of view of a particular religion to which we are committed. We seek to determine from the point of view of our religion what is acceptable and not acceptable in another religion. This is intellectually justifiable because we do not have a universal viewpoint and because, as we have said, the point of view of a scientific study of religion does not allow us to evaluate the truth of a religion.

To make an evaluation of another religion from the point of view of Christianity is to engage in the creation of a theology of other faiths. Such an examination often draws on the results of a scientific study of religion, but it differs from such a study because it goes further than an attempt to understand a religion from its own point of view, as does history of religion, or from a sociological, psychological, or philosophical point of view. It seeks to determine the validity of a religion's claims from the perspective of Christianity.

Most Christian theologians want to say that other religions have a valid and significant revelation. Christians can go quite far in this direction, but when we do, we encounter a dilemma. We cannot relinquish the claim that Christ is the Savior of the world. If Christ were our Savior only, he would be a parochial god, and that for Christians is impossible. Christ is either the one who died for the sins of the world or Christ is not a Savior at all. So we can either maintain Christ's uniqueness and indispensability for human redemption—and appear to condemn other faiths as inadequate—or we can accept other ways to God as equally valid at the cost of giving up Christ as the prime and indispensable mediator of redemption.

This dilemma was faced in the modern period because the search for trade routes to the East and the discovery of new lands led to a great interest in other cultures and religions. Many educated people did not want to say that because Christianity is true, other faiths must be false.

As we have seen, one major attempt at a solution was natural religion. It abandoned the distinctiveness of Christianity in favor of some generalizations that were allegedly based on reason and that were thought to be more or less present in all religions of the world.

In contrast to this solution, George Herbert (1593–1633), the poet and priest, met the dilemma by focusing on the distinctive feature of Christianity, the crucifixion of Jesus, and showing its universal significance. Unlike his brother, Lord Herbert of Cherbury, the founder of one variety of natural religion, English Deism, he retained the concreteness and particularity of Christianity.

This is a much more creative response because it enriches our understanding of our own religion. The centrality of Christ can be pictured as the point at the center of a circle. If we do not permit the challenge of new ideas from within our own culture or from other cultures to affect our understanding of Christ, we maintain orthodoxy but at the price of having a small circle. Christ's lordship does not extend terribly far. But if we reach out to new ideas and at the same time retain our commitment to Christ as the Savior of the world, then the result may be pictured as an elongated ellipse, with Christ as one focus and the material we have brought into relation with Christ as the other focus. Over a period of time, the two foci may be brought closer and closer together, until they coincide. When they do, we once again have a circle. But this time, the circle is much larger than before. This happened, for example, with Greek Stoicism. Stoicism was the most widespread philosophical-religious outlook in the hellenic world. It disappeared because anyone who might be attracted to Stoicism could find all that Stoicism had to offer and more in the Christian church.

A Christian theology of other faiths reaches out toward other faiths, retaining the conviction that Christ is the Savior of the world, and bringing another faith or aspects of it into a vital relation to Christ. This can enrich our understanding of Christ and extend Christ's significance into new domains. Ideally—and in some instances the ideal has been achieved—what at first was not at all connected to Christ becomes fully integrated and part of a greatly enhanced Christian faith. It may not happen in a single person's lifetime but take the effort of several generations. Even if another faith continues an independent existence, unlike Greek Stoicism, Christianity is enriched from the encounter, and the other faith is as well.

The generation of George Herbert and Lord Herbert was not the first to face the challenge of other faiths. In fact, Christianity developed in relation to another religion, Judaism. Those who received Jesus as the Messiah did not entirely repudiate the Jewish religion. Part of Israel's sacred writings became for Christians the Old Testament, an integral part of the Bible. The Old Testament is interpreted differently by Christians because everything is understood in the light of Jesus' life, teaching, crucifixion, and resurrection. When Christians read Psalm 23, they have Jesus in mind.

Christians also responded to the challenge of hellenic and Roman culture and religion. Much of it was rejected, but some was retained, and what was kept was transformed by being related to Jesus' person and deeds, as is evident in the Platonism of the Cappadocian fathers and Augustine. As I argued in another work, theology as a discipline results from the encounter of Christians with hellenic culture.[1] This happened in the High Middle Ages when many theologians were stimulated by the knowledge of lost Greek texts, transmitted to them by Islamic scholars. Thomas Aquinas was explicitly writing theology in a pluralistic situation, aware of both the Jewish faith and Islam. David Burrell has suggested that Thomas used "being" as a central term in his theology—rather than the traditional Father, Son and Holy Spirit—partly because it was a term shared with contemporary Jewish and Islamic theologians and philosophers. He was reaching out to make contact with their thought.

One of the great benefits of these encounters is that again and again we have been able to recognize our God's presence in other religions and cultures. We have been surprised as was Jacob, who had fled to a foreign country to get away from his brother: "Surely the LORD is in this place; and I did not know it" (Gen. 28:16b). If we too look, we are likely to find at least signs of our God and usually in a guise that surprises us.

I have spent some time in India, Thailand, Japan, and Egypt, attended services of some of the religions of those countries, and read parts of their sacred texts. But I am not an expert in any of the other various religions of the world. Even if I were, I could not complete the task of a Christian theology of other faiths since I do not know God's providence fully. As we noted in the Introduction, the apostle Paul could not fully understand the role those people of Israel who did not accept Jesus as the Messiah were to play in God's providence. He believed that it would be manifest some time in the future. So too we must be satisfied with at best only partial knowledge.

In this chapter we shall attempt to make a contribution to a theology of other faiths by drawing upon Simone Weil's understanding of the universal significance of the cross. Unfortunately she died before she had presented her ideas in a connected and orderly way. What follows is simply my understanding of her thought. I do not claim that Weil's views solve all our difficulties. But she has a fresh, original vision, and hopefully she will stimulate our imaginations to think our way through the dilemma other faiths present for Christianity and lead us to a better understanding of the gospel and of ourselves as Christian people. It will be necessary first to outline Weil's ideas and then to apply them to a Christian understanding of other faiths.

I

For Simone Weil the entire creation—physical, social, and psychic—is to be identified with the cross on which Christ died. The forces which form the fabric of the created universe are the same forces which led to the crucifixion. Christ's death has universality because the forces that came to a focus in Palestine to cause that death are also present throughout the universe.

A specific understanding of creation is embedded in this claim. We must therefore begin with her remarks about the nature of creation in order to understand her view of the cross. In the Genesis 1 account, God utters commands and one thing after another comes into existence. The fulfillment of God's commands instantly and without apparent effort on God's part suggests that God's might is not the same as any other power. Nothing can resist God, for whatever might anything else has actually depends on God's own power.

But more than a power is needed to create. As we mentioned earlier, Dorothy Sayers and Iris Murdoch, both creative writers, claim that the creation of characters for a story requires some renunciation on the part of their creator. Writers must restrain their own personality to create a personality which is not their own. For something to exist which is not themselves requires them to renounce themselves. Good literature, they claim, is not a "expression" of a writer's personality but involves self-renunciation so that something else might exist. Actors sometimes find their own identity becomes blurred for a time while portraying a character.

Weil applies this to God. When God creates, God causes something to exist that is not Godself. Creation requires an act of profound renunciation. God who was alone, with utter fullness in Godself, freely and out of love, chose to have something else exist and to exist in its own right, separate from deity, and not to satisfy divine needs. It is created to be itself, to exist as something of interest and value in its own right.

Nearly all that God has created operates as it does in regular patterns without any choice. This is also true of most human behavior. Our personalities and our social life operate for the most part as regularly as does nature. This entire order Weil refers to as the realm of "gravity."

Weil uses this term in a distinctive way. In science, gravity refers only to certain specific properties of matter. Weil, however, extends the term to refer to whatever acts automatically, according to its own nature.

One of the distinctive features of gravity is that everything goes as far as it can until it is prevented by some external factor from going any further—unless it is an organism. An organism is not only subject to external limitation, but a part of itself can check its expansion and limit its growth. All expansion and self-limitation of each organism are built into it, and every organism operates automatically without the exercise of choice. Even the actions of human beings frequently operate by gravity because we seek to gratify, protect, and enhance ourselves quite automatically.

In contrast to the realm of gravity, there is another realm, that of grace. Its basic characteristic is that it does not seek to go as far as it can; it does not expand until it is forced to stop by external or internal compulsion. Its mark is voluntary restraint. Restraint is exercised for the sake of other people and things. It respects their reality. It takes account of other people, even when it is not forced to, even when there is no reward for doing so. For example, there are people to whom I can easily respond when they express a need. Usually, the needs expressed are the kind I like to meet, and from my response I feel a kind of gratification, or fullness. The expenditure of effort gets replenished by the gratification. Sometimes, however, in the face of genuine need my initial tendency is to remove myself, to get away. In such a case I sense no possible return or gratification for my effort. I just know instinctively that something is about to be drained out of me, and I react automatically by trying to get away. It takes effort to overcome this automatic response.

The very creation of the world is an act of such grace. God does not seek to be all that there is, to spread Godself out, so to speak. But God graciously pulls back to allow a world to exist. God voluntarily restrains Godself so that there may be other realities. God holds back for the sake of the world. God is grace; the universe God made is gravity.

Within the world of gravity there is at least one creature that can operate with grace and not merely with gravity: a human being. But most of our life is dominated by gravity. The human personality is similar to a machine. Just as a machine needs fuel to keep it running, we need to have our energy for action constantly replenished. It will be replenished by the operation of either gravity or grace.

Simone Weil illustrates this with a family, one of whose members is an invalid. The invalid is indeed loved and cared for by the family. But in time resentment builds up because human love is limited. The family does not have enough energy supplied by human love to carry out the enormous task of taking care of the invalid day after day, year after year. He is loved to start with, but there just is not enough fuel supplied by human love to keep on looking after him without drawing upon the energy that comes from resentment and self-pity. The family members, for example, complain to each other and sympathize with each other. This gives them some energy, or "fuel," to keep going. Both the energy supplied by human love and that supplied by resentment and self-pity are part of gravity. One is attractive, the other is not. The amount of each form of gravity varies from person to person, but both spring from human temperament and make-up, and operate quite automatically.

People often begin with good motives. In taking care of a family member or helping a friend in need, people begin with the more admirable gravity of human affection. But if they are called upon to make more effort than their human love or affection can sustain, then people are forced to draw upon the energy supplied by less admirable motives. How often we have, for example, taken on a project from good intentions, and then, as the job becomes harder and harder, stick to it because we do not want the embarrassment of other people knowing we gave up?

In all our actions there is a need to receive the equivalent of what we give, even if it is only a smile or a feeling of self-praise. We cannot bear the emptiness that comes from giving without some compensation to help fill it up. We feel resentful and angry when we get nothing for all our efforts. Have we not all felt and said with bitterness, "He did not even say as much as 'Thank you' for all that I did!" We feel better for this expression of resentment. Energy is restored by the sense of superiority that comes from fixing our minds on the baseness of another person.

All this is the operation of our gravity. It dominates our actions and our thoughts. We act and think about ourselves and others in such a way as to protect our ego from irreplaceable loss and to compensate it for every expenditure of effort. We do this naturally, automatically. It is our gravity.

Gravity is created by God. It is created by God out of love, as we have seen. But it is also created by God to be a means to love. God seeks that we love God and each other. Even though we are gravity, we can receive grace, and we can have our own actions arise from this love. We are capable of belonging not only to the order of gravity but also to the order of grace. Just as a machine needs fuel to run, so too we need to find incentive and energy to act and live. The question is, What shall supply that energy, mere gravity or grace as well? In either case, we obey God; for God is the source of both realms. But we obey as slaves when we follow gravity only, operating like the world of nature; we obey God as children and heirs when we voluntarily consent to belong to the order of grace as well as to the order of gravity.

II

With the concepts of gravity and grace, we can now present Weil's understanding of the cross. Creation is an act of love because it involves God's voluntary renunciation of Godself as the only existent. The cross is the great act of Jesus' self-renunciation. He is the victim of the forces of gravity—the forces of self-expansion and of self-aggrandizement—which motivated the Roman Empire and the various aspirations of the Jewish people. These forces of gravity, which make a complex pattern of interlocking, conflicting systems, catch him up within their workings and crush him. As he is being crushed, he does not know why he must feel the presence of his Father leave him. Although feeling forsaken by God, he remains obedient to the order of grace. Christ lays his life down humbly instead of following the route of self-assertion.

This is why the disciples attributed to Jesus the statement, "No one takes [my life] from me, but I lay it down of my own accord" (John 10:18). Jesus' death is caused by the actions of gravity, but in the grip of gravity's vise, he yields himself up voluntarily. He accepts his vulnerability to the created forces of gravity, and he accepts the cross which is brought about by their action because he believes they are under the power, wisdom, and love of his Father. He therefore dies as a member of the order of grace, not as a slave to gravity.

The love of the Creator, which restrained itself for the sake of the existence of the universe, is answered from the cross by Christ. The Son restrains his own will by yielding it to the forces of a created universe that operates by gravity. In that crushing vise, Christ yields to the Father in faith that all this came from God for our sakes.

The cross of Jesus is both the wood to which he was nailed in Palestine and the forces of the created universe. The cross of Golgotha is the intersection of the forces of gravity, of which the universe consists, and grace. Gravity is represented by the nails which cause blood to flow and death to come, and the self-aggrandizing human institutions and human deeds which condemn Christ to the cross. Grace is that love which loves God in spite of being crushed and forsaken.

With this view of the creation of gravity, and Jesus as the incarnation of the Word of God, by whom and with whom and through whom all things were made, we have this picture: God, who created the universe, enters the order of gravity, is subject to what God made, and bears its full weight on Godself, humbly and as a creature. Divine love is not just a creative love that renounces its unique status as the sole reality but is a love that allows the creation to be itself even when it turns on God and crushes God.[2]

III

The gravity of the universe in its physical, social, and psychic forms is present everywhere, in all times and places. Gravity understood as the force which led to the crucifixion of Jesus on a wooden cross therefore means that something of the reality of Jesus' cross is present universally. Weil claims that many people who lived before Jesus or who did not know of Jesus, knew the cross under the form of gravity. They have perceived the force of gravity in its physical, social, or psychic forms as it grips and crushes people. They have renounced belonging to the realm of self-expansion and self-aggrandizement, and have given their allegiance to the realm of grace by a self-restraint that makes room for others. She spent much of her short life seeking to document this claim. Here and there, especially in Homer, Plato, and Aeschylus, she saw an honest recognition and portrayal of gravity and the way all people are subject to it, as well as a knowledge of grace. Let me illustrate this by examining her account of Homer's *Iliad*.[3]

Homer's account of the Trojan War shows the sway of might as it touches all people, both victors and victims, until it reduces both to things. The person who wields a sword and strikes another down becomes as much an object, acting mechanically, as the person who is struck down. "The true hero, the real subject, the core of the *Iliad*, is might. That might which is wielded by men rules over them, and before it man's flesh cringes."[4] Homer portrays both the Trojans, who are his enemies, and the Greeks, who are his compatriots, with the same sympathy and compassion. The *Iliad* is not a story of Greek triumph. It is about people who are subject to forces that even the gods, who are immensely stronger than people, cannot control or manage. As the events of the story unfold, gravity reveals itself more and more clearly, until victor and vanquished cease to be people and are reduced to things, obedient to forces that have established dominion over them.

It is this which makes the *Iliad* a unique poem, this bitterness, issuing from its tenderness, and which extends, as the light of the sun, equally over all men. . . . The destitution and misery of all men is shown without dissimulation or disdain, no man is held either above or below the common level of all men, and whatever is destroyed is regretted. The victors and the vanquished are shown equally near to us, in an equal perspective, and seem, by that token, to be the fellows as well of the poet as of the auditors.[5]

Weil claims that no one could so honestly portray people at war and have the whole work bathed by such beauty, compassion, and sense of solidarity with both victors and vanquished alike, as does Homer, without knowledge of a power utterly different from compulsion, of a power utterly different from gravity, namely grace. "In a certain way, Patroclus occupies the central position in the *Iliad*, where it is said that: 'he knew how to be tender toward all,' and wherein nothing of a cruel or brutal nature is ever mentioned concerning him."[6]

Again and again in various Greek writings she sees the contrast between gravity and grace, between brute power and social power that reduce people to things and a witness to another power. She claims that those who portray such forces have an intimation of grace. These authors see themselves as united to those who are reduced to rubble. They know that they could just as easily, despite all they could plan or do, become caught in the mechanism of gravity and be crushed by it as well. They are no more meritorious than those who are crushed. "The cold brutality of the facts of war is in no way disguised just because neither victors nor vanquished are either admired, despised, or hated."[7]

The humility of the ancient writers indicates that they have learned to think of themselves and others as limited, dependent beings. They have recognized the sway of gravity and yet have not given it their allegiance. To withhold one's allegiance from gravity, even when one knows of no power which can defeat it or redeem it, is the result of the presence of God's grace, whether it is realized or not.

Weil claims that this has happened in many faiths. She finds it in the ancient Babylonian epic of Gilgamesh and in sacred Hindu texts, as we shall see in the next chapter. Sometimes the intimations of Christianity she claims to have found may be exaggerated, such as intimations of the Trinity in Plato's *Timaeus*. But aside from some questionable interpretations, her basic claim that there has always been a witness to the cross of Christ in all places and times is generally persuasive. It was not known as a cross, because it was not known that the Word of God would become a person and endure the suffering caused by gravity. Yet the universe, which is gravity, is what led to Christ's crucifixion; it is those forces that killed him. So the cross of Christ is the forces of the universe, which came to a focus at Golgotha and pinned to a piece of wood the one by whom and through whom the universe was made.

In all places and times people have had the opportunity to know gravity and also the opportunity to refuse to give it their allegiance by showing compassion for those who suffer. They have had a witness to the cross of Christ, without having ever having heard of Jesus or the cross at Calvary. If Weil is on the right track, many ancient writings and religions give substantial warrant to the claim that the cross in another form has been perceived.

If the cross is a truth that can be known at least in part from the very intersection of gravity and grace, why does it matter that the Word of God came to earth? Weil tells us that the cross is not only a truth stretched out for all time on the rack of the physical, social, and psychic universe, but it is also an event at a point in time and space. At this point the cross is filled by God's own presence. The love which made the entire order steps inside that order, bears its full weight, and bears it as a creature.

In Christianity, our treatment of other faiths usually focuses on the doctrine of creation to find a tie between other faiths and our own but not on a doctrine of creation that has the cross integrally related to it. Or we emphasize the Logos or Word of God present in all people, hoping to discover a vital link. But Weil focuses on the cross, the cross which is a historical, particular crucifixion. It is with the most distinctive aspect of our religion that she seeks to uncover a vital unity between our faith and the faiths of other peoples. The cross may not be central to their religion; it may be buried and hardly noticed. But nonetheless, she says, it is there. God has not left Godself without a witness, nor has divine grace been unknown in lands far from historic Judaism and Christianity.

She believes that in the New Testament itself there is ample evidence for this claim. One of her favorite texts is the parable of the sheep and the goats (Matt. 25:31–46). Those who showed compassion for those who are thirsty, hungry, naked, and in prison were recognized by Christ as belonging to God and were welcomed into the kingdom, even though they did not recognize Christ as one to whom they had shown compassion, for Christ claimed to be present among those who were desperate. Those who are caught in the machinery of gravity share Christ's cross, whether they know it or not. Christ identifies with them because the forces which have left them without food and clothing are the same forces which left Christ nailed to a cross. To love them is to love God, whether or not we know the story of Jesus. The ability to show compassion for those who are desperate comes from the power given by grace; for to show compassion is to operate on a different basis than the physical, social, and psychological forces of the universe. But Jesus identified the capacity to love the oppressed—not the ability to prophesy, cast out demons, and work miracles—as the mark of a person who loved God.

Those of other faiths (or even of no faith) in Christian or non-

Christian lands may therefore belong to Christ. They may participate in the cross, without knowing that it is Christ's cross, nor that Jesus was ever crucified. They may only know of the gravity of the created universe which sometimes puts people on its rack and have compassion for its victims. In the parable these people are claimed by Christ as God's own.

Weil did not think it worthwhile to send missionaries to tell devout people of other religions that they belong to Christ. She was in favor of missions only to those who do not know God in any form.[8] Otherwise she thought missions were wrong. She believed that to convert a person from one religion to another is like asking him or her to address God in a foreign language; he or she would always be less fluent than when addressing God in his or her own tongue.[9]

I do not know how serious an objection this is. It does not seem to me to be very formidable. I believe that one who knows of the cross in the form of the adverse side of gravity is likely to rejoice to know that God came into the world to endure its effects in person. To know the cross is one thing; to know that God was crucified is another. If a person of another faith has the first, such a person would likely rejoice to learn the second. A mission to devout people is not a mission to the damned; it is to bring them something they already partly know, something about which they should delight to know more. The problem is: Do Christians who address others about God so understand the cross themselves?

At any rate, we have presented a way to recognize the universality of Christ. Something of the divine love Jesus exhibited by humbly enduring crucifixion in Palestine can be and apparently is known in other forms by people in times and places beyond the bounds of Christianity. A knowledge of Christ's cross in the form of the physical, social, and psychological gravity of the world is universally available, and so too is the grace of divine love.

Chapter Eleven

Incarnation in the Gospels and in the *Bhagavad-Gita*

Chapter Ten presented a way for Christians to make a valid place for other religions within their own faith. It sought to show the universality of the cross of Christ, that is how it and the grace of divine love are known in another form by people in times and places beyond the bounds of Christianity. In this chapter the focus is on the incarnation. It will focus on some features of the cross not previously treated and give us still another way to make vital connections between Christianity and other religions. Simone Weil believed that the Word of God has been manifest in human form in other religions. She maintained, however, that the Word of God that became Jesus Christ differs in two crucial respects from manifestations of the Word in human form in other faiths. First, in Jesus Christ the Word becomes a person and remains a person. The Word does not temporarily assume human form and then discard it. Second, Jesus suffers and dies because he is the mediator between a just God and unjust creatures. This is not true of other manifestations of the Word of God.

The other manifestations, however, do bring out aspects that are only implicit in the cross of Christ. They are important for those of us who are Christians because they make explicit what otherwise remains hidden in our own religion. It deepens our understanding of the atonement effected by Christ's incarnation and death. We shall illustrate this claim by discussing Weil's understanding of the *Bhagavad-Gita*. The existence of other faiths need not continue to erode our Christian faith, leading some theologians, such as John Hick, to treat the incarnation in a merely symbolic fashion, or to reduce Christ to the status of a Savior only for those who follow the route Christ opened to God (that route being only one of many possible routes).[1]

I

Weil's method of reasoning in religious matters is to focus on what is contradictory in earthly terms in order to lever ourselves above them into the realm of supernatural truth. She writes, for example, "It is contradictory that God, who is infinite, who is all, to whom nothing is lack-ing, should do something that is outside himself, that is not himself, while at the same time proceeding from himself."[2] That is to say, God inexplicably creates the universe. Every kind of human and animal mo-tivation—such as lack, need, or instability—is not a reason for God to create something that is not Godself, since an infinite, perfect being lacks nothing or needs nothing that cannot be supplied from *within*. As perfect, God is not forced by any instability to act. It is only a contradic-tion, however, on the plane of human and animal motivation. According to Weil (and Pascal), a contradiction presses us to rise to a higher level to gain understanding, which in this instance is the level of grace. At this level there is no contradiction between motive and action. There is a harmony between the motive of perfect love and the creation of some-thing outside oneself because creation is an utterly free gift.

Frequently Weil focuses on those matters which, because they are con-tradictory on a nonreligious plane, open the mind to receive supernat-ural or religious truth. A religious understanding does not remove all mystery, however. For example, the notion of grace—an utterly free gift—enables us to understand God's motive in creating what is not God-self. It does not enable us to understand how God creates, that is, the nature of the divine causality which produces finite existence, a matter we have already considered.

In the same way Weil writes of another mystery, the incarnation. "The supreme contradiction is the creator-creature contradiction, and it is Christ who represents the union of these contradictories."[3] Because we and God are on different levels, union between us is impossible. The incarnation of God makes it possible. The incarnate God is God, and yet God is on our level because God is human. In an earlier chapter, we said this could be pictured as a line resulting from the intersection of two planes. The incarnate one can raise us to the level of the Deity, because by making us holy or righteous, God raises us to the level of divine ho-liness or righteousness. The incarnation, which removes the contradic-tion that exists in the notion of union between beings which are on completely different levels—an infinite and holy being, and finite and sinful beings—does not enable us to understand how God became hu-man. The picture of intersecting planes is only an analogy, not an expla-nation of how divinity and humanity are combined in a single being who is both fully divine and fully human.

Union between God and human beings involves two items. (1) As we have seen, the infinite Creator exists on a different level from that of creatures. The incarnation of the Word of God brings God down to the human level. (2) God is perfect in righteousness or justice. We are not.

Christ raises us to the level of God by making us righteous. Paradoxically, it is this feature of traditional Christian theology—its most distinctive feature—which Weil uses to create a vital link with other faiths. Let us first see how she understands Christ's work of atonement, and then we shall see how she ties it to a Christian understanding of other faiths.

The key to understanding the way Christ is the mediator between unrighteous creatures and the holy, uncreated source of all is found in Weil's pregnant remark that we examined in Chapter Six, "We must ask that all the evil we do may fall solely and directly on ourselves. That is the Cross."[4] As we said there, many Christians are prone to accept too easily Christ as the bearer of our sins and evil. But if we seek to be just and to demand justice, then we ought in consistency to ask that all the evil we do may fall solely and directly on ourselves. That thought is too horrible to bear, but to think it is to gain access to what the cross involves. Let us see how.

Union with God or atonement for Weil means that we are to be assimilated to God. That is, we are to be made similar or like God. In order to bring together what is so disparate as God and human beings, there must be a mediator. Christ as a perfectly just or righteous person is like God.

Weil points out that in the *Phaedrus,* Plato tells a myth in which all intelligent creatures partake of food that resides in a realm that transcends the universe. They consume the reality of which this world is but a reflection. They nourish themselves with truth itself, justice itself, reason itself, and the other realities. This is indeed strange language, but I believe that we may say that by "justice itself" Plato means perfect justice. Moreover, perfect justice is a divine attribute. No human being is perfectly just. Perfection cannot be reached by adding more of the same to what we are.

Weil uses Plato's myth to show that there is not merely a quantitative difference between the Creator and creatures but a qualitative difference too. Perfect justice is not achieved by improving our behavior. Perfect justice is not a human characteristic. This may become evident to us if we meditate on the fact that we do not desire that all our evil fall solely and directly on ourselves. We flee from the thought. On the other hand, were God to be incarnate as a human being, God would be a perfectly just or righteous person. This is why Weil wrote, "Therefore, in spite of the fact that he was on earth, he would belong to those realities which lie on the other side of the sky."[5]

We do not become assimilated to God without a love of justice itself. As we saw earlier, when we are treated fairly, we find the treatment pleasant, but we do not love justice itself. Our attention is occupied by pleasure so that we do not attend to the goodness of justice itself. When we are treated unfairly, we are indirectly aware of the good of justice. We realize that justice matters because of the harm we suffer from injustice. But we do not yet love justice itself. To love it is to desire to become perfectly just, that is, to become like what we love. A way to test whether we do love justice itself, rather than demanding it because we desire other goods or because through injustice we suffer harm, is to ask God that the consequences of our evil fall solely and directly on ourselves. That would be to love justice itself. To reflect on this possibility honestly makes us aware of the fact that we also desire to be saved from justice. To a person caught in such a contradiction—loving justice and yet fearful of it—the need for a supernatural remedy is apparent.

God and human beings may meet in suffering. God, as transcendent Creator, cannot suffer as we do. God becomes human so that God is able to suffer as we suffer. The incarnate one saves us from having to bear the full consequences of justice by submitting to an unjust execution. Christ thus bears the consequences of God's mercy and forgiveness in Christ's own person and mediates the consequences of our evil into the very being of God.

To love justice itself, so that we ask that the consequences of our evil fall solely and directly on ourselves, and yet to shrink in horror from it, is the way we are assimilated to God. Justice puts us into a contradictory situation. It leads us to look to a reality which is on a higher level for relief. To have faith is to believe that we can be raised and belong to a transcendent realm by attending to God incarnate, a righteous one who suffers unjustly. To have faith is to believe that to love a righteous one, who is justice itself incarnate, makes us just, because we become like what we love. To have faith is to believe that to desire justice itself brings us nearer to it.[6]

II

Weil claims that the Word of God is the ordering principle of the world. This is a traditional notion in Christian theology. In Genesis 1 chaos is ordered into a cosmos by the Word of God; and John's Gospel begins with an identification of the Word of God with Jesus Christ. Weil's contribution is to show that the created world can be a medium for contact between God, who is the transcendent Creator, and human beings.

Weil (as others before her, notably Leibniz and Whitehead) was struck by Plato's remark in the *Timaeus* that the cosmos is the result of "good persuading necessity." This obscure remark can be understood by means of the Greek notion of "limit." The cosmos—which in Greek means an *ordered* world in contrast to chaos—is the result of limits being placed on things so that we no longer have amorphous stuff but specific things. To be a thing is to be limited, and the relations between things are the result of limitation. For example, the height to which waves wash up onto a shore is determined precisely by several factors, such as the shape and slope of the coastline. Waves can go only so far and then they reach their limit. The introduction of limitation, which is the introduction of necessity, gives us a cosmos rather than chaos.

Nature, however, is not to be understood simply in terms of necessary relations between its members. Things in nature have been given their specific limits with the intention of producing a harmonious whole, so that the universe is good as a whole and in every part. This is evident in the beauty of the universe as a whole and in every part, a beauty which is caused by nature's laws but which is not intended by nature's laws. For Plato, the beauty of the world points beyond the necessary relations between the members of the universe to a Mind that orders the universe with the intention of producing beauty (we should also remember that in ancient Greek the word *kalo* means either good or beauty).

Weil interprets the Christian claim that God creates the world by and through the Word to mean that God's Word is the principle of limitation or necessity that structures the world and orders things so structured into a harmonious whole. God's Word is the principle of its overall, harmonious order, which is spelled out in detail by our present-day sciences in the formulation of regularities as laws of nature. Nature's obedience to the Word of God is experienced physically by us as necessity. Weil calls the principle of nature's order an incarnation of the Word of God and the beauty of the world its smile.

This is not an incarnation in precisely the same sense that Jesus is the incarnation of the Word of God, because the Word of God is not identified with the cosmos of matter and energy as it is with Jesus Christ. The universe is not the Word of God; it is the continuous effect of God's Word. God is indirectly present to us in and through the world as the principle of its overall order. This implies that we can experience God indirectly or implicitly as we understand the world's laws by our intellects, as we perceive its beauty by our senses, and as we feel the effects of the operations of nature on our bodies.

For indirect contact with God through nature to elevate us, that is to mediate God's purifying presence (so that we are assimilated to God by being made righteous or just), we must attend to nature in the right way. This is also true with God's presence in Christ. As we have just seen, for contact with Christ to assimilate us to God, we must hunger and thirst for justice. Only so do we love Christ, the perfectly righteous one who was unjustly slain.

For contact with God to take place through nature, we must rise out of our particular point of view and come to love nature as a whole. We treated this in Chapter Six as the third aspect of faith. As we saw there, the natural world for all its beauty and goodness also injures us by its operations, causing pain, suffering, decay, and finally death. In its operations it does not make any allowance for our personal merits or demerits. If we are to have contact with God through nature, we must rise above an anthropocentric and an egocentric point of view. This means we must accept the indifference of nature and the injury it does to human beings and to us personally. Were it not for the beauty of the universe, we could not love it. But in loving nature, we are drawn out of our anthropocentricity and egocentricity. We are elevated or purified by our attentiveness to the beauty of the world because by attending to its overall harmony, we make contact with God. Then, says Weil, "Each sensation is like communion, that of pain included."[7]

To understand this more fully we must consider once again Weil's idea that contradiction on one level can enable us to reach a higher, supernatural level, which makes sense of the opposition. In *Gravity and Grace* Weil writes, "The word good has not the same meaning when it is a term of the correlation good-evil as when it describes the very being of God."[8] Necessity or the compulsion, which nature exercises on our bodies, is not the divine goodness that orders nature. When we face the truth of nature's indifference and accept our vulnerability to its operations, then we know in our very bones that the good we crave—happiness or well-being—is not to be found in this world.

There are moments of horror in facing the indifference of nature. But if we endure the horror of necessity, God becomes present to us. If we patiently wait for good to be done to us, we shall actually find ourselves being purged of evil precisely in proportion to our attentiveness to the necessities of nature. In that attentiveness we are in contact with God through contact with the realities of creation, both human and natural. Contact with God is purifying automatically, and we experience the relief of being rid of the burden of evil and the joy of being filled with charity.

By our attention to what is above we rise toward God; we become assimilated to God; we have an "at-onement." We thus belong to a different order from the necessities of nature or the interplay of human action. By our obedience, we belong to God's kingdom or rule. This is not to say that we are indifferent to human pain and to human injustice.

Quite the contrary, it is precisely because we are becoming assimilated to God that we can act more truthfully (and hence more fearlessly) in human affairs since we have a degree of detachment from the pluses and minuses that result from the world's natural and human operations.

III

There are two major sacred epics in Hinduism, the *Ramayana* and the *Mahabharata,* which tell the stories of the heroes of the Aryan race. Numerous additions and interpolations have been made to both of them. The *Bhagavad-Gita* ("the Song of the Lord") is one of the additions to the *Mahabharata.* The *Gita* consists of a long dialogue between Arjuna, a warrior, and his charioteer, who is actually Krishna, an incarnation of Vishnu (the name under which the ultimate reality, Brahman, is conceived in the *Gita*), just before a great battle. Arjuna sees many of his kinsmen and friends in the ranks of the opposing army and is filled with horror. He does not want to fight, but it is his duty to fight to protect others of his own people. His charioteer explains that salvation or union with ultimate reality is to be reached not only through asceticism, the renunciation of the world, but also through action that is in accord with *dharma* (which means roughly to fulfill the obligations which go with a person's place in human society), provided that the action is done with detachment and is offered to Krishna in a spirit of devotion or love (*bhakti*). The *Gita* became the most popular of all the sacred Hindu writings because it stresses the love of a personal god and because it opens a path to salvation in addition to the classic paths of salvation in the *Upanishads:* asceticism and scholarship.

As we shall see, there are vital differences in the understanding of incarnation and salvation in Christianity and Hinduism largely because there is some ambiguity concerning the relation between the supreme reality and creatures in Hinduism. Nonetheless, the incarnation and crucifixion of Christ and the story of Krishna and Arjuna address the same question: How may we rise above the level of the mixture of good and evil to the level of righteousness or purity so that there is union with God? In the Gospels Christ is a victim and, as we have seen, we may achieve assimilation to God with Christ as our mediator by love of that righteous incarnate one who suffers because of our unrighteousness. In the *Gita* Arjuna must wield the sword and kill his opponents—kinsmen, friends, and foes—indiscriminately. Yet Christ the victim and Arjuna the warrior are vitally alike in that both suffer from the effects of force. "Contact with force, from whichever end the contact is made (sword handle or sword point) deprives one for a moment of God. Whence the

Bhagavad-Gita. The Bhagavad-Gita and the Gospels complete each other." [9]

As we saw in the last chapter, force or compulsion has the power to turn us into things, that is, to reduce us for a moment wholly to items in the flow of causes and effects, both as victims and as users of force. We find ourselves facing cold necessity, which of itself operates blindly. It cuts us off from any contact with good, whether it be the good in the pair "good-evil" or transcendent good. This is why Christ in Gethsemane and Arjuna before a battle both shrink in horror before it. Just as Christ must submit to the necessity of crucifixion and become integrated into the flow of causes and effects, so too must Arjuna overcome his pity for those whom he must fight and, as a wielder of force, become integrated into the flow of causes and effects. In this way, both victim and actor become alike.

Jesus provoked the religious authorities of his day and, through them, the political authorities. Once events were in train, there was no recourse for him but to suffer penal execution. Christ believed that to submit to this chain of events was God's will. Arjuna is also in severely constraining circumstances. Whether he fights or refuses to fight, there will be evil consequences. He thus faces the question, How can an individual become righteous when to live in society means that an individual's actions, whatever they are, will have both good and evil consequences? The pair "good-evil" are produced by human action in a way that is similar to the pair "good-evil" produced by the operations of nature. Arjuna's situation is nicely rendered by Reinhold Niebuhr's title, *Moral Man in Immoral Society.*

In the midst of this highly circumscribed situation, Krishna brings enlightenment to Arjuna. He is to submit to obligation as to a necessity,[10] because at that moment there is no other course of action possible.[11] Just as Jesus consented to necessity because it was God's will, so too Arjuna is to consent to being a warrior.

There is, however, a clear recognition that even should society be altered and made more just, our actions have consequences, which are always a mixture of good and evil. In seeking to fulfill our obligations, we shall be caught in situations similar to the one Arjuna faced. No matter how we act—that is, whether we take part or refuse to take part in society—there will be both good and evil consequences. Righteousness cannot be achieved merely by meeting our obligations. Krishna explains to Arjuna that as we meet our obligations we ought to be detached from our actions. We are not to be in them, so to speak. Then we are free of their consequences. The concept of detachment from the consequences of our actions is unfamiliar to Christians and Westerners. What does it mean?

We need first to consider the Hindu doctrine that the ultimate ground of being in the self—the *atman*—is identical with the ultimate ground of reality in nature, Brahman. According to Weil, all of us perceive things from our own point of view, which is not only partial but also deeply distorted by our wishes and desires, so that most of our thoughts and actions are not in touch with reality. We do not perceive things as they are. One way to achieve liberation from this false perspective is to recognize and accept nature's indifference. As we have seen, if we accept our vulnerability to nature, we escape from our anthropocentricity and egocentricity. The entire universe becomes like the cane a blind person uses. A blind person has contact with that which is beyond the circumference of one's body through a cane. One is able to interpret or read the significance of what one touches by means of the cane.

This analogy is a crucial one for Weil. When we accept that the universe is a system of laws, indifferent but not hostile to us, and that we use the laws of nature to effect our ends, we may use all the universe—treating it as a whole because of its inner connections—as a blind person uses a cane. When we accept that the universe is indifferent to us, it becomes an extension of us, like a cane is an extension of a blind person's body. We have contact with what is beyond the universe by means of the universe, as a blind person has contact with what is beyond himself or herself through a cane. By achieving a detachment from our egocentric and our anthropocentric perspectives, our true selves are liberated; our true selves achieve a kind of identity with the universe as a whole. That enables us to have contact with ultimate reality. Our souls thus achieve union with Brahman.[12] Detachment is not indifference; it is freedom from illusions about what the universe is and attachment to a reality that is not the universe itself.

This identification with Brahman through the universe cannot be sustained. Disruption arises because one must continue to act as an individual and because one is not the only individual. The *Gita* deals with both: our need to act and our relation to other people.

Our relation to other people is different from our relation to the universe as a whole. Another person should never play a role in our lives analogous to that of a cane, that is an extension of ourselves. Another person is not merely a part of the universe but also one who like ourselves has a conception of the entire universe. How then is one to be properly related to another reality that also has a point of view?

The urge to use the universe to unite with what is beyond it is easily perverted. The urge leads every person and every group of people to feel that they have a right to possess the universe: their clan, their nation, their race should dominate. Weil connects war and various forms of domination and suppression to a misunderstood urge to find our true selves. We have a tendency to heighten our sense of uniqueness and importance by seeking to dominate others. War, the theme of the *Gita,* is an extreme form of seeking to establish our uniqueness and importance.

What is particularly horrible about war is that it deprives us of contact with God, just as suffering from the hands of nature's painful operations for a time snaps our identification with the universe. We are out of touch with our true selves, and even deprived of the good in the pair "good-evil."

However just the cause of the conqueror may be, however just that of the conquered, the evil caused, whether by victory or by defeat, is nonetheless inevitable. It is useless to hope to escape from it. That is why Christ did not come down from the Cross, and did not even remember, at the moment of supreme anguish, that he would return to life. That is why the other one [Arjuna] did not lay down arms and stop the battle.[13]

Under the impact of force—whether at the point of a sword or at its hilt—we lose ourselves, God, the universe, everything.[14]

In spite of the effects of war on himself and on those against whom he must fight, Arjuna's obligations to his own people mean that he must fight. Arjuna encounters in the most extreme form the reality of life in society. It obliges us in our actions to cause both members of the pair "good-evil."

But there is a way to righteousness. One may fight in a war and yet be detached from the force one wields. One is detached if one acts from necessity, if one's intention is to persuade the enemy to desire peace, and finally, if one pursues the war with restraint. One is then not identified with force or possessed by it because one does not seek to exterminate other points of view. How we are drawn into the sequence of causes and effects by participating in social life, including war, determines whether we are present or absent in the action. We are "missing" when our allegiance is not given to exterminating other points of view, though we indeed seek to kill. We, so to speak, step outside the necessity in which social situations involve us by recognizing that necessity with utter clarity and by restraining ourselves and not intending to exterminate other points of view or to gain at the expense of another's loss.

To act with detachment does not of itself raise us to a higher level. We merely refrain from evil. But by detachment we become a self which the ultimate reality can reach. We can be elevated to the level of righteousness through our love of the transcendent good in the form of Krishna, the incarnate Vishnu. To rely on Krishna is to go beyond the domain of moral obligations. It is similar to the Christian notion that we rely on Christ's righteousness.

Even war, if it is a necessity endured properly, can lead us toward righteousness. In action, and not just by enduring suffering as a victim in obedience to God, we may find righteousness. In our participation in social life we are to do what we must do, knowing that such actions of themselves do not elevate us to righteousness. But our love of righteousness itself or our love of righteousness present to us in the person of Krishna does raise us.

On this interpretation, detachment is not indifference. We care about the consequences of our deeds. We want to live and we want other people to enjoy life too. This is why the situation is one of duress. It is precisely when we realize that the situation is one from which humanly there is no resolution that we recognize that our only possible help is from a supernatural source.

IV

Throughout her *Notebooks* Weil voices her reservations with the *Gita*. She does not endorse all of it any more than she endorses all of the Old Testament. For example, she mentions that *dharma* "is only suitable in a stable society. Those people did not draw up rules for unstable societies. What becomes of dharma in a conquered country? And what are the duties toward the conquerors? (Must find out)." [15] It should be noted that her views on war and peace continued to develop, especially as she reacted to the continuing deterioration of the political situation in Europe and the outbreak of the Second World War. [16] In addition, she points out that Krishna is not an incarnation in the sense that Christ is because Krishna did not suffer. Krishna is a manifestation of deity (Vishnu is present), and so he is a revealer or enlightener. He is even a means of salvation (a *metaxu*). By loving him we can be raised to righteousness. But for justice itself to be incarnate entails suffering, and to be able to suffer requires that the divine become a creature. Among all the instances of alleged incarnations, Christ is the only one who suffered and suffered precisely because of his righteousness. We need not deny that Vishnu is one of the names of God, and that Krishna, as a manifestation of him, inspires, enlightens, and even enables people to reach the presence of righteousness itself in order to continue to maintain that

Christ is the righteousness of God *incarnate* and that through Christ's suffering God suffers the separation of the Word from Godself.

We must, however, recall that part of Weil's method is to find important analogies or likenesses. We have seen that the universe and Krishna are not incarnations of the Word of God in the same way that Jesus is. But Weil calls them incarnations because they are like Christ's incarnation in vital respects. They function as *metaxu* or mediators between God and human beings. Contact between us and God, which is a contradiction since we are on different levels of reality, is made possible by God descending to our level. The Word of God descends as the principle of nature's order and in human form in instances such as Krishna. Manifestations such as Krishna's provide a saving revelation, that is, show and mediate a path to righteousness. The prime incarnation, that of Jesus Christ, however, reveals the full depths of God's saving mercy since it is the actual endurance of the suffering which is the cost of God's mercy toward human unrighteousness, a suffering which is borne by very God.

One other very serious reservation, which we noted in passing, is that the distinction between ultimate reality and the universe is not clear in Hinduism. Attempts to clarify it have led to several schools of Hindu philosophic and religious thought. This lack of clarity affects the way salvation and incarnation are to be understood. As far as salvation is concerned, it is the difference between assimilation—being made like God, namely righteous—and identification. In addition, if there is an underlying ontological identity between the ultimate reality and human beings, salvation is a realization of identity, not the gift of an immortal status and participation in the life of God by creatures. So for Weil there is no transmigration of the soul from body to body, a major stress of the *Gita*. As Weil put it, "Plato: assimilation—India: identification." [17] As far as incarnation is concerned, if there is an underlying ontological unity between the ultimate reality and human beings, then an incarnation would not be a change in ontological status. In Christianity the divine and the creature are distinguished by the doctrine of creation *ex nihilo*. Only God is a necessary being who is wholly sufficient in Godself, in contrast to all else which exists contingently and adds nothing to God's being. For the Word of God to become human is to change in ontological status. It is a degradation—to move from one grade to another—so that the Word of God now is a human being.

For reasons such as these it is important that the exploration of a Christian theology of other faiths be pursued not only in terms of Christology but in such studies as David Burrell's. He compares Roman Catholic, Jewish, and Muslim medieval philosophical theologians whose common ground is Being. [18] The two approaches complement and interpenetrate; for were one to seek to study Being only, one would leave out the vital dimension of salvation in various religions. On the other hand, to examine salvation without the ontological dimensions of Being would be to fail to understand the nature of incarnation and salvation in Christianity and other faiths.

This venture into a theology of other faiths raises in a new way the question of the nature of revelation. It is clear that neither Christianity nor Hinduism has faced every kind of human situation for which religious enlightenment is needed. No religion has shed as much light on the significance of being a victim as has Christianity with its claim that God incarnate is a victim. That perspective, however, needs to be supplemented, as we have seen, by looking at righteousness from the point of view of one who acts. Our investigation thus opens up the possibility of developing new theories about the nature of revelation by allowing us to retain our Christian access to God in its full integrity while at the same time finding genuine revelations in other faiths, revelations which enlarge our own, just as our own enlarges theirs. But for this enterprise to be religiously and theologically fruitful for us it is necessary to approach other revelations from the point of view of seeking a Christian theology of other faiths. This contrasts with the approaches used by historians of religions, who seek to understand other religions from the inside, so to speak, to understand them as they understand themselves. But theologians and Christians must also seek to understand them from our point of view, from how they connect in vital ways to our understanding of God's revelation. And we might add that were a Hindu theology of other faiths attempted, we might then find a new appreciation of Christianity by Hinduism. The most ancient Vedas, accepted by all Hindus, have sacrifice as their foundation and hold that the world was brought into being by sacrifice. The Christian focus on God as the victim might open new vistas for that ancient faith. It might transform the Hindu view of love (*bhakti*) to think of love primarily in terms of a divine love that sacrifices itself for our redemption and does so from the very foundation of the world ("the Lamb slain from the foundation of the world," Rev. 13:8, KJV) so that there might be a world at all.

V

This is not a comprehensive study of other faiths from the point of view of Christianity. Only one Hindu holy book has been examined, and the classical paths to salvation in the *Upanishads*—asceticism and scholarship—have not been explored. Other faiths, such as Buddhism, have not been considered at all. Nor is what has been offered to be considered definitive. But enough has been shown about the nature of a Christian theology of other faiths for others to pursue it further.

In conclusion, let us review what has been learned from the examination of other faiths in the last two chapters. As far as method is concerned, we have seen that an examination of the relation of other faiths to Christianity is very fruitful when distinctive and centrally important features of Christianity, such as the cross and incarnation, are used to make an evaluation of another faith. This seems to be a more promising approach than one which drops the particularity of Christianity, as John Hick does.

In Chapter Ten we have seen that it is possible to maintain the universal significance of Christ's crucifixion without condemning people of other faiths by using a concept Simone Weil introduced, namely, gravity. It becomes possible to conceive of the entire created order in its physical, social, and psychical aspects functioning at times as a cross. It enables us to recognize that people such as Homer, who lived before Christ, received divine grace because of the compassion they have for those who suffer the negative effects of gravity, whoever the victims may be. When the grace of divine love, most fully realized in the crucifixion of Jesus, is shown to have been received and known under another form by people in times and places beyond the bounds of Christianity, the circle of our understanding of Christ's Lordship is extended. We not only affirm Christ's universal Lordship, we actually have more of it unveiled to our sight.

In Chapter Eleven we explicitly considered the person of Christ in the work of reconciliation and atonement by an examination of Simone Weil's comparison of Christ and Krishna as incarnations of God. We examined Weil's account of the atonement that Christ's crucifixion made possible, and then we showed how the identification of the Word of God, as the ordering principle of the universe, with the Greek understanding of limit leads to a view of nature's necessity and beauty functioning as a mediator between us and God. Since Jesus is the Word of God made flesh, by whose death the consequences of our actions are remitted, Jesus is the prime mediator from which other mediations, such as that performed by nature, have their validity.

Jesus reveals the path of righteousness through suffering. The *Bhagavad-Gita* reveals the path of righteousness which leads through the infliction of suffering. We saw, however, that a victim and a warrior are vitally alike in that both are under the dominion of force. So in spite of the difference in starting points, the gospel and the *Gita* complement each other. The *Gita* teaches that the way of righteousness for those who must act and so cause both good and evil by their actions is through detachment. This very distinctive Hindu religious way to righteousness, superficially alien to the activism of Western culture, is understood by Weil to be distinct from indifference toward the consequences of action. Detachment means that because we act from necessity, we are absent from the actions we perform. Weil makes room for the practice of detachment within Christianity because righteousness cannot be achieved by meeting our obligations with detachment. It does not of itself raise us to a higher level. But detachment, as an expression of our love of righteousness itself, connects us to Christ, the incarnation of righteousness itself.

Finally, we learned that incarnation as understood in the *Gita* is not the same as incarnation as understood in the Gospels. In the Gospels the Word of God not only becomes human and suffers but remains a human being. Arjuna's charioteer, Krishna, merely temporarily assumes human form and does not suffer. The full sense of the Christian teaching about incarnation requires the Christian teaching about creation, for without the particular ontological difference between Creator and creature that Christianity teaches, the nature of the degradation suffered by the Word of God in becoming a human being is not statable. This is the same thing as saying that the nature of the divine love taught by Christianity cannot be properly stated because the nature of divine love is stated in terms of what God has done. Comparison with the *Gita* enables Christians to recognize the distinctiveness of their own religion and to do so without condemning other faiths as not being viable ways to righteousness and without compromising the universal Lordship of Christ. Rather, the circle of our vision of Christ's Lordship is increased.

Conclusion

Most people do not come to have faith through the route that has been described: first an examination of the possibility of God, then a consideration of our need of God, and finally an experience of God's grace. The particular path each person follows is different, as an examination of biographies or autobiographies of Christians easily shows. Nonetheless, coming to faith usually involves exposure to Christian preaching, teaching, and worship; study of the Bible; and fellowship with Christians. The nourishment, guidance, and understanding received in these ways, and especially in prayer, frequently provide sufficient assurance for a person that he or she has contact with God. Elsewhere I have argued that faith arrived at in this way is fully reasonable and that no further ground is needed to justify adherence to the truth of Christian beliefs.[1] Although considerably more needs to be said to exhibit the reasonableness of this route to faith, it is today a recognized and frequently endorsed position in philosophy of religion among those who are free of the restricting boundaries of the Enlightenment's assumptions.[2]

My intention in this book is to give those who have no faith compelling rational grounds to become seekers and to those who have faith a greater degree of assurance and understanding than they can attain while constrained by the modern mentality. We therefore began by showing that the modern mentality, which, because of its reliance on classical physics and the philosophies of Hume and Kant, has been so hostile to Christianity, is now passing away. As we have seen, the book of nature, which was increasingly used against belief in God in the modern period, has now in both science and philosophy been seen actually to point toward God. The existence and order of the world pose questions that cannot be answered by science and which are not answered by philosophy (unless it relies on the disputed principle of sufficient reason).

Even though belief in God among the ancient Jews did not initially arise because of a desire to answer questions about the order and existence of the universe, God answers these questions (and many other ones as well, such as those which concern the meaning and goal of our lives). It is possible to believe in God rationally after all. It is a mistake to regard religious faith as a mere "personal preference" that does not call for serious consideration by every serious and rational person. The situation has so changed that there is no need to be on the defensive, as Christianity has been for several centuries. Rather, it is those who are not seekers who must account for not being so since there are fundamental questions concerning the existence and order of the universe that are vitally important to how we shall live and what we should hope for. A person who acts rationally ought to become a seeker. As Simone Weil put it,

The danger is not lest the soul should doubt whether there is any bread, but lest, by a lie, it should persuade itself that it is not hungry. It can only persuade itself of this by lying, for the reality of its hunger is not a belief, it is a certainty.[3]

In the Introduction and in Chapter Five, it was argued that the grounds for belief only become more accessible from the perspective of a seeker. Unfortunately it is still widely thought in philosophy of religion, among many practicing scientists and among those in other disciplines, that it is possible, without becoming a seeker, to conduct a complete, in contrast to a partial, examination of the grounds for Christian beliefs.

To have learned that nature's existence and order point toward God and to have become a seeker do not mean that one is able to find God without faith. It is rather that they give one sound reasons to expose oneself to the book of Scripture and to the Christian community in order to discern God's intentions for us. This gives us the opportunity to come to faith, that is, either to yield or to withhold our allegiance or consent to the realization of God's intentions.

Christian beliefs are adhered to by faith, not because there is a lack of evidence for them and we have to make do with faith. Faith is not a makeshift to overcome a gap between beliefs and evidence. Rather, faith is necessary because we must yield our allegiance to God's intentions and because we recognize that to be in a position to do so, we must move to a different order than that of the naked intellect. The order of the naked intellect is the use of our minds apart from our needs and especially apart from a search for that good in which we find our well-being.

The naked intellect forms a valid order. By trial and error we have learned that to deliberately restrict ourselves to it is appropriate for some of the questions we ask. But there are questions which push us beyond that order. It is irrational to limit ourselves to the order of the intellect because both the order and existence of the universe and our own human concerns push us beyond it to the order of the heart, that is, to a search for the good that would give us full satisfaction. It is by arguments formed within the order of the intellect that we have shown the limitations of the order of the intellect; that is, it is by argument that we have shown why we rationally ought to become seekers.

Kierkegaard pointed out that faith overcomes "offense."[4] When we are not being treated properly, we are offended. Those whose minds are well-trained are offended to be told that we must have faith to find our well-being or that we must hold to Christian beliefs by faith. To some it sounds like being told to abandon reason and evidence and to return to superstition, whim, and prejudice as the basis of our beliefs. But when we learn that it is rational to seek our well-being and that this cannot be found from the gratification we get from material goods or social success, or without a love of justice itself, we may realize that to be rational we must be open to what is above the order of the intellect. Once we have yielded our allegiance to the good we discern in Christian teachings and begun to receive the good God intends us to have, we realize that God has not abused our intellect by requiring faith. We can receive the good God intends for us only by consenting to receive it, only by actually participating in the life of God itself.

Faith does not replace critical thinking. Rather faith seeks understanding. It gains understanding only through reasoning. For example, it must examine evidence to determine whether a particular interpretation of a passage of Scripture or a commandment or a doctrine is plausible, likely, convincing, warranted. But to be critical is not the same thing as to be skeptical. All too often when people are exposed to unresolved issues in theology, they assume that until we can get a greater consensus among theologians and churches, we are to remain uncommitted to God. But in every field of inquiry there are unresolved issues. Advances in knowledge and understanding are possible only because everything has not been resolved. We can achieve sufficient discernment of God's intentions (such as that we are to love our neighbors as ourselves and to love justice itself) to yield our allegiance to God and to begin to receive from God nourishment, guidance, and understanding.

Faith does not rule out every kind of doubt. On the level of the intellect there is never sufficient evidence to prove rigorously any belief, as we know from the contingency of scientific theories and from critical philosophical thinking. Many beliefs are very well-grounded, but our grounds do not entail or prove that even well-grounded beliefs are true. Rigorous proofs are possible only in formal logic and pure mathematics but not in their application. According to Goedel's Theorem, there are limits to what we may prove even in pure mathematics. Therefore, if one is so disposed, one may doubt even in the face of excellent evidence.

This is also possible with religious beliefs, whatever the quality of the evidence may be. Within the order of the intellect, faith does not close whatever gap there is between evidence and a belief. Faith, however, overcomes doubt about the significance, worth, and rightness of our lives. Faith is actually to be receiving the good which, as we have discerned from Christian teaching, God intends us to have. As Simone Weil puts it,

When we are eating bread, and even when we have eaten it, we know that it is real. We can nevertheless raise doubts about the reality of the bread. Philosophers raise doubts about the reality of the world of the senses. Such doubts are however purely verbal; they leave the certainty intact and actually serve only to make it more obvious to a well-balanced mind. In the same way he to whom God has revealed his reality can raise doubts about this reality without any harm. They are purely verbal doubts, a form of exercise to keep his intelligence in good health.[5]

To have faith is indeed to "taste and see that the Lord is good!" (Ps. 34:8). It puts to rest doubt about where we shall find our well-being. Within faith there arises a particular kind of doubt which is inescapable. For example, in the tension between loving and at the same time fearing justice itself, we frequently suffer from doubt about our significance and worth. Also, when we suffer at the hands of nature and from injustice, we doubt that we shall find our well-being in obedience to God. Doubt that arises within faith is part of our movement toward a genuine and mature faith. This kind of doubt finds its resolution in faith and love. As George Herbert put it in "The Temper (I)":

> Yet take thy way; for sure thy way is best:
> Stretch or contract me, thy poore debter:
> This is but tuning of my breast,
> To make the musick better.

> Whether I flie with angels, fall with dust,
> Thy hands made both, and I am there:
> Thy power and love, my love and trust
> Make one place ev'ry where.

The next to the last line makes graphic the core of my position. God's power is at one end of the line, our trust at the other end; between them is love. It is because we encounter divine love—in the good God intends us to have—and yield our hearts to it that we trust in God's power as we are stretched or contracted by the course of our lives until God becomes present to us wherever we may be.

Notes

Introduction: The End of the Modern World

1. David B. Barrett, ed., *World Christian Encyclopedia* (Oxford: Oxford University Press, 1982), 6.
2. As found in E. E. Evans-Pritchard, *Theories of Primitive Religion* (Oxford: At the Clarendon Press, 1965), 100. Pritchard, one of the greatest field anthropologists of all times, critically demolishes the major theories in the social sciences that seek to undermine primitive and present-day religions with naturalistic accounts of the origin of religion, such as those to which Max Müller alludes and to theories formulated since Müller's day, such as Émile Durkheim's (1858–1917). Theologians, who are intimidated by Feuerbach's theory that divine beings are a projection of human nature, would do well to read Pritchard, as would philosophers of religion who refer uncritically to Sigmund Freud's theories on the origin of religion. Pritchard argues that these theories were bad science even in their own day.
3. See, for example, William L. Rowe, *The Cosmological Argument* (Princeton: Princeton University Press, 1975).
4. As we shall see in Chapter Seven, the philosophic views of reason that have dominated the modern period were so narrow that even science could not be conducted within their limited boundaries.
5. See Basil Mitchell, *Morality, Religious and Secular* (Oxford: At the Clarendon Press, 1980), and Alasdair MacIntyre, *After Virtue* (Notre Dame: University of Notre Dame Press, 1981). The summary of the nature of traditional morality is taken from Mitchell.
6. There are several important works which document the breakdown of the modern mentality and which also refer to our situation today as postmodern. See Romano Guardini, *The End of the Modern World: A Search for Orientation* (London: Faber & Faber, 1951); Frederick Ferré, *Shaping the Future: Resources for the Post-Modern World* (New York: Harper & Row, Publishers, 1976); Houston Smith, *Beyond the Post-Modern Mind* (New York: Crossroad, 1982); Harvey Cox, *Religion in the Secular City: Toward a Postmodern Theology* (New York: Simon & Schuster, 1984). Richard Rorty, *Philosophy and the Mirror of Nature* (Princeton: Princeton University Press, 1979), traces the breakdown of the Enlightenment understanding of reason, mind, language, and knowledge from Descartes to the end of the analytic tradition. A superb brief statement of the significance of this breakdown for Christianity and a criticism of Rorty's own relativism is given by Richard J. Neuhaus in "After Modernity," *The Religion and Society Report* 5 (February 1988). The *Center Journal* (Notre Dame: University of Notre Dame Press) is devoted to addressing the implications for Christianity and our culture at large of the transition to a postmodern world.
7. See David E. Klemm, "Toward a Rhetoric of Postmodern Theology: Through Barth and Heidegger," *Journal of the American Academy of Religion*

55 (Fall 1987): 443–69; Henry Staten, *Wittgenstein and Derrida* (Lincoln: University of Nebraska Press, 1984); David R. Griffin, *God and Religion in the Postmodern World* (Albany, N.Y.: SUNY Press, 1988).

8. Christopher Fry, *A Sleep of Prisoners* (London: Oxford University Press, 1951), 47–48.

9. Austin Farrer, *Saving Belief* (London: Hodder & Stoughton, 1964), chapter 1.

10. Ibid., 18.

11. Ibid.

12. Ibid., 22.

13. Austin M. Farrer, *Interpretation and Belief*, ed. Charles Conti (London: S.P.C.K., 1976), 1–6.

14. Ibid., 2.

15. Ibid., 5.

16. Ibid., 2.

17. Ibid., 6.

18. Ibid.

19. For an example in which the difference between a case for theism and its failure to provide a warrant for an actual religion see Gary Gutting, *Religious Belief and Religious Skepticism* (Notre Dame: University of Notre Dame Press, 1982).

20. Not everyone who thinks that theism is warranted would agree. Gutting, for example, argues for a religious skepticism in relation to an actual religion. We can give only an interim and not a decisive assent, as he puts it, to the rich outer belt of belief associated with our own religious tradition. For a perceptive evaluation of Gutting's position, see the review by George I. Mavrodes in *Faith and Philosophy* 1 (October 1984), 440–43.

Chapter One: The Christian Roots of Modern Science

1. Herbert Butterfield, *The Origins of Modern Science, 1300–1800* (New York: The Macmillan Company, 1951), viii.

2. Michael B. Foster, "The Christian Doctrine of Creation and the Rise of Modern Science," *Mind*, vols. 43, 44, 45; 1934, 1935, 1936.

Foster's influential work was anticipated by the great physicist Pierre Duhem (1861–1916) in his monumental ten-volume work *Le système du monde: les doctrines cosmologiques du Platon à Copernic*. The first five volumes were published between 1913 and 1917, but the remaining five were delayed until 1954 to 1959. From the very first volume, it was clear that Duhem's work ran counter to the prevailing secularist interpretation of history, in which science owed its origin to the de-Christianization of the West. Duhem shows, among other things, that the Christian belief in creation enabled any number of people before Galileo to break with the debilitating Aristotelian physics of motion. See Stanley L. Jaki, "Science and Censorship," *Intercollegiate Review* (Winter 1985–86): 41–49, and Harry W. Paul, *The Edge of Contingency: French Catholic Reaction to Scientific Change from Darwin to Duhem* (Gainesville: University of Florida Press, 1979), chapter 5, especially 156–61 and 176.

3. See Gary B. Deason, *The Philosophy of a Lord Chancellor: Religion, Science, and Social Stability in the Work of Francis Bacon* (Ph.D. diss., Princeton University, 1977).

4. See, for example, the review by James L. Gould of *The Growth of Biological Thought* by Ernst Mayr (Cambridge, Mass.: Belknap Press/Harvard University Press, 1981), in *The New York Times Book Review*, 23 May 1982, 7.
5. James Jeans, *Physics and Philosophy* (Cambridge: At the University Press, 1943), 1.
6. See E. M. W. Tillyard, *The Elizabethan World Picture* (New York: The Macmillan Company, 1944), which firmly refutes this widespread claim.

C. S. Lewis notes,

> Nor was it generally felt that earth, or Man, would lose dignity by being shifted from the cosmic centre. The central position had not implied pre-eminence. On the contrary, it had implied, as Montaigne says (*Essais*, II. xii), "the worst and deadest part of the universe," "the lowest story of the house," the point at which all the light, heat, and movement descending from the nobler spheres finally died out into darkness, coldness, and passivity. The position which was locally central was dynamically marginal: the rim of being, farthest from the hub. Hence, when any excitement was shown at the new theory, it might be exhilaration. The divine Cusanus (1401–64), who was an early believer (for his own, metaphysical, reasons) in earth's movement, rejoiced in 1440 to find that she also is "a noble star" with her own light, heat, and influence (*De Docta Ignorantia*, II. xii).

See C. S. Lewis, *English Literature in the Sixteenth Century* (Oxford: At the Clarendon Press, 1954), 3.

It is also worth noting this remark by Peter Brown on Augustine's world: "The world in which they lived was situated 'in the lowest depths of the universe,' a tiny pocket of disorder beneath the harmonious stars. This world was ruled by hostile 'powers,' above all, by the 'Lord of this world,' the Devil." See Peter Brown, *Augustine of Hippo* (Berkeley and Los Angeles: University of California Press, 1967), 244.

7. See, for example, Jacob Bronowski, *The Ascent of Man* (Boston: Little, Brown & Co., 1973), chapter 6, and Bertolt Brecht, *Galileo*, in *Seven Plays*, ed. Eric Bentley (New York: Grove Press, 1961).
8. See Carl Becker, *The Heavenly City of the Eighteenth Century Philosophers* (New Haven: Yale University Press, 1932), and *Carl Becker's Heavenly City Revisited*, ed. Raymond O. Rockwood (Ithaca: Cornell University Press, 1958).
9. Arthur Koestler, *The Sleepwalkers* (New York: The Macmillan Company, 1959), 425.
10. Ibid., 425–26.
11. *New Catholic Encyclopedia* (1967) 6:253. It may well be that Roman authorities such as Bellarmine did not want to expose themselves to the accusation that they tolerated a free-and-easy attitude toward biblical interpretation because in Protestant polemics the Roman Church was charged with failing to follow the teachings of the Bible.
12. See, for example, Reijer Hooykaas, *Religion and the Rise of Modern Science* (Edinburgh: Scottish Academic Press, 1972); Stanley L. Jaki, *Science and Creation* (Edinburgh: Scottish Academic Press, 1974), *The Road to Science and the Ways to God* (Chicago: University of Chicago Press, 1978), and *Cosmos and Creator* (Edinburgh: Scottish Academic Press, 1980); Eugene M. Klaaren, *Religious Origins of Modern Science: Belief in Creation in Seventeenth-Century Thought* (Grand Rapids: Eerdmans, 1977); and Harold P. Nebelsick, *Theology and Science in Mutual Modification* (New York: Oxford University Press, 1981).

Chapter Two: Has Science Replaced God?

1. "That Rule which is necessary to our future Happiness, ought to be generally made known to all men." Charles Blount, *The Oracles of Reason* (1693) as quoted in J. M. Creed and J. S. B. Smith, *Religious Thought in the Eighteenth Century* (Cambridge: Cambridge University Press, 1934), 23.
2. For example, see Immanuel Kant, *Religion Within the Limits of Reason Alone* (1790). Kant himself lost confidence in the book of nature and in its place developed a moral argument for God's existence in his *Critique of Practical Reason* (1788).
3. See Maurice Wiles and Mark Santer, eds., *Documents in Early Christian Thought* (Cambridge: Cambridge University Press, 1975), 4.
4. See, for example, the *Leibniz-Clarke Correspondence, 1715–16,* ed. H. G. Alexander (Manchester: Manchester University Press, 1976; New York: Barnes & Noble, 1976).
5. For the various developments which led to a demand for clarity and the effects it has had on Christianity in the twentieth century, see Michael B. Foster, *Mystery and Philosophy* (London: SCM Press, 1957). Foster gives a masterful description of what is meant by "mystery" in both biblical and Greek thought, how they differ from each other, and how both are to be distinguished from superstition and occultism. Few books are as important for understanding the way science and philosophy have so shaped the modern mind that it continues to misunderstand religion. This will be considered more fully in the discussion of the "hiddenness of God" in Chapters Six, Seven, and Eight.
6. See Samuel L. Bethell, *The Cultural Revolution of the Seventeenth Century* (London: Denis Dobson Ltd., 1951), which illustrates this with detailed comparisons of late sixteenth- and seventeenth-century figures.
7. David Hume's attack on miracles is more subtle and far-reaching than these crude arguments, as we shall see. We shall consider the subject of miracles in Chapter Nine.
8. Roman Catholics relied on Scripture and tradition, as well as on Scholastic philosophy, but did not read the book of nature as it was described by classical science.
9. Pascal's exact words were "'God of Abraham, God of Isaac, God of Jacob' [Exod. 3:6], not of philosophers and scholars." Pascal's remarks include scientists since in the seventeenth century they were called "natural philosophers." See *Pensées,* trans. A. J. Krailsheimer (Harmondsworth, England: Penguin, 1966), 913. Pascal did not complete the *Pensées.* After his death, the fragments were variously numbered by different editors. The numbers given here refer to those used in Krailsheimer's edition.
10. For a fuller account, see Tillyard, *The Elizabethan World Picture.* See Ch. 1, n. 6. For its theological significance see Bethell, *The Cultural Revolution of the Seventeenth Century.*
11. *On Nature Itself* in G. W. Leibniz: *Philosophical Papers and Letters,* 2d ed., ed. Leroy E. Loemker (Dordrecht, Holland: D. Reidel Publishing Co., 1969), 499.
12. I shall give my own view of divine agency in Chapter Nine.
13. See Robert Jastrow, *God and the Astronomers* (New York: Norton, 1978).

Chapter Three: The Order of the World

1. G. K. Chesterton, *Orthodoxy: A Personal Philosophy* (Glasgow: William Collins & Sons, 1961), 53–54.
2. William P. Alston, "Teleological Argument for the Existence of God," in *The Encyclopedia of Philosophy*, ed. Paul Edwards (New York: The Macmillan Company, 1967), 8:86–87.
3. G. W. Leibniz, *Discourse on Metaphysics*, section 19.
4. This phrase was used by Owen Gingerich, an astrophysicist at the Smithsonian Astrophysical Observatory in Cambridge, Massachusetts, and Professor of Astronomy and of the History and Philosophy of Science, Harvard University, in his lecture "Let There Be Light: Modern Cosmogony and Biblical Creation," delivered at the University of Pennsylvania, 6 April 1982.
5. Immanuel Kant, *Critique of Pure Reason*, Book II, chapter 3.
6. Lynn Barber, *The Heyday of Natural History, 1820–70* (Garden City, New York: Doubleday & Company, 1980), 13.
7. Ibid., 21.
8. In Germany a reaction to the narrow view of reason based on the mechanistic interpretation of nature led to a stress on the imagination, emotions, and tradition as bearers of deep truths. Many philosophers and theologians turned their backs on what appeared to them the simpleminded argument from design. Samuel Taylor Coleridge, an admirer of the Germans, burst out, "Evidences for Christianity! I am weary of the word. Make a man feel the want of it [religion]; rouse him, if you can, to the self-knowledge of his need of it." Quoted by Basil Mitchell in *The Scope and Limits of Reason in Religion*, the first of the Nathaniel Taylor Lectures, Yale University, 1986.

   German idealist philosophers such as Goethe, Fichte, Schelling, Schopenhauer, and Hegel tended to spiritualize nature, rather than to treat it as a machine. This not only spawned pantheistic tendencies but also encouraged the treatment of God solely as an immanent spirit. With the decline of German idealism in the mid-nineteen hundreds, the book of nature ceased to play a significant role in German-speaking Protestant theology for more than a hundred years.

   In France the demise of Paley's type of argument caused no distress. The main concern among Roman Catholics was to defend the spiritual nature of human beings and the unity of the human race. For the reception of Darwinism in France, see Harry W. Paul, *The Edge of Contingency*, 45, 64, 74. See Ch. 1, n. 2.
9. The Aristotelian view was greatly reinforced by Carolus Linnaeus (1707–78), the influential eighteenth-century systematizer in biology, who stressed that species were absolutely fixed since the time of creation.
10. See, for example, Roland M. Frye, ed., *Is God a Creationist? The Religious Case Against Creation Science* (New York: Scribner's, 1983). For an excellent summary of Christian positions on the interpretation of the creation stories in the history of Christian thought, see Ernan McMullin's introduction to *Evolution and Creation*, ed. Ernan McMullin (Notre Dame: University of Notre Dame Press, 1985), 1–56.
11. John D. Barrow and Frank J. Tipler, *The Anthropic Cosmological Principle* (Oxford: Clarendon Press, 1986), 5.
12. Ibid.

13. Ibid., 3.
14. Fred Hoyle, a Cambridge University astrophysicist, who in the past has been an outspoken opponent of religion, has recently argued that *impersonal* explanations are not sufficient to account for the existence of life on earth. He calculated that, given the constants of nature and the basic notion of biological evolution, the earth is not old enough for life to have originated on this planet. At first he postulated that some of the building-blocks of life developed in other parts of the universe and were transferred to earth by perhaps comets or other heavenly bodies. Later he calculated that the time since the Big Bang is not long enough either because it is exceedingly *improbable* that the right set of circumstances should have occurred in that time span for life as we know it to have evolved. He therefore postulated the activity of some *intelligence*. See Fred Hoyle, "The Universe: Past and Present Reflections," *Engineering and Science* 45 (November 1981): 8–12; and "The Sciences," *Spectrum* (November 1982): 9–13.

    Hoyle is not taken seriously on this issue by scientists, and it is not difficult to see why. It is another instance of a God of the gaps: the postulation of a deity because of a present lack of knowledge of the relations between the members of the universe. Hoyle does not address the fundamental issue nature's order raises. He works *within* the framework of the Big Bang theory and various biological theories of evolution. He claims that for life as we know it to arise *within the parameters* of these theories is highly improbable. But whether nature's order is intended applies to his framework itself—the Big Bang theory and evolutionary theories—and that question arises because nature's order is contingent, not because some feature of nature is improbable.

15. Simone Weil, *Pensées sans ordre concernant l'amour de Dieu* (Paris: Gallimard, 1962), 11.

Chapter Four: The Existence of the World

1. David Hume, *Dialogues Concerning Natural Religion,* ed. Norman Kamp Smith, in the Library of the Literary Arts series (Indianapolis: Bobbs-Merrill, 1947), 189.
2. This was first argued effectively by Norman Malcolm in his article "Anselm's Ontological Arguments," *Philosophical Review* 69 (1960): 41–62. This is to say, after Malcolm's article, two senses of "necessary being" came to be widely accepted by analytic philosophers who had hitherto supported Hume's objection to the concept of a necessary being.
3. See Patterson Brown, "St. Thomas' Doctrine of Necessary Being," *Philosophical Review* 73 (1964): 76–90.
4. Hume, *Dialogues Concerning Natural Religion,* 190–91.
5. See Rowe, *The Cosmological Argument.* See Introduction, n. 3. It is worth noting that Rowe himself is an agnostic and is in the analytic philosophic tradition.
6. William L. Rowe, "Two Criticisms of the Cosmological Argument," *The Monist* 54 (July 1970): 456–57, reprinted in B. A. Brody, ed., *Readings in the Philosophy of Religion* (Englewood Cliffs, N.J.: Prentice-Hall, 1974). It was later incorporated in Rowe's book *The Cosmological Argument.*
7. Originally a BBC debate in 1948 reprinted in *The Existence of God,* ed. John Hick (New York: The Macmillan Company, 1964), 175.

8. Rowe, "Two Criticisms of the Cosmological Argument," 448.
9. Ibid., 449–50.
10. Ibid., 450–51.
11. Stanley L. Jaki, "Teaching of Transcendence in Physics," *American Journal of Physics* 55 (October 1987): 884–88.
12. Kant's own solution to the antinomies is a secular variation of Augustine's. For Kant, the entire cosmos, including time and space, are not ultimate reality either, but unlike Augustine for whom they are creatures, Kant treats the world as immediately dependent on things-in-themselves or *noumena*, about which we can know nothing whatsoever by pure reason.
13. See Immanuel Kant, *Prolegomena to Any Future Metaphysics*, 356–60.
14. See my *Philosophy for Understanding Theology* (Atlanta: John Knox Press, 1985), 143–44, 217.
15. Hume, *An Inquiry Concerning Human Understanding* (1748), Part XII, as found in *Hume on Human Nature and the Understanding*, ed. Antony Flew (New York: Collier Books, 1962), 163.
16. For a discussion of the principle, see Rowe, *The Cosmological Argument*, chapter 2.
17. Milton K. Munitz, *The Mystery of Existence: An Essay in Philosophical Cosmology* (New York: New York University Press, 1974), 6.
18. Gerhard von Rad, *Old Testament Theology,* trans. D. M. G. Stalker, 2 vols. (New York: Harper & Brothers, 1962), 1:121–28, 136–53.
19. The distinction I have given between an answer and an explanation, as well as the duality of "whence" and "whither" in the answer, is based on Nicholas Lash's essay, "Production and Prospect: Reflections on Christian Hope and Original Sin," in *Evolution and Creation*, ed. Ernan McMullin, 173–89. See Ch. 3, n. 10.
20. For an excellent discussion of this point see Robert Sokolowski, *The God of Faith and Reason* (Notre Dame: University of Notre Dame Press, 1982), especially chapter 2.
21. Ludwig Wittgenstein, "A Lecture on Ethics," *Philosophical Review* 74 (January 1965): 7–8, and reprinted in *Philosophy Today No. 1,* ed. Jerry H. Gill (New York: The Macmillan Company, 1968), 4–14. As a matter of interest, see also Michael Murray, "A Note on Wittgenstein and Heidegger," *Philosophical Review* 83 (October 1974): 501–503.
22. Paul Tillich, *Systematic Theology,* 3 vols. (Chicago: University of Chicago Press, 1959), 1:110, 113, 163–64, 186. It is important to note that Tillich sometimes characterizes the question posed by the existence of the universe as the "shock of non-being." This suggests that what we experience in the contingency of the world—that it might not be—is some tendency toward nihilation.

This is not implied in Thomas Aquinas' understanding of being. For Thomas, there is no potency toward non-being. A being's potency is toward actualization. When a seed eventually becomes a tree, and then when the tree eventually dies and decays (and so ceases to be), what was a tree now has become something else (earth), and that earth has the potency (capacity) to become various things (given the requisite conditions). To experience the contingency of the universe is not to experience the "threat of non-being." In addition, Thomas does not refer to "an experience" in his "Third Way" but to the prosaic fact that various caused beings begin to exist and cease to exist. This is the starting point of his argument that there must be a necessary being which is not dependent on anything for its existence. See David Burrell, *Knowing the Unknowable God* (Notre Dame: University of Notre Dame Press, 1986).

Chapter Five: The Need for God and the Book of Nature

1. This phrase is from Robert Sokolowski, *The God of Faith and Reason*. See Ch. 4, n. 20.
2. This desire and its significance is the subject of my book *Finding Our Father* (Atlanta: John Knox Press, 1974).
3. See Simone Weil, *The Need for Roots*, trans. Arthur Wills (New York: Harper & Brothers, 1952), 295.
4. See Simone Weil, *Intimations of Christianity Among the Ancient Greeks*, ed. and trans. Elisabeth Chase Geissbuhler (London: Routledge and Kegan Paul, 1957), 90.
5. Simone Weil, "God in Plato," in *On Science, Necessity and the Love of God*, ed. and trans. Richard Rees (London: Oxford University Press, 1968), 132. A watch can be a work of art, but Weil is considering the design argument in which the beauty of the watch is not a consideration.
6. Weil, *Intimations*, 89–91.
7. See Oliver Sacks, *A Leg to Stand On* (New York: Summit Books, 1984). Sacks, a well-known neurologist, documents his mental and spiritual development during the course of a bad injury. It is an excellent example of someone whose affliction leads him to question whether this world is ultimate. He writes,

> To be deaf to metaphysical implications is one thing, but to be deaf to anguish is another; and this was my indictment of classical neurology. . . . Classical neurology has no room for such matters, and will not admit them, except as occasional, colorful "figures of speech."
> . . . [There is] a refusal to hear or allow significance to the experiential, and an insistence on confining matters to the purely mechanical.
> Neuropsychology had crashed in ruins about me—it retained all of its practical uses and powers, but it had lost all its promise of anything deeper. And if empirical science had failed me as a guide to the musicality of action and life, so did Hume and the philosophy of empiricism, on which empirical science was founded.
> What I felt so intensely, in these two years of dark, was a need to assert and affirm the living subject, to escape from a purely objective, and "robotic" science, to find and establish what was missing—the living "I." If Sherringtonian neurology was the study of "trigger puppets," and Laurian neurology the study of "self-activating robots," I had to go beyond these to a *neurology of the soul*. Sacks, *A Leg to Stand On*, 209, 214, 217, 218–19.

8. Weil, *On Science, Necessity and the Love of God*, 170–98.
9. Epictetus, *Arrius' Discourses of Epictetus* (Cambridge, Mass.: Harvard University Press, vol. 1, 1967), Part I, Book VI.
10. Weil, *On Science*, 197.
11. Ibid., 196.
12. Ibid., 197.
13. William James, "The Will to Believe," reprinted in many places including *Classical and Contemporary Readings in the Philosophy of Religion*, ed. John Hick (Englewood Cliffs, N.J.: Prentice-Hall, 1964), 226–42.
14. John Bunyan, *The Pilgrim's Progress* (New York: Pocket Books, 1957), 11.

Chapter Six: The Experience of God's Grace

1. For the harmony between Thomas Aquinas and John Calvin, see A. Vos, *Aquinas, Calvin, and Contemporary Protestant Thought* (Grand Rapids: Eerdmans, 1985). See also the penetrating review of Vos' book by Jesse de Boer in *Review of Metaphysics* 40 (December 1986): 406–8.
2. Pascal, *Pensées*, 308. See Ch. 2, n. 9.
3. Consider this remark by Ludwig Wittgenstein: "In religion every level of devoutness must have its appropriate form of expression which has no sense at a lower level. This doctrine, which means something at a higher level, is null and void for someone who is still at the lower level; he *can* only understand it *wrongly* and so these words are *not* valid for such a person." *Culture and Value*, ed. G. H. von Wright, trans. Peter Winch (Oxford: Basil Blackwell, 1980), 32e.

    Even *within* the order of the heart there are levels of understanding, so that an increasing purification of the heart is necessary for a greater and greater understanding of the nature of the good God intends us to have.
4. Farrer, *Interpretation and Belief*, 2. See Introduction, n. 13.
5. Simone Weil, *Gravity and Grace*, trans. Emma Craufurd (London: Routledge and Kegan Paul, 1952), 64.
6. Wittgenstein, *Culture and Value*, 32e.
7. This test of our love of justice and the view of faith is based on Simone Weil, *Gravity and Grace*, 88, and *First and Last Notebooks*, trans. Richard Rees (London: Oxford University Press, 1970), 306–7.
8. The subtlety and power of those three temptations are brilliantly presented in Dostoevski's chapter "The Grand Inquisitor," in his novel *The Brothers Karamazov*. Austin Farrer also has a fine study of them, *Triple Victory: Christ's Temptations According to Saint Matthew* (London: The Faith Press, 1965; New York: Morehouse-Barlow, 1965), and I myself have tried my hand in *Temptation* (Cambridge, Mass.: Cowley Publications, 1986).
9. Another instance is Jesus' reference to an incident in which the fall of the tower of Siloam killed eighteen people. Jesus asked rhetorically, "Do you think that they were worse offenders than all the others who dwelt in Jerusalem?" (Luke 13:4). His blunt reply, "Neither," to his disciples' question, "Who sinned, this man or his parents, that he was born blind?" indicates that misfortune is at least not always a punishment (John 9:2–3). The parable of Lazarus and the rich man also made it clear that prosperity in this life is not necessarily a mark of God's favor and abject poverty a mark of God's disfavor (Luke 16:19–31).
10. See, for example, the comment of Nancy Mairs, "Cancer removed myself from the center of the universe," *New York Times*, 6 August 1987.
11. Simone Weil, *The Notebooks of Simone Weil*, trans. Arthur Wills, 2 vols. (London: Routledge and Kegan Paul, 1956), 394.
12. See Alvin Plantinga, *God and Other Minds* (Ithaca: Cornell University Press, 1967), Part II.
13. This point is fully discussed in my book *The Reasonableness of Faith* (Washington: Corpus Publications, 1968), chapter 7.
14. Weil, *Gravity and Grace*, 89.
15. See Antony Flew, "Theology and Falsification," in *New Essays in Philosophical Theology*, eds. Antony Flew and Alasdair MacIntyre (London: SCM Press,

1955). It has been reprinted in many anthologies on the philosophy of religion.

16. Simone Weil, *Waiting for God,* trans. Emma Craufurd (New York: G. P. Putnam's Sons, 1951), 68–69.

17. See, for example, Edith Barfoot, *The Witness of Edith Barfoot: The Joyful Vocation to Suffering* (Oxford: Basil Blackwell, 1977); Iulia de Beausobre, *Creative Suffering* (Westminster, England: Dacre Press, 1940), and *The Woman Who Could Not Die* (New York: Viking Press, 1938); Laurens Van der Post, *The Prisoners and the Bomb* (New York: William Morrow and Co., 1971), 12–13; John Bowker, *Problems of Suffering in the Religions of the World* (Cambridge: Cambridge University Press, 1970), especially 89–97; Helmut Gollwitzer, et al., eds., *Dying We Live: The Final Messages and Records of the Resistance,* trans. Reinhard C. Kuhn (New York: Pantheon Books, 1956). The German title, literally translated, is even more impressive: *Thou Hast Sought to Bring Us Home by Night.*

18. Consider a frequently quoted passage from the penultimate paragraph of Steven Weinberg's book on cosmology, *The First Three Minutes: A Modern View of the Origins of the Universe* (New York: Basic Books, 1977), as found in Jeremy Bernstein, "Cosmology," *The New Yorker,* 6 June 1988, 118:

> As I write this I happen to be in an airplane at 30,000 feet, flying over Wyoming en route home from San Francisco to Boston. Below, the earth looks very soft and comfortable—fluffy clouds here and there, snow turning pink as the sun sets, roads stretching straight across the country from one town to another. It is very hard to realize that this all is just a tiny part of an overwhelmingly hostile universe. It is even harder to realize that this present universe has evolved from an unspeakably unfamiliar early condition, and faces a future extinction of endless cold or intolerable heat. The more the universe seems comprehensible, the more it also seems pointless.

The beauty and the indifference of nature are both perceived, but they are only *thought* about. Nothing is done. Without action, an interaction with God that would give an assurance that all is not pointless does not take place.

19. Its relevance for philosophical discussion of the problem of evil is shown in detail in my article, "Natural Evil and the Love of God," *Religious Studies* 19 (December 1980): 439–56.

20. Weil, *The Need for Roots,* 265. See Ch. 5, n. 3.

21. Weil, *Gravity and Grace,* 87.

22. Weil, *The Notebooks,* 386–87.

23. For a fuller response to recent philosophical discussion of the problem of evil, shaped so as to meet the charges of the opponents to the Christian conviction of the goodness of God, see my article, "Natural Evil and the Love of God," and my book *Traces of God in a Frequently Hostile World* (Cambridge, Mass.: Cowley Publications, 1981).

24. See Henry Snyder Gehman, ed., *The New Westminster Dictionary of the Bible* (Philadelphia: Westminster Press, 1970), 824.

25. Recently the disobedience of Adam and Eve has been explained as a result of their inexperience. They had to learn from experience the consequences of their action. Their "fall" was therefore not a fall but in the long run a good thing because it represents a valuable step in their growth toward maturity. See John Hick, *Evil and the God of Love* (New York: Harper & Row, 1966).

But, as we have seen, we experience the reality of good and evil by doing good actions and refusing to do evil ones because we must check our desire to get our own way. This check is not experienced in committing evil deeds. ick and others are, therefore, mistaken in thinking that to commit evil actions is to grow toward maturity. Only if one repents of evil acts, does one grow toward maturity. Repentance is a good action.

26. Wittgenstein, *Culture and Value*, 6e.
27. Robert N. Bellah et al., eds., *Habits of the Heart: Individualism and Commitment in American Life* (New York: Harper & Row, 1986).

Chapter Seven: The Reasonableness of Faith

1. Hume, *Dialogues Concerning Natural Religion*, 134–35. See Ch. 4, n. 1.
2. Thomas Kuhn, *The Structure of Scientific Revolutions* (Chicago: University of Chicago Press, 1962).
3. See Martin Rudwick's superb essay, "Senses of the Natural World and Senses of God: Another Look at the Historical Relation of Science and Religion," in *The Sciences and Theology in the Twentieth Century*, ed. A. R. Peacocke (Notre Dame: University of Notre Dame Press, 1981), 141–61.
4. Sallie McFague, "An Epilogue: The Christian Paradigm," in *Christian Theology*, ed. Peter C. Hodgson and Robert H. King (Philadelphia: Fortress Press, 1982), 323.
5. Ibid., 324.
6. Propositions in formal logic and pure mathematics do not constitute counter examples because they are not propositions about the world.
7. McFague, "An Epilogue: The Christian Paradigm," 323.
8. These criticisms do not imply that I oppose the author's claims that we use models and metaphors in theology, that some newer ones may have merit, and that older ones have negative features. It is rather that the theological consensus the author gives voice to has got itself into a tangle.
9. Basil Mitchell, *Reason Restored*, the second Nathaniel Taylor Lecture, Yale University, 1986.
10. This is taken from a summary of Polanyi's position by Thomas F. Torrance. See Thomas F. Torrance, ed., *Belief in Science and in Christian Life: The Relevance of Michael Polanyi's Thought for Christian Faith and Life* (Edinburgh: Handsel Press, 1980), 9.
11. This paragraph is a paraphrase of Aage Petersen, *Quantum Physics and the Philosophic Tradition* (Cambridge, Mass.: M.I.T. Press, 1968), 2–34.
12. See W. Jim Neidhardt, "The Creative Dialogue Between Human Intelligibility and Reality—Relational Aspects of Natural Science and Theology," *The Asbury Theological Journal* 41 (Fall 1986): 59; and "Faith and Human Understanding," *Journal of the American Scientific Affiliation* 21 (March 1969): 9–15.

For a suggestive application of Owen Barfield's *Saving the Appearances: A Study in Idolatry* (London: Faber & Faber, 1957; New York: Harcourt, Brace & World, 1965) to the similarities and differences in reasoning in physics and theology, see Walter R. Thorson, "Realism and Relevance," *Journal of the American Scientific Affiliation* 38 (June 1986): 75–87.

Perhaps the most illuminating account of similarities and differences between physics and theology is Russell Stannard's nontechnical account of the experiments in which he took part that confirmed the existence of the theoretical particle "Charm." See *Science and the Renewal of Belief* (London: SCM Press, 1982), chapters 10–12.

13. See John W. Bowker, *The Sense of God* (Oxford: Clarendon Press, 1973), and *The Religious Imagination and the Sense of God* (Oxford: Clarendon Press, 1978), especially 1–30, which states the above thesis that is then exhibited in an examination of several major religions of the world.

14. Pascal, *Pensées,* 172. See Ch. 2, n. 9. This may appear to contradict Pascal's famous Wager Argument, which does seem to rely on fear. It is easily harmonized when one realizes that the Wager Argument is directed toward those who are kept from Christianity because they belong to the order of the body. Motives which are valid currency in that order, such as crude self-interest and fear, are used to show the inconsistency of rejecting Christianity on the basis of self-interest. The Wager Argument shows such people that they cannot comfortably remain members of that order. The intent is to turn them into seekers. As seekers, their passions are increasingly purified and their understanding and appreciation of the good God seeks to give them increase.

15. Socrates is puzzled in a similar way. For example, Socrates asks in the *Phaedrus,* "Am I a monster more complicated and swollen with passion than the serpent Typho [who led the Titans in a rebellion against the gods], or a creature of a gentler and simpler sort, to whom Nature has given a diviner and lowlier destiny?" See Plato, *The Dialogues of Plato, Phaedrus,* trans. Benjamin Jowett, ed. Raphael Damos, 2 vols. (New York: The Macmillan Company, 1892, 1920; New York: Random House, 1937), 230.

16. I have simplified the account by leaving out the intermediate form of existence, the ethical, because it does not affect the main point being made concerning faith. See my *Three Outsiders: Pascal, Kierkegaard, and Simone Weil* (Cambridge, Mass.: Cowley Publications, 1983).

Chapter Eight: Reason and Revelation

1. John Baillie's *The Idea of Revelation in Recent Thought* (London: Geoffrey Cumberland, 1956; New York: Columbia University Press, 1956) helpfully describes the transition from a view that God reveals propositions or statements to the view God reveals Godself primarily in a person, Jesus Christ.

Michael Foster's *Mystery and Philosophy* (London: SCM Press, 1957) is a more profound study of the nature of revelation. He carefully characterizes mystery (or revelation), distinguishes between the Christian and Greek senses of mystery, and defends it against the assumptions of the logical positivists and other analytic philosophers.

Austin Farrer in *The Glass of Vision* (Westminster, England: Dacre Press, 1948) brilliantly examines both general revelation (what we may know of God through nature and history) and special revelation (what we may know of God through Israel's history and the New Testament accounts of Jesus). Farrer argues that the prime medium of knowledge in philosophy and in both general and special revelation is images. His comparison of the role of the imagination in the composition and reading of the Bible to the role of the imagination in the composition and understanding of poetry is a pioneering effort that has not been surpassed in the recent stress on a literary approach to biblical interpretation.

The studies by Foster and Farrer are a far better place to start one's study of the nature of revelation than the much better known work by H. Richard Niebuhr, *The Meaning of Revelation* (New York: The Macmillan Company, 1941).

2. See the superb treatment of this New Testament episode by Charles A. Ryerson III, "Evangelism in an Exploding World," *Princeton Seminary Bulletin,* New Series 5 (1984): 235–39. Ryerson is a historian of religion, specializing in Hinduism, with considerable experience of intercultural and interreligious dialogues.

3. See Rorty, *Philosophy and the Mirror of Nature.* See Introduction, n. 6.

4. In the philosophy of religion today, one of the major positions concerning the reasonableness of Christianity is based on a rejection of foundationalism. See Alvin Plantinga and Nicholas Wolterstorff, *Faith and Rationality* (Notre Dame: University of Notre Dame Press, 1983), with whom this position is most usually associated. For an earlier position, which describes how faith arises and the role of reason in faith and in the formulation and criticism of Chrisian doctrines, see my *The Reasonableness of Faith.* See Ch. 6, n. 13.

5. Iris Murdoch, "Metaphysics and Ethics," in *The Nature of Metaphysics,* ed. David Pears (London: The Macmillan Company, 1957), 99–123.

6. From a conversation with M. O'C. Drury, as reported by Drury in his *The Danger of Words* (London: Routledge and Kegan Paul, 1973), xiii.

7. Other religions tell of divine beings *appearing* in human form, but only Christianity has claimed that the divine *became* a human being (and indeed has remained one, "at the right hand of the Father"). This is treated more fully in the final chapter.

8. Herbert Butterfield, *Man on His Past* (Cambridge: Cambridge University Press, 1955), 139, 141.

9. Wittgenstein, *Culture and Value,* 31e. See ch. 6, n. 3.

Chapter Nine: Divine Agency in a Scientific World

1. David F. Strauss, *Life of Jesus,* ed. Peter C. Hodgson, trans. George Eliot (1835; Philadelphia: Fortress Press, 1972). As found in the article "Miracles" by Antony Flew, in *The Encyclopedia of Philosophy,* 5: 346–347.

2. Rudolf Bultmann, *Jesus Christ and Mythology* (New York: Scribner's, 1958), and *Kerygma and Myth,* ed. H. W. Bartsch, trans. R. H. Fuller (London: S.P.C.K., 1953, 1972).

3. See C. C. Gillispie, *The Edge of Objectivity: An Essay in the History of Scientific Ideas* (Princeton: Princeton University Press, 1960).

4. Pierre Duhem, as quoted in Harry W. Paul, *The Edge of Contingency,* 145–46. See Ch. 1, n. 2.

5. See G. E. M. Anscombe, *Intentions* (Ithaca: Cornell University Press, 1958), 37ff., and Robert I. King, *The Meaning of God* (Philadelphia: Fortress Press, 1973), especially chapter 3. King's book is an excellent treatment of many of the issues concerning the intelligibility of divine agency and deserves much more attention than it has so far received.

6. William G. Pollard, *Chance and Providence* (New York: Scribner's, 1958).

7. These simple examples, of course, do not establish human freedom. But since arguments for determinism today usually are based on psychoanalytic theories of unconscious motivation, brain physiology, or some version of the

principle of sufficient reason, and not on scientific accounts of the relations between large scale objects, we need not consider them. Those who want to follow up the topic, however, may consult the excellent defense of human freedom by Richard L. Franklin in *Freewill and Determinism* (London: Routledge and Kegan Paul, 1968). For my own position, which supplements Franklin's, see "Freedom and Human Fulfillment," *Theology Today* 28 (October 1971): 295–308, and "Deliberation and the Regularity of Behavior," *American Philosophical Quarterly* 9 (July 1972): 251–57.

8. See Gordon D. Kaufman, *God the Problem* (Cambridge, Mass.: Harvard University Press, 1972), and Maurice Wiles, *God's Action in the World* (London: SCM Press, 1986). For an excellent discussion which compares them unfavorably to Austin Farrer's treatment of the topic, see Brian Hebblethwaite's "Providence and Divine Action," *Religious Studies* 14 (June 1978): 223–36. Although I differ slightly from Hebblethwaite's understanding of miracles, I have been greatly influenced by his discussion of God's providential activity in bringing about specific events.

9. This is treated at length in my book *Temptation*, especially chapter 2. See Ch. 6, n. 8.

10. See Thomas H. Gainer, Jr., *A Theoretical Investigation of M2 Constituent of the Tide in the Gulf of Mexico* (Master's Thesis, United States Naval Postgraduate School, 1966). Gainer supplied me with this account of his work for those with a scientific interest in the subject:

This work was undertaken to use basic theory and first principles to explain sudden shifts in the astronomical tidal patterns on the northeastern coast of the Gulf of Mexico. Here, in relatively short distances, tides change from one high and one low daily (New Orleans to Cape San Blas) to two highs and two lows (Cape San Blas to Cedar Key) and then to mixed tides. Tides are constituted of 67 astronomical factors of varying periods. Two of the most significant are those of 12- and 24-hour periods caused by the moon and the moon and sun together respectively. By studying the distribution of the 12-hour period, one can see the patterns that contribute to the whole. Beginning with basic physics, Newton, Kepler, et al., differential equations were developed which would represent tidal height and phase (time relationship to the moon's passing a given meridian of longitude). Gravity, coriolis effects, friction, current velocities, and boundaries were included. These various differentials were then approximated by finite differences and the equations were set up for 504 points 30 miles apart from each other in the Gulf of Mexico. This is an old and early study. Input card errors accounted for repeated flooding of the Rocky Mountains. The solution on the computer was analogous to pressing all the air uniformly out of an air mattress: the computer was to solve for tidal height and phase at each point, repeatedly revising its answers until it reduced residual errors to a specified tolerance. The computations were not inherently stable, and there was a real possibility that they would not converge on a solution, but after 37 iterations (about 35 minutes running time), the solution was complete. Its accuracy or applicability was not demonstrable until tidal amplitudes and phases could be plotted for each point and the whole analyzed. The remarkable and reassuring revelation was that in the northeast corner of the Gulf, the tidal constituent pivoted full circle. This could not be analyzed (drawn as in a weather map) otherwise. Physical theory would require that tidal amplitudes reduce to zero at such a pivot point (technical term: amphidromic point) and the solution reflected this. This analysis was an exhilarating moment for the researcher!

This study was an early attempt and has been improved upon immensely by others, but it did succeed in using physical theory ($F = MA$ and its derivatives) to relate to the observed data. For many years the procedure has been to extrapolate based on observations and relationships to nearby data. Here theory results in explaining data and could therefore be used to predict tides in reshaped or reconstructed basins.

11. I am here paraphrasing Russell Stannard's comments to me at the Center of Theological Inquiry, Princeton, New Jersey, 15 June 1988. His point is the same one as Leibniz makes with his celebrated distinction between two kingdoms, nature and grace. According to Leibniz, the laws or rules that govern the normal course of events express God's intentions, and they are included within and subordinate to those laws or rules that express God's gracious intentions and purposes for the salvation and eternal destiny of human beings. See Leibniz's *Theodicy* (1710) and *Principles of Nature and Grace* (1714).

Chapter Ten: A Christian Theology of Other Faiths

1. See my *Philosophy for Understanding Theology*, 1–6. See Ch. 4, n. 14.
2. There are other aspects of Weil's discussion of the cross. The nature of Christ as the prime mediator was considered in an article, "Suffering at the Hands of Nature," *Theology Today* 37 (July 1980): 183–91. In that article, Christ's affliction as the one who became sin for us is the focus; here, the universality of the cross is stressed.
3. Simone Weil, "The Iliad, A Poem of Might," in *Intimations of Christianity Among the Ancient Greeks*. See Ch. 5, n. 4.
4. Ibid., 24.
5. Ibid., 48–49.
6. Ibid., 44.
7. Ibid., 50.
8. For example, see Weil, *Waiting for God*, 185 (see Ch. 6, n. 16):

> If one is born into a religion which is not too unsuitable for pronouncing the name of the Lord, if one loves this native religion with a well directed and pure love, it is difficult to imagine a legitimate motive for giving it up, before direct contact with God has placed the soul under the guidance of the divine will itself. After that the change is only legitimate if it is made in obedience. . . .
> If the imperfection of the religion in which one is born is too great, or if the form under which it appears in one's native surroundings is too corrupt, or if, through special circumstances, love for this religion has never been born or has been killed, the adoption of a foreign religion is legitimate. It is legitimate and necessary for certain people; probably not for everybody. This is the same with regard to those who have been brought up without the practice of any religion.

9. Ibid., 182.

Chapter Eleven: Incarnation in the Gospels and *Bhagavad-Gita*

1. John Hick, ed., *The Myth of God Incarnate*.
2. Weil, *The Notebooks*, 386. See Ch. 6, n. 11.
3. Ibid.
4. Weil, *Gravity and Grace*, 88. See Ch. 6, n. 5.
5. Weil, *The Notebooks*, 384.
6. Weil, *First and Last Notebooks*, 306–7. See Ch. 6, n. 7.
7. Weil, *The Notebooks*, 394.
8. Weil, *Gravity and Grace*, 89.
9. Weil, *The Notebooks*, 25.

10. "For things outside our power, 'Thy will, not mine, be done' is clear. But for things within our power? Not to regard them as such. To read the obligation as a necessity." Weil, *The Notebooks,* 40–41.
11. "*At a given moment* one is not free to do anything whatever. And one must accept this internal necessity; accept what one is, at a given moment, as a fact, even one's shame." Ibid., 56.
12. Ibid., 19, 21, 23.
13. Ibid., 25.
14. Ibid., 27.
15. Ibid., 49.
16. See Simone Weil, *Formative Writings, 1929–1941,* ed. and trans. Dorothy Tuck McFarland and Wilhelmina Van Ness (Amherst: The University of Massachusetts Press, 1987), 227–78.
17. Weil, *The Notebooks,* 65.
18. David Burrell, *Knowing the Unknowable God.* See Ch. 4, n. 22.

Conclusion

1. For a discussion of the role of reason in a faith that relies on the assurance of the nourishment, guidance, and understanding given through Christian beliefs as its ground, see my earlier book *The Reasonableness of Faith,* especially Part II. See Ch. 6, n. 13.
2. For example, see Austin Farrer, *Faith and Speculation* (New York: New York University Press, 1967), and Nicholas Wolterstorff, *Reason Within the Bounds of Revelation* (Grand Rapids: Eerdmans, 1976).
3. Weil, *Waiting for God,* 210. See Ch. 6, n. 16.
4. Søren Kierkegaard, *Training in Christianity,* is completely devoted to this theme.
5. Weil, *Waiting for God,* 212.

Index

Abraham and Sarah, 39, 78–79, 81, 121, 127, 149–50, 152, 163, 220
Adam and Eve, 36, 106–7, 121–23, 157, 226; *see also* Garden of Eden
act, 44, 96, 105, 119, 151–52, 203–4, 209–11
action(s), 85–86, 105–7, 115, 160–62, 164–181, 190–91, 203–5, 207, 211, 226, 227, 229
affliction, 92–93, 95, 231
agency, divine, 18–19, 46, 48–49, 157, 164, ch. 10, 229
agent, rational, 86, 93, 95–96, 99, 111, 167–70
Almighty, 15
Alston, William P., 51, 221
An Essay Concerning Human Understanding (title), 16
analogy/analogies, 48, 75, 90–91, 123, 128, 136, 158, 198, 205, 208
analytic philosophy, 67, 217, 228
Anscombe, G. E. M., 169–170, 229
anthropic principles, 60–62
anthropomorphism, 75, 92
antinomies (Kantian), 70–72
Aquinas, Thomas, 66, 70, 75, 188, 223, 225
Arjuna, 203–4, 206, 211
Aristotle/Aristotelian, 25, 27–28, 30–31, 33, 36, 40–45, 57, 59, 75, 146, 221
aspiration(s), 3–4, 13, 19, 40, 86–90, 93–95, 99, 154, 192
atheist, 82, 123–24, 128, 161
atonement, 199–200, 202–3, 208, 210
Augustine, 48, 72, 162, 188, 219, 223

Bacon, Francis, 26, 42, 125, 218
Barbour, Ian, 27
Barrow, John D., 221
Barth, Karl, 6, 217

beauty, 89–91, 93, 95–96, 113, 115, 117, 119, 155, 194, 201–2, 224, 226
being, 66, 73, 83, 208–9, 223; *see also* ontology
Bellah, Robert, 125, 227
Bethell, Samuel L., 220
Bhagavad-Gita, 197, 203–16
Bible/biblical, 7, 16, 18, 31–32, 35–36, 38–40, 45, 79–80, 85–86, 94, 96, 99–102, 108, 111, 123, 133, 140, 144–45, 147, 156–64, 166–67, 174–75, 178, 180–81, 188, 195, 213–15, 219, 220, 228
Big Bang, 47–48, 61, 70, 74, 222
biology, 2, 25, 29, 60, 89, 136, 156, 222
Bohr, Niels, 138
Bowker, John, 139, 156, 226, 228
Boyle, Robert, 42
Brahe, Tycho, 31
Brecht, Bertolt, 219
Buddhism, 2, 209
Bultmann, Rudolf, 167, 229
Bunyan, John, 95, 224
Burrell, David, 188, 208, 223, 232
Butterfield, Herbert, 23, 160–61, 218, 229

Calvin, John, 58, 225
Catholic Church, Roman, 28–34, 77, 157, 161, 165, 208, 218, 219, 220, 221
causality, 48, 51, 56, 68, 72–75, 80, 152, ch. 9, 198, 203–4, 206; in Hume, 129–30; in Kant, 72–74, 130
chance, in contrast to design, 44–45, 50, 55–57, 59–60, 65
Chesterton, G. K., 50–51, 221
Christ, 13–15, 17–19, 35–36, 38, 99–100, 105, 108–10, 115–21, 127,

140, 143, 147, 150, 162–63, 180, 186–89, 192, 195–96, 197, 199–204, 206–8, 211, 228; *see also* Jesus

Clarke, Samuel, 65–66, 73–76

community, 19, 26, 96, 99–100, 106–8, 120–23, 125–27, 139, 146, 154–56, 162, 213–14

Confessions (title), 72, 162

contemplation, 87

contingent/contingency, 5, 14, 25–26, ch. 3, ch. 4, 85–88, 91, 93–96, 140, 144, 149, 152, 156, 160, 165, 173, 208, 213–16

Copernicus/Copernican, 27–28, 30–33

Copleston, Father, 68

cosmological argument, 55, 64–66, 72–74, 76–77, 84, 217, 222–223

cosmology, 3, 47, 70–71, 74, 130–31, 174, 221, 222, 226

craftsman, 25, 44

creation, 25–26, 35–36, 45–48, 56, 58–59, 72, 74–75, 78–83, 90–91, 119, 129, 141, 149–50, 152, 160, 165–66, 171–73, 175, 177, 189–93, 195–96, 198–200, 202, 208, 210–11, 218, 219, 221, 223

Creator, creator, 7, 10–14, 18, 25–26, 35–36, 45–48, 50, 56, 58–59, 72, 74–75, 78–83, 90–91, 105, 109–111, 115, 119, 129, 141, 149–50, 152, 160, 165–66, 171–73, 175, 177, 189–93, 195–96, 198–200, 202, 208, 210–11, 218, 219, 221, 223

cross, 109, 189, 192–97, 199, 206, 210, 231

crucifixion, 38, 118, 126, 150, 158, 188, 193–96, 203–4, 210

Darwin, Charles/Darwinism, 29, 54, 57–60, 81, 218, 221

death, 87–88, 113–14, 120, 126, 139–41, 155, 158–59, 177, 180, 192, 197, 202, 210

Deism, *see* natural religion

Derrida, Jacques, 6, 151, 218

Descartes, René, 27–28, 37, 40, 42, 44, 125, 134, 140, 151, 167–68, 217

Design (order of the universe), 55–57, 60, 62, 81–82, 165, 173, 221

designer, 38, 45, 55–63, 90, 111–12, 115; *see also* craftsman

determinism, 135, 168–69, 229

Dialogues Concerning Natural Religion (title), 54–55, 57, 65, 75–76, 91, 111, 113, 129, 222

Duhem, Pierre, 169, 218, 229

Einstein, Albert, 46, 70–71, 103, 110, 130, 138

Eliot, T. S., 79

empirical, 51, 60, 71–88, 122, 151, 224

Enlightenment, 2–19, 133, 160, 163, 185–86, 213, 217, 219

Epictetus, 92, 224

epistemology, 41, 134

ethics, 4, 12–14, 16, 18, 39, 41–42, 112, 124, 153, 165–67, 185, 204, 206–7, 223

Evans-Pritchard, Edward Evans, 217

everlastingness of the universe, 40–41, 72–73, 76–77

evidence, 10–12, 14–16, 23, 35–36, 39, 51–52, 78, 128, 134, 145–48, 214–16, 221

evil, 5, 18, 39, 55–56, 62, 82, 91–93, 105–7, 109–12, 114–17, 121, 123, 126, 139, 155, 199–200, 202–4, 206, 211, 226, 227; problem of, 114–117, 226

existence (God's), 11–18, 35, 38–39, 44, ch. 3, ch. 4, 101, 147, 185, 220

existentialism, 6, 153

experience, 18–19, 70–71, 75–76, 83, 89, 91, 96, 99–100, 104–7, 113–15, 122–24, 129–31, 136, 138, 150–51, 153, 201, 213, 223, 226

faith, 1, 7; and knowledge, 10–18, ch. 1, ch. 2, 62–63, 85–86, 92, 95–96, ch. 6, ch. 7, ch. 8, 202; and reason, 10–18, ch. 1, ch. 2, 62–63, 85–86, 92, 95–96, ch. 6, ch. 7, ch. 8, 202, 229, 232

Fall, the, 106–7, 121–23, 140, 143, 226

Farrer, Austin, 11–15, 85, 95, 101,

105, 110, 157, 172, 176, 218, 225, 228–229, 230, 232
Feuerbach, Ludwig, 217
Fichte, Johann Gottlieb, 221
fideism, 7
final cause, 43, 93; *see also* teleology
Flew, Antony, 114, 225, 229
formal cause, 43–44
Foster, Michael B., 23, 27, 218, 220, 228–29
freedom, 71, 113, 123, 153, 167–171, 177, 189, 205, 229–230
free will, 86, 123, 153, 167–171, 177, 205; free choice of God/freedom of God, 150, 151
Freud, Sigmund, 101, 140, 217
Fry, Christopher, 8, 217

Gainer, Thomas H., Jr., 230
Galileo, Galilei, 26–34, 40, 44, 168, 218–19
Garden of Eden, 39, 106–7
Gibbon, Edmund, 103
Gillispie, Charles Coulston, 167, 229
Gnostics/Gnosticism, 25, 125
God, *see* existence of God; image of God; intentions of God
good, 5, 10–16, 18, 39, 44, 54–58, 80–81, 83–85, 92–93, 100–17, 120, 122–23, 125, 139–40, 143, 145–49, 152–56, 200–4, 206, 211, 214–16, 225–27; form of the Good, 155
Gorgias (title), 88
grace, 9, 18–19, 79, 99–100, 111, 116–17, 120–21, 123, 140, 167, 172, 190–98, 200, 208, 210, 225, 231
happiness, 87–88, 96, 99–101, 110, 114, 122–25, 139, 143, 145–48, 152–56, 162–63, 177, 202, 214–16, 220
Hartshorne, Charles, 6
heart, 1, 11, 13–15, 85, 103–5, 108–9, 111, 114, 116–17, 120, 123, 139–40, 145–47, 150, 153–54, 178, 216, 225
Hegel, Georg Wilhelm Friedrich, 151, 221
Heidegger, Martin, 6, 217, 223
Heisenburg, Werner Karl, 138

Herbert, George, 115–16, 119–20, 124, 187, 216
Herbert, Lord of Cherbury, 39–40, 187
hermeneutics, 6, 16
Hick, John, 197, 210, 222, 226, 231
hierarchy, 41–42, 75, 222
Hinduism, 2, 185, ch. 11, 229
history, 10, 14–16, 18–19, 29, 38–40, 49, 96, 131, 133, 147, 150–52, 154, 157–64, 166–67, 170, 174–80, 185, 195, 228; critical history, 157–64
Homer, 193–94, 210
Hoyle, Fred, 222
humanism, 5
Hume, David, 3, 6–7, 40, 45, 52, 54–57, 63–68, 70, 75–77, 80, 83, 91, 111, 113–14, 128–31, 133, 175–76, 213, 220, 222, 223, 224, 227
humility, 109, 124, 193–94

illumination, 142–46, 202, 209
image of God, 110–11, 140–41, 143
immortality, 39, 41, 101, 141, 155, 208
incarnation, 109–10, 119, 147, 150, 152, 157–59, 161–62, 192, 195–96, ch. 11, 229, 231
innate ideas, 16
intentions of God, 25, 36–38, 52–63, 79, 80–81, 99–100, 102, 107–8, 110, 116, 122, 124, 126, 141, 149–52, 154, 157, 162–64, 166, 169–81, 174, 201, 214–15, 231
intuition, 83, 134, 137
Israel, 17, 35–36, 38, 79, 94, 99, 118, 143, 147, 149–52, 154, 162, 174, 178, 188, 228

Jaki, Stanley L., 218–19, 223
James, William, 94–95, 224
Jastrow, Robert, 47–48, 220
Jesus, 13, 16–17, 35, 38, 59, 99–100, 102, 104, 109–12, 117–18, 120, 123, 126, 134, 147, 151–52, 157–63, 166–67, 174, 177–78, 180, 187–88, 192–93, 195–97, 200–1, 204, 208, 210, 225, 228; *see also* Christ
Jew/Jewish, 15, 78–79, 107–8, 120–

21, 150, 159, 166, 168, 188, 208, 213
Judaism, 15, 35, 187, 195
justice, 100, 108–12, 114, 116–19, 125, 154–56, 198–200, 204, 206–11, 215–16, 225

Kant, Immanuel, 3, 6–7, 40, 52, 57, 63–65, 68, 70–77, 80, 83, 128, 130–31, 133–34, 151, 167–68, 213, 220, 221, 223
Kaufman, Gordon, 174–77, 179, 230
Kepler, Johann, 26, 29–30, 33, 42, 230
Kierkegaard, Søren, 146–48, 153, 215, 228, 232
Koestler, Arthur, 29–30, 219
Koyré, Alexandre, 45
Krishna, 203–4, 207–8, 210–11
Kuhn, Thomas, 131, 227

language, 196
Laplace, Pierre, 47
Lash, Nicholas, 223
laws, scientific, 1, 29, 36, 51, 53, 59, 76, 78, 81, 85, 113–15, 130, ch. 9, 201, 205
Leibniz, Gottfried Wilhelm, 44, 53, 200, 220–221, 231
Leibniz-Clarke Correspondence, 1715–16 (title), 220
Locke, John, 16, 151
logic, 16, 131, 134, 227
logical positivism, 131, 133, 151, 228
Logos, 151, 195, 215
love, 13, 90, 107–11, 113–15, 117, 119–21, 124, 125, 156, 189–93, 195–98, 202–3, 207, 209–11, 215–16, 225, 226, 231
"Love" (poem), 115
Luther, Martin, 58

machine, world as a, 36–37, 39, 44, 47, 55, 90
Malcolm, Norman, 222
Marx, Karl, 28–30, 87–88
Marxist countries, 10
material cause, 43
materialism, 125

matter, 44–45, 130, 165–66, 167, 175, 201
McFague, Sallie, 227
mechanistic universe, 28, 39–40, 42–45, 52–53, 81, ch. 9, 224
metaphysics/metaphysical, 76, 136, 153, 219, 229
Mind, divine, 53, 201
miracles, 38–39, 158, 166–67, 175, 181, 195, 220, 230
Mitchell, Basil, 7, 19, 128, 136, 217, 221, 227
Munitz, Milton K., 77, 223
Murdoch, Iris, 90, 153, 189, 229
mystery, 36, 40, 48, 152, 198, 220, 228
mysticism, 83, 163
myth, 11, 37, 156–57, 167, 229

natural law, 36–38
natural religion, 35–36, 38–40, 45, ch. 3, 129–30, 144, 163, 165–66, 175–76, 178, 185–87
natural theology, 57–59, 221
nature, 10, 14–16, 25–26, 29, 35–36, 38–42, 44–46, 49, 51–53, 55, 58–63, 80, 82, 84–85, 89, 91, 93–94, 96, 100, 111–19, 132–33, 138, 140–41, 143, 150, 157, 163, 166–80, 190–92, 201–5, 210, 219, 220, 221, 222, 228
necessary being, 55, 65–66, 71, 73–77, 208, 222
necessity, 50, 65–66, 113, 129–30, 134–35, 167, 200–4, 206–7, 210–11
needs, human, 1, 85, 88, 94, 96, 99, 190, 213–14
Neidhardt, W. Jim, 139, 227
Neoplatonism, 41, 162
Newton, Sir Isaac/Newtonians, 37, 45–47, 49, 65, 123, 130, 134, 165, 179–80, 230
Niebuhr, Reinhold, 204
noumena, 71, 75, 167, 223

ontological argument, 73, 222
ontology/ontological, 83, 208–9, 211
order of the world, 25–26, 38, 45, 47,

ch. 3, 78, 80–82, 84–85, 89–91,
94–95, 114–15, 129, 137, 144, 165,
200–201, 208, 210, 213–15; *see also*
design

Paley, William, 57, 90, 221
pantheism, 221
Pascal, Blaise, 39, 102–3, 109–11,
127, 140–43, 146, 198, 220, 225,
228
Phaedo (title), 52–53, 155
Phaedrus (title), 155, 199, 228
phenomena (appearances), 43–46, 71–
72, 75, 130, 135, 167
philosophes, 28–34
philosophy, 2–4, 9–10, 14–15, 18, 35,
37, 39, 44–45, 47, 52, 62–64, 72,
75–78, 80–86, 96, 101, 107, 113–
14, 136, 138, 140–41, 146–47,
151–52, 154–56, 164, 186–87, 208,
213–16, 220, 221, 225–26, 228, 229
physics, 2, 10, 23–34, 44–48, 54, 60,
89, 130–31, 136, 138–39, 156–57,
167, 169, 171, 174, 227
Planck, Max, 6
Plantinga, Alvin, 113, 225, 229
Plato, 37, 52, 88, 104, 154–56, 193–
94, 199, 201, 224, 228
Platonism, 188
Plotinus, 41
pluralism, 1, 9–10, 126
Polanyi, Michael, 136–37, 227
Pollard, William G., 171, 229
potency, 44, 223
Prime Mover, *see* Unmoved Mover
Principia Mathematica (title), 31
progress, 5, 29, 82, 125–26
proofs, 37–38, 78, 215
providence, 17, 116–17, 160, 174,
178–79, 188, 229, 230
Ptolemy, 30, 40–42

rational, 3–4, 25–26, 37, 40, 45, 51,
59, 76, 78, 84–89, 93–95, 99–100,
112, 127, ch. 7, 213–15
Ray, John, 56
reason and faith, *see* faith
Redeemer, 7, 10–14, 78, 119, 143; *see
also* salvation

redemption, 26, 110, 119, 143, 186;
see also salvation
relativism, 1, 9–10, 107, 133–36, 152,
217
religions of the world, 17, 19, 78, 139,
150, 156, ch. 10, ch. 11, 217, 229
Renaissance, 163; *see also* humanism
repentance, 38–39, 105, 123, 155,
227
Republic (title), 155–56
resistance (original sin), 80, 110, 122–
24, 126, 160, 172
revelation, 18, 35–36, 38, 128, 137,
143, ch. 8, 185, 209, 216, 228–29,
232
Rorty, Richard, 217, 229
Rowe, William L., 67–70, 83, 217,
222, 223
Rudwick, Martin, 132, 227
Russell, Bertrand, 68–69, 151

salvation, 17, 100, 186–87, 197, 200,
203, 207–9
Sartre, Jean-Paul, 88
science, 2–11, 14, 17–19, ch. 1, ch. 2,
50, 52, 59, 62–64, 70, 74–75, 77–
78, 80–82, 84–85, 123, 127–28,
130–32, 134, 136–39, 144, 147,
154, 156–57, 160–61, 164, ch. 9,
186, 190, 213–14, 218, 219, 220,
227–228, 229–230
Shakespeare, William, 33, 41, 133
sin, 79, 108–110, 121–26, 143, 159–
61, 198–99, 223, 226, 231; *see also*
resistance
Socrates, 4, 52, 155, 228
Sokowlski, Robert, 223, 224
soul, 115, 155, 208, 214
space, 71–72
Spinoza, Benedict de, 87, 104, 134,
151
Stannard, Russell, 227–228, 231
Stoics, 92, 187
Strauss, David F., 166–67, 229
suffering, 91–93, 100, 109–20, 139,
154–55, 159, 177, 193–95, 197,
200, 202, 206–11, 225, 226, 231
sufficient reason, principle of, 65, 75–
78, 80–82, 84, 144, 213, 230

technology, 4, 23–24, 42
teleological argument, 4, ch. 3, 84, 90–91, 224
teleology, 3–4, 43–44, ch. 3, 79, 85–86, 93, 95, 146, 153–54
theism, 15–16, 67, 78, 92, 96
theodicies, 116, 231; *see also* evil
theology, 6–9, 16–17, 19, 39, 45, 47–48, 72, 74–75, 80–82, 86, 95–96, 112, 120, 128–29, 133–34, 137–39, 146, 148–53, 156, 166, 175, 181, ch. 10, ch. 11, 215, 217, 219, 221, 223, 227
theories (scientific), 1, 27–34, 46, 53–54, 58, 60, 78, 85, 130, 132–33, 138, 140, 167, 215, 217, 222, 231
Tillich, Paul, 83–84, 223
Timaeus (title), 37, 194
time/timelessness, 71–73, 130, 168, 172
Tipler, Frank J., 221
Torrance, Thomas F., 227
transcendent, 78, 156–57, 199–200

union, 198–99, 203, 205, 208
Unmoved Mover, 40, 44, 75

Voltaire, 28, 39
Von Rad, Gerhard, 78, 223

Weil, Simone, 62, 90–93, 112–17, 188–211, 214, 216, 222, 224–26, 228, 231, 232
Weinberg, Steven, 226
Whitehead, Alfred North, 6, 200
Wiles, Maurice, 174–76, 179, 220, 230
William of Ockham, 81
wisdom, 109–10, 121
witness, 19, 86, 94–96, 108, 194–95
Wittgenstein, Ludwig, 83, 109, 125, 157–58, 161–62, 223, 225, 227, 229
Word, the, 109–10, 119, 150, 157–59, 162, 180–81, 192, 194–97, 200–1, 208, 210–11; *see also* Incarnation